Childhood Stress

Childhood Stress

Don't Let Your Child Be a Victim

BARBARA KUCZEN, Ph.D.

Delacorte Press/New York 𝒹𝓅

Published by
Delacorte Press
1 Dag Hammarskjold Plaza
New York, N.Y. 10017

ACKNOWLEDGMENTS
Reprinted with permission from the *Journal of Psychosomatic Research*, Volume 11, T. H. Holmes and R. H. Rahe, "The Social Readjustment Rating Scale," Copyright 1967 Pergamon Press, Ltd.

Excerpts from *Temperament and Development* by Alexander Thomas, M.D., and Stella Chess, M.D., reprinted with permission of the publisher, Brunner/Mazel, Inc.

Excerpts from the book *How to Raise Independent and Professionally Successful Daughters* by Dr. Rita Dunn and Dr. Kenneth J. Dunn. © 1977 by Dr. Rita Dunn and Dr. Kenneth J. Dunn. Published by Prentice-Hall, Inc., Englewood Cliffs, New Jersey 07632.

"A Glossary of Measurement Terms," a Test Service Notebook published by The Psychological Corporation. Used with permission.

Reprinted by permission of Warner Books/New York from *Al Ubell's Energy-Saving Guide for Homeowners*. Copyright © 1980 by Jeffrey Weiss, Alvin Ubell and George Merlis.

Manufactured in the United States of America

First printing

Designed by Richard Oriolo

LIBRARY OF CONGRESS CATALOGING IN PUBLICATION DATA

Kuczen, Barbara.
  Childhood stress.

  Bibliography: p.
  Includes index.
  1. Stress in children—Prevention.   2. Parenting.
I. Title.
BF723.S75K82   649′.1   82-4976
ISBN 0-440-01368-2   AACR2

This book is dedicated to
my parents,
Jennie and Lee Schaller,
who taught me the meaning
of unconditional love and support.

Acknowledgments

I am deeply grateful to a number of individuals for their assistance and support. Without them this book would never have been written. I thank Cynthia Vartan, my editor at Delacorte, who contributed large measures of enthusiasm, effort, and expertise, and I am indebted to my agents, Arthur Pine and Richard Pine, for their many ideas—but most of all for keeping me going when I was ready to quit. I also extend my gratitude to Charlotte Barr, Dan Byron, G. E. Cronin, David Falk, Barbara Kardas, Lynn Kissel, Pat Moroney, Glen Noren, Linda Noren, Vaso Papadopulos, Laurette Paredes, and Carol Schaller for their suggestions and motivating force. Lastly, I thank my husband Ken, and daughter Carly for coping with the life-style stress this book generated in our family.

Contents

Introduction

In the past sixty years life has changed from a relatively simple existence to a fast-paced, technological rat race. Stress wasn't a major threat to our grandparents, but times are different today. Studies show a dramatic increase in stress-related disorders or so-called life-style illnesses. Nonetheless, stress can be prevented or managed. And yet, most parents have not altered their child-raising practices to train children to cope.

Stress can be either personal or environmental. Personal stress is associated with social situations such as divorce, job pressure, or personal antagonisms. Environmental stress results from the effects of external influences such as noise, pollution, or temperature. Both types of stress disrupt the individual and cause a series of physical reactions that are basically the same, regardless of the nature of the stressor. In other words, the physical response to the stress of job pressure does not differ greatly from the response to noise. Frequent reaction to stress produces wear and tear on the body which experts believe is linked to a large number of diseases, including hypertension, heart attacks, ulcers, diabetes, colitis, tension headaches, backaches, and even the common cold. It can also break down the personality.

Stress is inevitable. It is encountered almost everywhere, so no one can avoid it. Driving a car, overcrowded conditions, dieting, or boredom can cause it. So can travel, moving, changing family structures, or hospitalization. Although, fortunately, humans are capable of adapting to stress, adjustment is a slow process. The rapid pace of societal change does not allow time for natural adaptation.

Adults are not alone in experiencing the stresses generated by modern living. No child can grow up without stress. And understanding it less, children are even more susceptible to feelings of insecurity and helplessness. Children as young as six years old have developed ulcers. Adolescent death by suicide has tripled since 1958. In fact, suicide is the second leading cause of death among adolescents. (Accidents are first.) Depression in children is an area of increasing concern for health care specialists, and more than one in every ten children suffers from an emotional or mental illness. Too many young people have not learned to cope.

As adults we engineered our own coping systems through sometimes painful trial-and-error. Considering what is known about stress, it seems highly inefficient to leave children on their own in developing stress defenses.

Stress can be compared to "the force" in the popular *Star Wars* movie. Those familiar with the plot will recall that there are two sides to "the force"—one good, one bad. Stress is a force that every child must learn to control. If the bad side of this force takes over, children can develop such problems as irrational fears, bed-wetting, tics, overeating, rashes, nail biting, eczema, or asthma. Older children may drop out or turn to alcohol or drugs. But there is another, more positive side to stress. Nearly any activity can produce stress—giving a party, crossing the street, or going on a date. Stress can give a student the extra energy needed to earn an A on an exam. The individual just has to know how to deal with it. The same stressful situation which stimulates one child can destroy another.

One of the goals of this book is to help parents harness the positive energy generated by this powerful force. The key is control and amount. The body can make short-term adjustments to minor amounts of stress. Throughout childhood the measure and duration of controllable stress should be increasing by tiny increments. The well-adjusted adult has built a coping system through dealing successfully, within the security of the family, with stressful childhood experiences. Coping with childhood stress means providing children with the freedom to develop, while simultaneously recognizing when stress is approaching the danger level.

A second goal of this book is to help parents acquire that skill to recognize the warning signs which signal that the child is beyond the tolerance level. Ignoring these indicators can ultimately result in incapacitating physical, emotional, social, or intellectual crises.

A third goal is to help parents determine what is causing their child's stress. Children face potential stress-provoking situations daily. In order for stress to be controlled, minimized, or prevented, it must first be identified. Sources of childhood stress are not always obvious and often go undetected by parents.

Finally, this book seeks to reduce the isolation and helplessness parents experience in understanding and coping themselves with the sometimes heartbreaking stresses of their children. Although each child is unique and ultimately arrives at a coping system that is distinctly personal, all parents share the dilemma and frustration that come with sensing that something is wrong but having only the vaguest notion of what it is. In some cases the stressful life-style of the parents is a prime source of the child's difficulty. Techniques for minimizing life-style stress are an important part of the book. Widely accepted relaxation and stress-management approaches are also given. The book, which concentrates on the stresses of children between the ages of approximately two and twelve, is divided into three parts. Part I, ''Prepare to Cope with Childhood Stress,'' provides background information regarding stress, parent coping, and your child's individuality. In Part II, ''Minimize and Prevent Stress,'' suggestions are provided for dealing with a wide variety of childhood stressors. Part III, ''Control and Manage Stress,'' includes ideas for organizing your family life-style and managing inevitable stressors.

Children can learn to cope with stress, but they need good teachers, and *you* are your child's most important teacher.

PART I

Prepare to Cope with Childhood Stress

Chapter One

Understand Stress

Betty used to think her life was relatively normal and her family reasonably well adjusted. Suddenly, everything seemed to fall apart. Her six-year-old daughter began to wet the bed, and the pediatrician blamed "stress." Almost overnight her sixteen-year-old daughter became unbearably rude, sassy, and prone to speaking to her mother as if she were her private maid. The high school counselor advised restraint and attributed this sudden superiority complex to the "stresses" of dating. Betty's son, aged seventeen, borrowed half a gallon of vodka, the keys to the family car, and phoned from the police station. His only explanation was that he just couldn't take the pressure—too much stress in all those honors classes. Her husband arrived home from work one day to announce that he had ulcers and must enroll in a "stress-prevention" course as part of his doctor's prescription. Even her best friend blamed "stress" for her son's serious stuttering problem. Betty sits alone—glass of wine in one hand, bag of caramels in the other—trying to understand stress, this diabolical force which has so disrupted her once happy, peaceful home. Little does she know that she is the latest victim.

What Is Stress?

Stress. You hear the word almost as often as you hear about inflation or the energy crisis. The problem is that the term *stress* is one of those imprecise words which is easily and often used, but not clearly understood. We hear about executive stress, college stress, homemaker's stress, and assembly line stress. The term regularly creeps into newspapers, magazines, television programs, and conversations. It seems that stress is more widespread than the common cold—but what *exactly* is it?

The concept of stress originated in physics and engineering, where it refers to physical forces and the ability to withstand strain. In this regard, stress is measured with relative precision. In bridge construction, for example, experts can calculate just how much stress a structure can take before trouble sets in. More recently, psychologists, sociologists, and medical practitioners have borrowed the term. However, in dealing with people, we have only begun to define what stress is and what it does. It is a much more complex term when applied to human beings—and while stress in engineering can be neatly measured, people react in a multitude of ways, depending upon their own perceptions and coping systems. Unlike a bridge, the human response is difficult to predict.

Stress is often thought of as tension, anxiety, burnout, frustration, pressure, or distress. It is blamed for temper tantrums, overeating, alcoholism, and acts of aggression. Everyone realizes that it can produce harmful effects on an individual, but they may not comprehend how or why.

In the late nineteenth century physiologists began preparing the foundation for the study of stress which was to follow. They suggested that man had an inner balance which had to be maintained. When changes occurred in the environment, the body made adjustments to bring things back into balance in order for the organism to remain healthy. In the 1930's an American named Walter B. Cannon termed this tendency to maintain a sort of equilibrium *homeostasis*. Then he took one additional giant step forward by presenting the "fight-or-flight response" as an explanation of the body's reaction to stress. It seems modern humanity has inherited a rather out-of-date response system of biological reactions to perceived threats. We react with the same patterns as did our primitive ancestors.

Today, as in prehistoric times, certain sights, sounds, smells, and situations serve as danger signals. In early times the signal might have come from a wild beast, while today it could come from the boss. A complicated series of events within the body's autonomic nervous system causes hormones to be released and chemical changes to occur which result in alterations in the normal state of the body. We have all experienced these changes. The heart beats faster and breathing speeds up, increasing the amount of oxygen consumed. Blood flow is directed to the brain and skeletal muscles, providing a sense of alertness and energy. The pupils of the eyes dilate, making them more light-sensitive. Even our hearing becomes keener. Our hands become sweaty, and we know we are aroused.

This stimulated condition was highly appropriate for our ancestors, facing an attacking wild animal, hostile neighbor, or rockslide. It enabled them to launch a vigorous attack or mount a speedy retreat.

In modern times this automatic response, often associated with anger or fear, is much less efficient. The situations we face rarely call for a fight-or-flight response. We can hardly engage in hand-to-hand combat with the surly plumber or run and hide when called upon to speak at school meetings. Nonetheless, inherited biological equipment prepares us for this means of coping. The normal body can tolerate these hormonal, chemical, and physical changes for short periods. Extended arousal of our fight-or-flight reaction can cause problems ranging from a mild headache to a heart attack.

Respected physician Hans Selye is often credited with borrowing the term *stress* from physics to refer to the human adjustment to danger signals. Dr. Selye was very interested in the body chemistry and physical changes that occur when an individual reacts to stress, and he conducted much of the earliest research on the subject. He defined stress as "the nonspecific response of the body to any demand," and as "the rate of wear and tear on the body." Selye wrote that stress was not necessarily unpleasant, and that pleasure could produce the same need for the body to make biochemical changes in order to readjust. For example, a passionate kiss may cause the same biochemical changes in the body as a spider bite. Selye termed this adjustment process the "general adaptation syndrome," in which the body defends itself against stress by certain adaptive reactions. After conducting very technical studies in which he measured the biochemical changes that accompany adapting to stress, he concluded that the defense of the body against stress-producing situations causes hormones that are normally in balance to work against each other. If this condition is prolonged, "adaptation diseases" result.[1]

More recent scholars in the field usually anchor their work in Selye's theories. However, most have adopted a wider definition of stress. Many contemporary stress-experts feel that Hans Selye's heavy emphasis on the stress reaction overlooks the extremely significant role of individual perceptions in the stress-provoking situation. They argue that the stress reaction is not automatic but is largely determined by the interpretation of the person involved. Consider the example of twins, Susan and Sara. They are seated in the same room. The telephone rings. Susan very naturally extends her arm to pick up the nearby receiver, hardly giving her action a thought. Sara instantly reacts with a tightness in the chest and pounding heart. Her hands become clammy and she begins to breathe rapidly. Unlike Susan, Sara perceives the ringing telephone as potentially threatening. Before leaving work she placed a letter of resignation on the desk of her employer of the past fifteen years. Sara expects him to return later in the day, read the letter, and phone to question her loyalty. The ringing telephone does not in itself produce stress. It is the interpretation of the event that is crucial.

Coming to Terms with Stress

One of the most confusing aspects of stress is keeping the terms straight. You know your child is troubled—but is it stress or distress? The teacher says it's anxiety—is that the same as fear? Your child seems angry—or should you call it being aggressive? You want your child to cope—unless having tolerance would be better. No doubt about it. Groping for exactly the right word can prove to be a real stressor (and what in the world is a stressor?). Stress, as previously discussed, occurs when the child experiences a situation that is perceived as threatening, thereby causing an internally triggered physical and emotional reaction. (The situation precipitating that reaction is called the stressor.) Total freedom from stress is impossible, and stress is actually vital to a healthy person. If it becomes uncontrollable, some experts say, stress has become distress. Often, however, the two terms are used interchangeably, with *stress* referring to the entire range of beneficial to harmful outcomes. This latter meaning will be the one used in this book.

The fight portion of the fight-or-flight response is reflected in anger. When the anger results in acts of hostility, these acts are called aggression. Anger is the emotional state—aggression is the outward display. Neither anger nor aggression is very effective in dealing with stress. The angry child is less apt to listen to reason. Constructive attempts to work out interpersonal conflicts usually fall by the wayside, and angry words and deeds can impart a sting more potent than intended. Unfortunately, sex-typing in our society imparts the impression that it is appropriate for males to react to stress with aggression. (This topic is explored more fully in Chapter Four.)

Anxiety is associated with the flight portion of the fight-or-flight response. An individual experiences anxiety when the evaluation of the stressful situation results in a sense of helplessness to prevent harm. The harm might involve physical injury, embarrassment, a blow to the ego or to emotional security. Anxiety is extremely hazardous. The child is not able to actually "flee" and may remain in a keyed-up condition, causing physical, social, and emotional deterioration over the long run.

Fear can translate into either the fight or the flight response, depending on the appraisal of the situation. If the child believes that it is possible to handle the threat, fear results in anger and aggression. However, if the threat is judged overwhelming, anxiety is the outcome.

Tolerance refers to just how much stress the child can keep under control before distress sets in. Tolerance is not fixed. Vulnerability to stress is determined by many factors, including personality type, age, state of general health, and recent dosages of stress and anxiety. Coping is an individualized process and involves a system of selectively controlling some stresses, while minimizing and preventing others.

Is Less Stress Best?

Many parents view stress the way they do sin—as something to be avoided. It is considered disagreeable, uncomfortable, and hazardous to one's health. In fact, stress is not always detrimental. Some stress is actually good. Controllable stress motivates and can increase creativity and productivity. For example, test taking is a notorious stress provoker. Stress prompts the student to study and can activate peak performance during the actual examination. Only if there is too much stress, and the student becomes overly anxious and is unable to prepare, or "blanks out" and forgets the answers, is there a problem. Hans Selye has pointed out that "complete freedom from stress is death." Suppose the impossible—that you were able to eliminate nearly all stress from your child's life. You would seriously retard the child's ego development. A world devoid of tension and pressure would be dull and would stifle all ambition. Consider a common situation: A preschooler just can't get a puzzle piece to fit. As the youngster becomes visibly stressed, some concerned adult rushes over and inserts the piece. At this point the child usually becomes perplexed. The stress is over. The puzzle piece is safe in its spot. Yet, somehow, the child doesn't quite feel satisfied and can't understand why. It is much more beneficial for children themselves to learn to control stress in gradually increasing amounts than it is to have stress-interference run by overzealous parents.

Recipe for Childhood Stress

Our recipe for childhood stress has four ingredients. We begin with the child. Every child is different—and in dealing with childhood stress, you must be thoroughly familiar with the child's individuality. Chapter Three tells how to plot your child's individuality profile. Next, a potentially stressful situation is introduced to the child's environment. The range of these possible stress provokers is enormous and many are often overlooked. A large portion of this book is concerned with getting potential stress producers out in the open and into full view. Third, the child must actually interpret the situation as being, in fact, threatening. And once the child makes such a determination, the fourth ingredient—the physical and emotional stress reaction—is biologically and chemically programmed into the child.

Warning Signs—Stress Alert

The warning signs that signal childhood stress can be compared to a smoke alarm in your home. Although you are alerted by the alarm in time to escape disaster, it would be far better to avoid the fire altogether. Signs of stress are easily spotted (a detailed list is given later in this chapter) and give notice to the parent that stress is already a problem and has become a destructive force affecting the health of mind and body. Parents who mistakenly assume that stress is under control until the telltale symptoms are evident delay in minimizing or eliminating stressors. It is much wiser to deal with stress before there is evidence of a problem, but if warning signs do appear, it means that something must be done immediately!

The first step in recognizing warning signs is to note the obvious. The following anecdote might help to make this point. In 1965 there was an unusual upset at the Los Angeles County hog calling contest. The contestants presented impressive calls—ranging from ''WHOOOooooooooeeeeeeeeee,'' to ''ERGH ERGH RRrkie.'' However, four-year-old John Magrich defeated nearly two dozen adults when he employed the rather obvious cry of ''Here, piggy, piggy,'' and six pigs walked right up.[2] Many parents have a tendency to overlook the obvious. They don't feel qualified to identify stress and feel ill-prepared to launch a coping campaign. As a result of this sense of helplessness they ignore their own potential and seek outside aid. I recall a speech I made in an affluent suburb on Chicago's North Shore. At the conclusion a woman approached the podium to ask if I could suggest a technique that would stop her preschool son from throwing sand in the toilet. I asked her if she had firmly laid down the law and told the child sand in the toilet was absolutely intolerable. The woman replied: "Why, no. I thought I had better get some professional advice. He seems so intent on throwing that sand in the toilet."

As a parent you have two qualifications that provide a great source of information concerning childhood stress and its effects. First, you yourself have experienced some childhood stresses. In interpreting your child's warning signs, rely on your own recollections of childhood. Try to slip into your child's way of thinking, feeling, and reacting, for although the world has changed—changing childhood with it—it is possible to vividly recapture many earlier emotions, values, and reactions. Consciously clear your mind and ask yourself questions, such as "How would I have responded to that situation when I was in Mrs. Turner's second grade?" or "How would I have felt had that happened to me when I was an eighth-grader?" Use the knowledge it took your whole childhood to acquire and don't forget to *ask* your child to describe what's happening. Many parents don't know how their children are reacting because they simply don't ask "How do you feel?" Second, when it comes to your child, *you* are the expert. No professional has had the opportunity to get to know your child that you have had. So, trust your common sense and don't ignore the obvious. Should you find, in some cases, that you are not able to empathize with your child's problems or assist in solutions, you might need professional assistance. But don't sell yourself short. You have a vital role to play in the prevention and management of stress in your child's life.

Following is a list of common childhood stress signals. It is normal for children to demonstrate a *few* of these characteristics at some period of their childhood. They can be symptomatic of typical growing pains or the process of wrestling with a temporarily troublesome problem. If, however, your child exhibits a number of the signs simultaneously, and the symptoms persist beyond an isolated frustrating or disappointing incident, suspect trouble. A number of signs, persisting over an extended period of time, and evident even when there is no apparent cause, usually signals that stress is becoming a threat to the well-being of the child.

Guard against overassigning these characteristics to your child. By the same token, a child who appears free from symptoms today might exhibit many of them within a short time span. I am reminded of one extremely conscientious mother. Each August she took her child for a complete physical which included a vision test, hearing examination, and dental checkup. When the child was given a good report, she mentally crossed off these possible problem areas. In early November the child was diagnosed as having sixty

WARNING SIGNS

Bed-wetting

Boasts of superiority

Complaints of feeling afraid or upset without being able to identify the source

Complaints of neck or back pains

Complaints of pounding heart

Complaints of stomach upset, queasiness, or vomiting

Compulsive cleanliness

Compulsive ear tugging, hair pulling, or eyebrow plucking

Cruel behavior toward people or pets

Decline in school achievement

Defiance

Demand for constant perfection

Depression

Dirtying pants

Dislike of school

Downgrading of self

Easily startled by unexpected sounds

Explosive crying

Extreme nervousness

Extreme worry

Frequent daydreaming and retreats from reality

Frequent urination or diarrhea

Headaches

Hyperactivity, or excessive tension or alertness

Increased number of minor spills, falls, and other accidents

Irritability

Listlessness or lack of enthusiasm

Loss of interest in activities usually approached with vigor

Lying

Nightmares or night terror

Nervous laughter

Nervous tics, twitches, or muscle spasms

Obvious attention-seeking

Overeating

Poor concentration

Poor eating

Poor sleep

Psychosomatic illnesses

Stealing

Stuttering

Teeth grinding (sometimes during sleep)

Thumb-sucking

Uncontrollable urge to run and hide

Unusual difficulty in getting along with friends

Unusual jealousy of close friends and siblings

Unusual sexual behavior, such as spying or exhibitionism

Unusual shyness

Use of alcohol, drugs, or cigarettes

Withdrawal from usual social activities

percent hearing loss in both ears, following a September infection. The mother was stunned and embarrassed at her failure to recognize what was wrong. She prided herself on the topnotch health care she provided. However, once she mentally eliminated hearing as a possible problem, she never considered it again until it was time for the yearly hearing test the following August. Freedom from stress today is obviously not a once-and-for-all matter. Do not, based upon current status, dismiss the long-range possibility of debilitating stress.

It's Just a Stage

In the process of normal development nature provides children with an opportunity to deal progressively with a variety of stressors. Each stage of development produces social and emotional changes that require the youngster to cope. Of course, all children are unique, and any chart of normal development is intended to serve as a rough guide, at best. The individual differences among children create wide variations, and it is perfectly normal for children to develop in advance of or at a slower rate than is suggested by the age levels. In addition, some stressors—such as parents' divorce, death of a loved one, personal illness, or a family move—affect children at any age.

Following are some typical sources of stress experienced at each stage of development. It is important to note that some of the stressors listed begin at one age level and continue for a number of years. For example, a two-year-old child begins resisting parent influence in order to demonstrate independence. This behavior continues throughout childhood. Conflict among friends also begins at about two years old and continues throughout life. Differences in temperament (discussed in Chapter Three) also influence the intensity with which a child demonstrates a typical childhood trait, such as negativism.

It is important for parents to view the difficult aspects of each stage of development as a learning experience for the child. As the child grows and matures, valuable coping skills are gained.

Sources of Stress for the Two-Year-Old:

- Negativism—doesn't like to take orders; may be downright contrary
- Rigidity—wants own way; is upset when rituals are disrupted; dislikes interference
- Lack of sociability—engages in solitary or parallel play but is generally disinterested in socializing

- Self-centeredness—believes the world revolves around her or him; doesn't want to share; may dawdle
- Separation anxiety—fears loss of parents
- Stranger anxiety—fears strangers; is shy
- Toilet training
- Bedtime—dislikes being ordered to bed; may fear bed-wetting or separation from parents; may have terrifying dreams
- Tantrums—may revert to temper tantrums or destructive behavior; may hit or bite
- Security object—may have a security object that, if lost or misplaced, leads to great emotional upset
- Overdoing—may become overstimulated or overtired
- Fears—in particular, may include animals or anything that makes a loud noise
- Hospitalization—may prove especially stressful at this age
- Doctors—visits to the pediatrician may prove extremely stressful

Sources of Stress for the Three-Year-Old:

- Infantile behavior—reverts to babyish ways; can't completely let go of babyhood
- Stubbornness—although the child is developing an interest in social relationships and a concept of "we," the child may lapse into uncooperative behavior
- Possessiveness—guards belongings and may be bossy about them
- Jealousy—particularly when it comes to parents' love
- Separation anxiety
- Stranger anxiety
- Confusion—can't always discriminate between fantasy and reality
- White lies—may result from wishful thinking, fantasy, and desire to please or impress
- Imaginary playmate—often blamed in the white lies
- Fears—may be precipitated by imagination; may also fear dogs or other animals
- Speech—may stutter or stumble over words
- Activity level—seems to be in perpetual motion; may exhaust himself or herself

- Toilet accidents
- Eating—may forget to eat or lose interest in food
- Nap or bedtime—may fear bad dreams, the dark, or missing out on some fun while asleep
- Destructiveness—may enjoy wrecking or destroying
- Questions—continually asks "why," and is upset if trusted adults do not respond or do not know the answer

Sources of Stress for the Four-Year-Old:

- Insecurity—may develop nervous habits such as nail biting, facial tic, thumb-sucking, genital manipulation, eye-blinking, or nose-picking; may insist on bringing a familiar item from home to preschool
- Exaggerations—may attempt to boost self-image with boasts
- Companionship—enjoys interacting with friends, although there may be many quarrels
- Silliness—tends to engage in rambunctious, silly play; likes words and is fascinated by rhyming syllables or foul language; is disciplined for lack of control
- Property rights—protects belongings; may become bossy
- Sex—interested in the human body; may engage in exhibitionism
- Activity level—enjoys running, jumping, and slamming doors; may be punished for disruptive behavior
- Fears—picks up fears from adults; may fear dark room, snakes and lizards, or anything perceived as "creepy"
- Attention—likes to talk and is frustrated if ignored or put off; whines to get own way

Sources of Stress for the Five-Year-Old:

- Approval—parents' love and acceptance are vital; seeks praise
- School—may have difficulty adjusting to kindergarten
- Separation anxiety—particularly fears loss of mother
- Infantile behavior—may occasionally lapse into babyish behavior as a result of realizing that babyhood is ended
- Worrying—may develop irrational fears, take information out of context, or fret over a misinterpreted, overheard conversation
- Masturbation—is concerned about being "bad"

- Belongings—protects possessions
- Showing off—performs in order to gain praise
- Procrastination—may dillydally now and then
- Name calling—insults others to boost self-image, but is upset when she or he is the victim of mockery

Sources of Stress for the Six-Year-Old:

- Expectations—parents, teachers, and other adults begin to demand more
- School—first grade introduces the child to the more formal, academic setting; it may be the child's first experience away from home all day
- Activity level—may find it difficult to sit still for long periods of time; may have frequent accidents, such as spilling milk
- Competition—the child wants to be "first" or best
- Shyness—may initially be shy in a new situation, but usually recovers quickly
- Aggression—may become hostile or aggressive; temper tantrums peak
- Sensitivity—begins to read body language or facial expressions and becomes upset when disapproval is sensed
- Teasing—engages in teasing, but becomes upset when on the receiving end
- Decisions—has difficulty coping with increasing independence
- Jealousy—sibling rivalry is common
- Fears—usually center around newly found independence and might include fear of getting lost or fear of making an embarrassing social blunder

Sources of Stress for the Seven-Year-Old:

- Moodiness—is often moody, unhappy, or pensive
- Approval—continues the need for praise and approval from peer group and parents
- Modesty—demands privacy when in the bathroom or dressing
- Organization—is comfortable with rules, regulations, routines, and order; becomes upset when they are disrupted

- Interruptions—hates to be disturbed when intensely involved in an activity
- Idols—has a desire to be more like an admired idol
- Friendships—becomes more selective about playmates

Sources of Stress for the Eight-Year-Old:

- Self criticism—is very critical of personal ability and performance
- Parental authority—is beginning to resent parental authority
- Loneliness—likes frequent interaction with friends; may hate to miss school
- Praise—continues to seek approval but can identify when praise is not genuine
- Independence—may begin to stay alone for brief periods of time while parents run errands, with resulting feelings of uneasiness

Sources of Stress for the Nine-Year-Old:

- Rebelliousness—occasionally tests independence by rebelling
- Opposite Sex—engages in sex-segregated play; expresses an aversion to the opposite sex
- Fair play—has a keen sense of what is fair and is vehement in demanding personal rights when a situation is perceived as unfair
- Interruptions—continues to dislike interruptions but will usually resume an activity after an interruption
- Propriety—has a sense of propriety and will often be upset if siblings or parents offend the child's notion of decorum or dignity

Sources of Stress for the Ten- to Twelve-Year-Olds:

- Sexual maturation—girls, in particular, may become self-conscious regarding obvious signs of development
- Social issues—a new level of awareness can generate concern regarding pressing societal problems
- Size—both boys and girls may be upset by the fact that the girls are taller; the extremely small or extremely large child may be concerned about his or her size
- Shyness—if the child already has a problem in this area, it is likely to become more pronounced at this stage

- Opposite Sex—may become interested, yet shy, around members of the opposite sex
- Confusion—too much freedom can cause the child to flounder
- Health—it is not uncommon for a child to become a hypochondriac during this period of development
- Money—child is anxious to earn and handle money, but often uses poor judgment
- Competition—continues to be highly competitive and looks to peer group for prestige
- Burnout—may become vigorously involved in so many activities that the child finally becomes exhausted
- Self-concept—may engage in teasing, scapegoating, or vicious attacks to temporarily boost his or her self-image; guilt often ensues; may be self-conscious about attempting a new skill
- Parents—often becomes highly critical or intolerant of parents
- Idols—continues hero-worshipping
- Fair play—continues to have a highly developed sense of fair play
- Drugs and Sex—may be tempted to experiment with drugs or sex because everyone is doing it
- Peer pressure—becomes a powerful motivating force
- Self-criticism—child may be highly critical of personal performance

The preceding list is far from complete, but it does highlight a few of the more common potential stressors at each age level. The following pages will deal with many of those listed, as well as some associated with crises of modern times.

Guaranteed to Produce Stress

The parent is highly instrumental in the formation of a child's self-image and value system, both of which influence the child's interpretation of a stressful situation as being actually threatening. In an informative book entitled *Stress, Sanity, and Survival,* Robert Woolfolk and Frank Richardson discuss some basic perceptions that can lead to adult stress.[3] Many parents unwittingly preach a doctrine loaded with similar beliefs to their children. Following is the childhood version of common stress-producing adult beliefs:

**Doctrine 1:
I'm not as
good as
everyone
else, and I
never will
be.**

Children are not born with a self-image. They learn about themselves and their worth through the accumulated impressions they receive from others. The reactions of people to them are like a mirror—reflecting back important information about the self. If the child is constantly told: "Bad girl! Don't ever touch that again. No, no, no," she begins to believe that she *is* bad and that many of the objects in her environment are more valuable than she is. In Chapter Five specific techniques for enhancing self-image and improving a negative self-concept are suggested. At this point suffice it to say that the child who doesn't like him or herself is not a happy child. The child probably won't like many people—including parents, teachers, and authority figures—and will probably do poorly in school. Feelings of inferiority are guaranteed to produce stress, since basic self-esteem is constantly in a state of attack.

**Doctrine 2:
It's not how
you play
the game;
it's whether
you win or
lose.**

Ambition and competition are fine—better for some children than for others. But children who grow up experiencing constant pressure to be "best" or to "win" are under constant stress. No one can always be on top. The parent who continually bombards children with questions such as "Who made the top grade on the test?" or "How many points did you score? Were you the high-scorer?" or "Why did you stop reading? There is still an hour before bed. Don't you want to win the reading contest, again?" is making impossible demands. Children become stressed when they don't always win. They may worry because they don't even care about perpetual success. They feel there must be something wrong with them—since ambition and competition are not only part of their parents' dream, but also part of the American ideal. Your child's daily life shouldn't be like the Olympics, with one competitive event after another in which self-image is at stake.

**Doctrine 3:
You owe**

In an effort to develop a sense of responsibility, some parents exaggerate the child's commitment

me . . . and Grandma, and your coach, and your sister, and your music teacher, and . . . and . . . and . . .

to a huge number of people. Many of these commitments are real and important. However, children are not capable of an infinite number of demanding relationships. Moreover, many of these "commitments" are not nearly so crucial as the child is taught to believe. For example, missing Great-grandma's eightieth birthday in favor of attending an NFL football game might, indeed, violate a child's commitment to Grandma. However, "letting the scoutmaster down" by not attending a meeting in favor of the football game could be an exaggeration. Close relationships are bound to create stress. They are accompanied by a certain vulnerability. Sometimes the parent has led the child to imagine that the child is closer, or owes more, to someone than is actually true. When the second party in the relationship does not demonstrate the same closeness, the child experiences hurt, rejection, disappointment, and stress.

Doctrine 4: Stress is noble. Noble deeds cause stress.

Children imitate their parents. The parent serves as a model for many types of behavior, including coping. If the parent tells the child through word or example that virtuous behavior and good deeds create stress, or that worry which generates stress is noble, you can expect the child to react similarly. For example, every time Mom is involved in a charity project or "good works," she acts as if she is doing something at great personal expense and under great stress. Her children may wind up thinking that stress is a natural part of doing good. Likewise, some parents think that worry is a good way to prevent problems. Consider Dad, who insists on checking, rechecking, and triple-checking every detail prior to a vacation. His unnecessary thoroughness results in great stress, but Dad gives the impression that the stress is part of a productive, precautionary measure. In either case, preventable stress is the result.

Doctrine 5: The world's all wrong,

There is no doubt that the world is not in the best condition. However, some parents spend inordinate amounts of time dwelling on what's wrong in

**and it af-
fects you
personally.**

society. They show their children that they are unhappy, frustrated, and powerless to do much about
it. Their stress is evident, and children internalize
the tendency to take too much personally.

**Doctrine 6:
. . . and I
expect the
same from
you.**

No two human beings are exactly alike, and while
most parents give lip service to accepting their
children as individuals, in practice it is not the case.
Subconsciously, parents expect children to live up
to the same standards that they, as well as older
siblings, met. In some cases it simply is not possible. The child is doomed at the start. There is no
way the expectations can be met. Self-esteem is
naturally threatened, and the child experiences a
preventable stress.

**Doctrine 7:
You de-
serve a
break to-
day.**

Everyone wants their children to have the best.
However, children who grow up believing that they
deserve the best of everything—with little personal
expenditure—are destined for stress. No one has
the inherent right to be entirely happy, comfortable, and satisfied. These needs must be met
through work. The child who regards life's little
setbacks as a personal affront will walk the earth
with a perennial chip on the shoulder.

**Doctrine 8:
There is
nothing you
cannot do.**

Children need self-confidence and faith in their own
abilities. However, there is a realistic limit beyond
which a child cannot achieve. Parents who create
an inflated concept of what is actually possible are
preparing the child for a painful fall—which might
permanently damage the child's self-concept. One
warning: Most children are capable of far more than
we expect or demand. The wise parent must know
when enough is enough, something much easier
said than done.

**Doctrine 9:
"You and
me against
the world."**

The home should be a place where the child is
totally accepted and loved. It should be warm, safe,
and secure. The emotionally healthy child experiences the closeness of family and home without
becoming overdependent. If the child begins to put
all the eggs in the home basket, and is unable to

find fulfillment in people and situations away from the family, stress is bound to occur. The home and family are an important part of life, but other aspects of existence should also have something to offer. The family does not make the child happy. The child finds happiness within himself or herself.

Doctrine 10: Look out for number one. The past ten years have witnessed a tremendous surge in self-interest. You have to look out for yourself. A positive self-image, concern about physical and mental health, and opportunities to enjoy leisure are one thing. Selfishness is another. The "me-generation" philosophy has dangerous implications. Children need to believe in the importance of things beyond themselves—such as relationships, religion, or commitment.

Doctrine 11: This too shall pass. The stresses of life are never-ending. It is stress-provoking to teach children that if they wait and are patient, stresses will finally subside. Coping is a daily part of life and doesn't end until life does.

Will Your Child Be a Victim or a Victor?

Beth has just returned from morning kindergarten. She enters the house exhausted, but happy to be home and away from the first- and second-graders who tease the younger children as a matter of policy. She quickly goes to her blocks and begins to build a city. Beth had tried to construct a city that morning during free play, but the other children kept using the blocks she needed. Just a few more blocks and her masterpiece will be complete. Suddenly disaster strikes. Eleven-month-old Jason toddles over and laughingly collapses in the center of town. Beth explodes, screaming and kicking the blocks all over the floor. She runs to her room, throws herself on her bed, and weeps. Mother attempts to soothe her, saying: "Now, Beth, you know Jason didn't mean it. You must be nice to him. Jason was sent to us from heaven." Beth looks her mother squarely in the eye and with surprising calm replies: "Jason wasn't sent. They kicked him out."

Exasperated little Beth is facing but one in a lifelong series of stressful situations. Every individual experiences the stress and strain of daily living. Beth, as well as your child, will grow up in a world marked by the most rapid change in history. Growing up has never been easy, but it has never been harder than in today's society. Children face stressors everywhere. Parents and friends cause stress. Teachers cause stress. Your child spends approximately thirty hours per week in school, and one study has reported that as many as three million children are assigned to classrooms in which the teachers are so emotionally disturbed that they should not be around children. Air, noise, and water pollution all contribute to stress, as can diet, television, moving, or changes in family structure. The body is constantly experiencing some sort of stress.

There were, of course, stressors a hundred years ago. Illness, failing crops, and poverty were recurring threats. However, the culture of the time was relatively fixed. People learned early in life exactly what their role was to be. The blacksmith's son grew up and took over the family business. His wife had a full-time job caring for the home and family in the absence of labor-saving devices. Individuals were born to a station in life, accepted it, and worked hard to fulfill their role. Current society transmits a new set of values to young people. The self-made executive is admired, and youth are taught to compete and overcome difficulties, rather than to accept them. There is social pressure to keep up with the Joneses more often than to help them, and I ask you, who would watch a setting sun when there is television?

Family structures, male-female roles, and confidence in government, business, and religion have changed. Your children cannot even be certain that their offspring will have clean air, safe water, or adequate energy.

The Turks have a holiday when for one entire week children are allowed to eat all the candy they want to. No one tells them when they've had enough. Many of them learn the hard way, by becoming ill. In some households the situation with childhood stress is much like the candy holiday in Turkey. Children make coping decisions on their own and engineer their own coping system. Considering what we already know about coping and what knowledge is available from experts, does it make sense for our children to reinvent the wheel? A well-rounded education should include coping skills. Nevertheless, even the most conscientious parents, who dutifully monitor their children's progress in school and spend hours each week driving them to a multitude of extra lessons and recreational activities, do little to ease the coping process.

Pause for a moment to reconsider your child-raising priorities. There is no doubt that the lessons and events you program into your child's life build important intellectual, motor, and social skills. But ask yourself, isn't it equally important to raise your child to cope with stress?

Chapter Two

Be a Coping Parent

Coping is a skill parents teach children—directly and indirectly. However, it is hard to be an effective teacher if you are ineffective in dealing with your own stress. If stress in your life is galloping unchecked, it can adversely affect your physical and emotional health. In addition, it is contagious, and one family member's stress can play havoc with the entire household. A parent suffering stress overload is often in a helpless condition and unable to fully meet the needs of offspring. This lack of effectiveness is particularly noticeable in the failure to provide an indirect, imitable coping model, or to offer more direct, concrete guidance and suggestions for dealing with everyday childhood stresses. Understanding your own methods for coping is vital in teaching children coping skills that enable them to face the inevitable stresses of childhood and to grow with them.

We have seen that stress is not all bad. Too little stress can produce dissatisfaction, low self-esteem, fatigue, boredom, or even illness. Consider the many lonely senior citizens, who live out their lives in a state of greatly reduced stress. On the other hand, many individuals in our society remain in a prolonged or chronic state of intense stress. They suffer illnesses, exhaustion, depression, irrational thinking, and even death. Somehow we must find the middle ground between these two extremes, where we are able to handle stress and use it to our best advantage. We are then well equipped to help our children.

In this chapter you will have an opportunity to examine the stress in your own life, as well as the personality traits that make you more vulnerable to stress's ill effects. Finally, approaches for reducing and coping with parent stress are offered.

Let's Clear the Air

In order to assure that your underlying attitude is not tainted, there are a few common falsehoods which merit debunking:

Fallacy: It's a jungle out there, and individuals occupied outside the home are more susceptible to stress than those sheltered at home.

Fact: Stress is a real threat to everyone. Housewives, in particular, have a high vulnerability because of the unrelenting demands of their life-style.

Fallacy: New, inexperienced parents face more parental stress than parents with years of seniority.

Fact: Stress is a personal reaction to an intricately inter-woven set of variables. Brand-new parents might actually experience much less stress than parents with older children, each of whom is generating a unique set of problems.

Fallacy: Admitting that stress gets you down is a sign of weakness.

Fact: Parents who refuse to admit that stress is becoming a debilitating force begin to lose control. They are not only hurting themselves, but probably con-tributing to a stressful home environment, while simultaneously failing to assist their children in coping. Acknowledging stress is not synonymous with failure as a parent. It is a sign of self-aware-ness and concern for your children.

Fallacy: Stress is a big-city problem.

Fact: Although urban living undoubtedly has stress-pro-voking potential, suburban and rural settings also have stress-generating capability. Remember, stress is a personal response which cannot be generalized by locale.

Fallacy: If you are basically a nervous person, there is little you can do to reduce or control stress.

Fact: Understanding your patterns of behavior, stress re-actions, and coping system can enable you to live more effectively.

Fallacy: Once you learn to control stress, the ability gen-eralizes to all areas of your life.

Fact: Stressors must be tackled one by one. For example, learning to deal with the stress of entertaining at home does not automatically transfer to meeting deadlines at work. However, the knowledge that you were able to control stress in one area might give you the incentive to keep trying.

Fallacy: You can rise above stress.

Fact: Stress is an unavoidable part of life. You can learn to prevent, reduce, and cope with it. Sometimes when you think you "really have it together," you might find yourself lapsing back into patterns of behavior you thought you had changed. Don't dismay—keep plugging away.

Fallacy: You have to go it alone.

Fact: If you are determined to improve your effectiveness in dealing with stress, ask those most near and dear for their assistance, understanding, and support. Unexplained sudden changes in your behavior might even be cause for their concern.

What Kind of Person Are You?

Even the most casual observer of human characteristics can easily spot major differences in behavior patterns. Some individuals are identified as movers or dynamos, while others earn the label of easygoing or even-tempered. Researchers have classified these two extremes as types A and B and have attempted to relate behavior type to stress, heart attacks, and illness.

During stress, the hypothalamus triggers the autonomic nervous system, which controls metabolism and usually keeps the body in balance, or equilibrium. The stress reaction causes the autonomic nervous system to speed up heartbeat, slow down digestion, and stimulate the pituitary and thyroid glands to release hormones. These hormones cause an increase in blood pressure, metabolism, and level of blood sugar. In addition, adrenaline and noradrenaline are released, which prepare the body to handle emergencies by stimulating the cardiovascular system. Since the stress reaction is accompanied with increases in both cholesterol level and heart rate, many physicians conclude that chronic stress increases the risk of heart disease. The immune system is also impaired by the release of hormones under stress, and the individual becomes more susceptible to bacteria and viruses.

The following descriptions portray the classical type A and type B personalities:

Case study:
Type A

Fran Jeffrey sometimes reminds you of a movie in fast-forward. She moves quickly, eats in a hurry, and has ritualistic habits which govern the route she drives to work and the way she organizes her desk each morning. She often does two things at once, such as talking on the telephone while reading her mail. Fran seems driven by a desire to accomplish more and more in less and less time. She feels guilty when she is doing nothing. Fran is highly competitive and has a history of achievement in academics and past employment. She sets high standards and demanding goals and usually brings her work home. Fran is competent, but her impatience and short fuse are legendary. She is always rushed, and even when her head is pounding, and she is obviously fatigued, Fran keeps going.

Case Study:
Type B

Jim Janus is a very intelligent fellow. Although his grades in college were respectable, he never earned honors. It didn't seem to bother him, either. Jim is ambitious, but you'd have to work closely with him for quite a while to notice. He is a steady worker and rarely irritates anyone. Jim seldom takes work home. He loves to garden and watch sporting events. Jim takes things one at a time. His colleagues always understand his directions and experience a sense of confidence working closely with him. Jim Janus is very flexible and accepts change easily.

Evidence indicates that when type A's face the frustration of a highly stressful situation that they cannot control, they stand a greater risk of heart attack than type B's in a similar situation. Certainly, not all type A individuals will suffer a heart attack. However, stress generated from disagreeable life experiences can have a cumulative effect resulting in poor physical and emotional health.

Although a professional interview technique is necessary to determine behavior type, the following questionnaire can assist you in spotting typical type A traits. Check each statement that applies to your behavior more often than not.

TYPE A OR TYPE B? ANSWER AND SEE

_____ 1. It is difficult for me to relax after a hard day.

_____ 2. I love competition and want to win.

_____ 3. People who know me think I have a short fuse.

_____ 4. I often do two things at once, such as scanning reading material while on the phone or at a meeting.

_____ 5. I hate to wait in line and soon become restless or impatient.

_____ 6. I have been told, or suspect, that I eat too fast.

_____ 7. I usually spend at least fifty hours per week working on matters related to my employment.

_____ 8. I often take less than my allotted vacation time.

_____ 9. I often set deadlines for myself.

_____ 10. I sometimes experience irrational rage over minor frustrations, such as a cabinet door that won't open or a knot in my chain necklace.

_____ 11. I am usually punctual for appointments.

_____ 12. I am prone to talk business at social gatherings.

_____ 13. Most of my friends are business-related.

_____ 14. I hate to be kept waiting.

_____ 15. I usually make detailed plans for vacations and trips— laying out a specific itinerary.

_____ 16. My hobbies and leisure activities are carefully organized.

_____ 17. Either currently or in the past, I have worked more than one job.

_____ 18. I frequently stay up late or get up early to accomplish more.

_____ 19. I am often irritated if someone interrupts me when I am in the middle of something.

_____ 20. I sometimes fill in words or thoughts for others while in conversations simply to move the discussion along.

_____ 21. I always seem to be in a hurry.

_____ 22. People who know me think I have an extra supply of energy.

_____ 23. I have been advised to relax or slow down.

_____ 24. I seem accident-prone.

_____ 25. I have a tendency to accumulate things but rarely seem to have the time to use or enjoy them.

_____ 26. I have strong opinions on most subjects.

_____ 27. I often take on my limit of projects (or even more).

_____ 28. I talk rapidly.

_____ 29. I rarely have enough time to keep up on my reading.

_____ 30. I use gestures and strong inflections in my speech.

_____ 31. I don't have many hobbies or outside interests.

_____ 32. I seek recognition.

_____ 33. When I tackle any job, I feel compelled to make it a success.

_____ 34. I hate to waste time.

_____ 35. I sometimes feel work causes me to neglect my family.

If you checked fifteen or more of the statements above, you are likely to be a type A person. The characteristics listed are not all bad. In fact, most people demonstrate at least five or six. The real significance of this exercise is to make you aware that a large number of type A behaviors usually translates to a genuine health hazard. In addition, many of the behaviors are also associated with workaholism, in particular the last trait.

Workaholics have allowed work to become the dominant force in their lives. They no longer maintain a healthy balance. The problem of workaholism becomes even more serious when it creates a phantom parent. Childhood is short and children need warm, close, daily interaction with real, here-and-now parents.

Do You Know Stress When You See It?

Connie Martin glanced nervously at the clock. Her six-year-old daughter, Vickie, was twenty minutes late arriving home from school. Vickie had never been late before, but Connie resisted the temptation to panic. "She probably stopped to play," thought Connie. "No need to get alarmed." But when Vickie was nearly forty-five minutes late, Connie was really concerned. She phoned the homes of the children with whom Vickie usually walked. None of the children remembered seeing her daughter. Connie decided to walk the route between home and school. She returned home frightened—she had found no trace of Vickie. Connie called the school and the principal contacted Vickie's first-grade teacher, who reported the girl had left school on time, with her class. By now Vickie was over an hour and a half late, and the principal urged Connie to notify the police. She took the principal's advice and two officers arrived at the Martin home within minutes. The officers were extremely concerned and told Connie that a suspicious car had been reported near the school. Connie's heart began to pound; she became weak in the knees and collapsed in tears on the sofa. When the officer went to comfort her, he could hear Connie breathing rapidly and noticed that her hands were clammy. Time dragged endlessly as the Martin family waited for news. Suddenly the doorbell rang, and Connie rushed to answer it. There stood a muddy little Vickie with the two officers. It seemed she had stopped to peek into the basement window of a new home under construction and accidentally dropped her school bag into the basement. She enterprisingly found a long stick, stretched through the window to hook the bag, leaned too far, and toppled in. Once inside, she was trapped until the police found her—cold and crying. When Connie saw Vickie, her heart began to pound; she became weak in the knees and collapsed in tears on the sofa. When Vickie ran to the sofa, she could hear her mother breathing rapidly and noticed that her hands were clammy.

Connie's physical reaction to the fear of her child's disappearance was nearly identical to the joy of her safe return. Pleasant and unpleasant situations generate similar stress reactions. Drs. Thomas Holmes and Richard Rahe, psychiatrists at the University of Washington Medical School, developed a well-known rating scale which gives weighted value to common pleasant, as well as unpleasant, stressors. They then established a correlation between one's score on their rating scale and the possibility of becoming ill within the next two-year period with anything from a common cold, to colitis, or even heart attack. The probability of illness determined by this scale is amazingly accurate. However, I believe that rating oneself according to this scale serves an even more useful purpose by clearly focusing on the many diverse sources of stress individuals face in the course of ordinary existence and what their effect can be. To obtain your own rating, simply circle the value points for any event which you have experienced within the last year.

Add all values circled to find your total score of Life Change Units. Research indicates the following possibility of illness, based on your score:

SOCIAL READJUSTMENT RATING SCALE[1]

Rank	Life event	[Life Change Units] LCU value
1.	Death of spouse	100
2.	Divorce	73
3.	Marital separation	65
4.	Jail term	63
5.	Death of close family member	63
6.	Personal injury or illness	53
7.	Marriage	50
8.	Fired from job	47
9.	Marital reconciliation	45
10.	Retirement	45
11.	Change in health of family member	44
12.	Pregnancy	40
13.	Sex difficulties	39
14.	Gain of new family member	39
15.	Business readjustment	39
16.	Change in financial state	38
17.	Death of close friend	37
18.	Change to different line of work	36
19.	Change in number of arguments with spouse	35
20.	Mortgage or loan for major purchase (home, etc.)	31
21.	Foreclosure of mortgage or loan	30
22.	Change in responsibilities at work	29
23.	Son or daughter leaving home	29
24.	Trouble with in-laws	29
25.	Outstanding personal achievement	28
26.	Wife begins or stops work	26
27.	Begin or end school	26
28.	Change in living conditions	25
29.	Revision of personal habits	24
30.	Trouble with boss	23
31.	Change in work hours or conditions	20
32.	Change in residence	20
33.	Change in schools	20
34.	Change in recreation	19
35.	Change in church activities	19
36.	Change in social activities	18
37.	Mortgage or loan for lesser purchase (car, TV, etc.)	17

SOCIAL READJUSTMENT RATING SCALE[1]

Rank	Life event	[Life Change Units] LCU value
38.	Change in sleeping habits	16
39.	Change in number of family get-togethers	15
40.	Change in eating habits	15
41.	Vacation	13
42.	Christmas	12
43.	Minor violations of the law	11

SCORING: ____

149 points or less	thirty-seven percent chance of illness in the next two years
150 to 299 points	fifty-one percent chance of illness in the next two years
300 points or more	eighty percent chance of illness in the next two years

Can You Cope with 437 Questions a Day?

Parents cope daily with an assortment of varied stressors which includes their own children to a large degree. Stress is as natural a part of parenthood as warming bottles or taking temperatures. Physical stress begins before the baby is born and continues during the many years of providing care—day and night. However, even more significant are the emotional stresses. Children usually change the nature of many of the parents' relationships. Husband and wife may not find time for the intense intimacy once shared. One spouse may become jealous of the bond forming between the other parent and child. Employment may also be influenced. If a parent quits a job in order to provide child care, a decline in self-worth may emerge. Having children also influences adult friendships for better or worse. During a baby's infancy many parents find they don't have time for socializing or money for a baby-sitter. Sometimes mothers form a new type of friendship with their mother or other relative, who is able to provide care and expert advice. As children mature, parents find themselves thrust into social situations with parents of their children's friends. Old friendships gradually fade. Parents also experience stress associated with their perceptions of the overwhelming responsibility of parenting. It is frightening to realize that you will play a highly significant role in shaping your child's future. When the child is under stress, parents may be stressed by the frustration of wanting to help but of being unable to do so. It is difficult to watch your child trying futilely to cope.

Children themselves are stressors. Consider the wear and tear generated by the average four-year-old, who asks 437 questions a day. Parents with older children are not immune—children as young as ten or eleven can enter early adolescence, with changes in disposition that make this childhood stage most trying. Daily stress can contribute to radical mood swings in children of any age. They are confronted by peer pressure, conflicting moral standards, and the urgency to grow up faster than nature intended. Their confusion is reflected in ups and downs which are impossible to predict and difficult to tolerate. It is not easy to cope with rebellion, rage, disrespect, or carelessness—especially when they are interpreted as evidence of parenting failure or a foreboding indication that the child is "off the track" and headed for trouble. There is no doubt about it—children have substantial stress-generating potential, which is reflected in parent anger, frustration, and worry.

If you have ever muttered under your breath, "I'm going to kill that kid," felt the steady buildup of parenting pressure until you thought you were going to explode, or lashed out at your child, only to regret it later—welcome to the club. You would be an unusual parent had you never reacted in any of these ways. It comes as no surprise—the "normal" child often seems rather abnormal. The most innocent laugh, mimicked from Sesame Street's Ernie or Mr. Kotter's Arnold, can cause teeth grinding in the parent who is listening to it for the eightieth time. While there is no substitute for the ultimate calm you experience when all the children are tucked safely in bed, it is often accompanied by guilt at the dislike or resentment you experienced during the day. As one anxious mother put it: "Sometimes I really scare myself. Every once in a while I find myself thinking, I can understand how some parents abuse a child."

Effective coping with your children is important for the health and happiness of the entire family. It yields a less stressful home life. It also provides children with an imitable model which eases the stresses of childhood and ultimately contributes to successful adjustment as an adult. For example, psychologists have found that an alarming number of children who are abused by parents unable to cope later resort to child abuse themselves.

Stress Fitness Program

Coping with the typical stresses of adult life, as well as with the special parenting stresses, is difficult. One government study has estimated that seventy-five percent of the visits to family doctors are related to unrelieved stress. Stress is a precipitating and sustaining factor in the high blood pressure that affects forty million Americans. Some experts believe that the women of today are more stressed than men, as a result of their diverse range of responsibilities—ranging from motherhood to employment. Keep yourself in shape for handling stress by:

1. Getting enough exercise.
2. Eating three healthy, well-balanced meals a day. Reduce intake of coffee, tea, and other stimulants that provide short bursts of energy, and drink six to eight glasses of water per day instead.
3. Drinking no more than an average of two alcoholic drinks per day, but no more than four in any one day.
4. Keeping your weight at the suggested level.
5. Breaking the smoking habit.
6. Getting enough sleep each night.
7. Not letting stress build up. Vent your anger and emotions so the slate is clear. Unresolved stress can intensify new stressors. Find someone you trust to confide in.
8. Going on strike and taking time for yourself.
9. Paying attention to the stress signals your body sends you, such as a headache or upset stomach, and slowing down.
10. Taking time to relax, *especially* when it seems you're too busy to take a break. Learn a relaxation technique that works for you. (See last chapter.)
11. Accepting that which you are incapable of changing.
12. Programming success into your life by establishing realistic goals and organizing your life.
13. Walking—not running—through life. Force yourself to think positive thoughts, listen to others, enjoy a hobby, and drive the speed limit.

. . . And They Lived Happily Ever After

In many instances parents intensify their stress in their effort to live up to a fairy tale notion of what an ideal parent should be. The exemplar exists solely in the minds of adults determined that their children will have nothing but the best, particularly when it comes to parents. They tackle their new career as a parent with a firm commitment to do everything just right and according to their ideal model. However, in short order they realize they are not living up to their prototype. They begin to experience stress and turmoil resulting from a sense of being out of control. Parenting is genuinely one of the most important components of their lives. "How then," they question, "is it possible to keep goofing the whole thing up?" The easiest, most direct means for reducing the stress associated with raising children is to weed out impossible parenting goals that keep parents in a stressful cycle of unfulfilled striving, failure, and unrealistic determination to do better. Trying to be a perfect parent is as futile as vowing never again to fall behind in your work. Following is a list of the more common stress-producing ideals:

There is a set of rules to follow in raising children.

Just as you can't learn to play tennis by reading a book, you can't raise children by following a list of rules in some book. The so-called rules in this volume, or any other, are meant to serve as guidelines, tempered by your own experience, common sense, and good judgment. Books can provide carefully researched child development findings, valuable insights, and worthwhile suggestions. However, experience remains the best teacher.

There is one right answer for every problem.

All parents, including child care experts, experience the frustration and uncertainty of not knowing the best way to handle occasional troublesome situations. In some cases it is impossible to know, since there are important variables that are unknown or yet to emerge. Don't worry about attaining perfection. A mistake here and there won't hopelessly damage your child. Children need a model of real parents, rather than perfect parents, and real people rely on instincts, make mistakes, and recover from them.

Coping with children is entirely different from coping with adults.

Coping with your children involves the same basic process as coping with adults. The key ingredients are mutual understanding, communication, and a continuous effort to maintain and improve the close relationship. If you rely on confrontation coping, someone is always a loser. When dealing with your children ask yourself, "Would I treat an adult in a similar fashion?" Children need, and are entitled to, respect, information, and the right to express themselves. When adults face problems with other adults, they usually attempt to work them out in a mutually satisfying manner. Yet it is not unusual for parents to bark commands and demands with no explanation whatsoever. Children are not second-class citizens. I am concerned when adults adopt a double standard when it comes to treatment of children. For example, if an adult accidentally knocked some papers off a co-worker's desk, retrieval of the papers and an apology would certainly be in order. However, I have witnessed adults in the same situation with children, their only response being a harsh "Well, pick them up!" You are a model for your children. If you show them poor manners, disrespect, lack of concern for opposing points of view, and confrontation coping, expect them to cope in a similar fashion.

I must treat all my children alike to treat them fairly.

Every child is born with a unique set of genes which has never been duplicated. Your children have special personality traits, interests, and abilities. If all children were born alike, it would be fair to treat them just alike. However, since each child has very specialized needs, treating all your children alike is actually unfair. During my tenure as an elementary school teacher, I learned that fair discipline was a personal, individualized matter. The same technique might prove mild with one student and unduly harsh with another.

I can avoid parent-child clashes.

Conflict is bound to occur in any family. If accepted as a natural phenomenon, it needn't destroy the relationship but can serve as an important lesson in problem solving and coping. Children and adults will differ in their perceptions, opinions, and wants. Unless the child has been taught to "keep still," these differences will periodically erupt into full-scale battles.

It is sometimes necessary to hide true feelings.

Children have an invisible antenna that picks up on parents' feelings. If you are disturbed, it is difficult to hide that fact—even from an infant. In relationships with your children it is better to discuss your feelings rather than attempt to conceal them. Tell your children you are coping with a problem, even if you are not able to explain it in detail. Your children can profit from watching you work out your stresses and learn to recognize their own. You might even ask for their support and assistance.

Children must be treated with consistency.

Parents are not the only important influences in children's lives. A number of other people have a share. Since there are vast differences in personalities, there are similar treatment children receive. For example, Mom might react with delight at Junior's desire to assist with the diapering of his new baby sister, while Dad attempts to divert the child's attention to a more masculine endeavor. Recognizing and coping with individual differences is an important skill learned throughout life. There will be differences between adults, between parents, and occasionally even in the same parent over time. The identical situation might prompt a violent reaction from an overstressed parent one day and a mild warning the next.

The parent should always be in control.

Many parents believe that it is their duty to control and train their children. I have always found the use of the word *train* objectionable. We train dogs or seals. Our goal in raising children should be to assist them in developing self-control and positive coping skills. It is not enough for children to do as they are told. Parents obviously possess physical, psychological, and monetary power. However, forcing, manipulating, or coercing children into obedience or compliance gives them little coping experience. I have found that children who are kept "under control" usually erupt once they are away from the controlling influence. In fact, they often seem bent on finally accomplishing whatever behaviors the adult has prevented. Since there has been little practice in self-control, difficult new situations are dealt with ineffectively.

I must insist on respect. Respect is earned—not legislated. Some parents confuse respect with fear. It is easy to make children fear you, but much more challenging to gain their respect.

I should always feel good about my children. Adults don't always feel good about themselves, so it is little wonder they sometimes experience mixed feelings about their offspring. Children can annoy, frustrate, and anger even the most even-tempered of parents. Don't feel guilty if feelings of dislike, disgust, or disappointment sneak up on you. Your negative response will probably be duplicated by individuals outside the household at some point in the future. Assisting your child to cope with the behavior that illicited your response will help smooth the rough edges. You may also find that you react differently to each of your children. It may disturb you to realize that you favor the company of one child over the others, or that you are more prone to look the other way with one child, while you jump all over another. You may not be satisfied with your actions, but at least you can understand them. Just as you have preferences in adult friendships, personality traits in your children can make one child more appealing or easier to get along with than another.

Does Your Coping Model Need a Tune-up?

You may already sense that stress is getting the best of you—or realize that you are prone to some bad stretches, in which you have difficulty coping. If you experience a perpetual state of physical and emotional exhaustion with a decline in your outlook, stress may be the cause. Parents with coping problems are depressed by their lack of enthusiasm and overall out-of-sorts condition. The most distressing consequence is the realization that the joy of parenthood is fading. The stress backlash can make parents less tolerant of normal childish behavior. Sometimes they are shocked by temporary dislike—or even momentary hatred—for their own children. This whole discouraging scene heaps on additional feelings of guilt and inadequacy for the already troubled parents. In response, some turn to pills, tranquilizers, alcohol, drugs, overeating, or isolation from the family.

The first step in tuning up your coping model is to recognize the presence of problems in the breeding stage. Following is a twenty-point check for obvious signs:

TWENTY-POINT CHECK

___ Lack of enthusiasm for children, family, work—or life in general

___ Withdrawal into increased privacy and solitude

___ Steady weight gain or loss

___ Continual fault-finding in others

___ Increased number of interpersonal conflicts

___ Speech becoming gradually louder and more excited; uncharacteristic frequent screaming

___ Undue irritation over rather minor aggravations

___ Development of a tic or nervous mannerism

___ General feeling of uneasiness

___ Increased use of cigarettes, alcohol, drugs, tranquilizers, or pills

___ Difficulty sleeping and/or getting up in the morning

___ Frequent minor illness, such as colds; frequent urination/diarrhea, or backache

___ Headaches or dizziness

___ Tendency to let things "go to pot"

___ Explosive anger or crying

___ Poor concentration or forgetfulness

___ Depression or irrational sense of dread

___ Impatient tendency to interrupt others during conversation

___ Easily startled

___ Hyperactivity or nervousness

Now that you have run through the checklist, don't be like Chicken Little, who thought the sky was falling because she never stopped to consider what was really dropping on her head. Don't terminate your introspection with the knowledge that stress is present without pinpointing your specific coping crisis.

Do You "Pop Your Cork" or Silently Seethe?

Having identified some of the major causes of stress in your life, it is time to analyze your reactions to them. The two basic responses detailed in Chapter One were fight or flight. In modern terms, fight usually boils down to anger, while flight translates into worry and anxiety. The body's prolonged arousal for fight or flight can prove unhealthy and reduce your effectiveness as a parent. Understanding and control are the best defenses.

The flight response is perfectly normal. It involves a set of physical changes accompanied by worry over a situation viewed as personally threatening. In mild doses worry is both natural and productive. It assists us in adapting and improving our performance. Unfortunately, worry can easily get out of hand. We can't seem to draw the line between justifiable worry and worry for worry's sake. We begin to habitually experience anxiety over the most unthreatening and minor of life's events. There is no simple cure for the worrywart. However, once you are aware that you have the tendency to create calamities, you will begin to recognize that many situations aren't really catastrophic at all. Of course, it is easier to talk about controlling worry than it is to accomplish the job. However, by forcing yourself to consider the exact dimensions of a perceived threat, as well as the actual probability of occurrence, you are moving in the right direction. Start by asking yourself, "Just what is the worst that could happen in this situation?" or "What will this all matter a few months from now?" If the worst is really a cause for alarm, productive worry is a valid response. Nevertheless, if you let it take you over, you will find worry debilitating rather than stimulating. If you decide that the whole matter really isn't very important, relax and forget it. Either way, you must make your worry work *for* you rather than *against* you, by exercising control via rational thinking.

Anger—or the fight response—is handled in one of two ways. Either we "pop our cork" or silently seethe. There is inherent danger in both of these reactions. Everyone has experienced the alienation or regret caused by words spoken in anger. We have also stewed in the frustration of having lost the battle by withholding arguments and retorts during a confrontation. If anger is left to fester long enough, it can turn to hostility. No one likes to be around someone with a chip on the shoulder—and rarely can others figure out what put it there. Suppressing anger results in poor communication. Not only are we unable to express ourselves clearly, we often hide our true feelings with indifference. Tension headaches, stomachaches, and high blood pressure can follow.

If anger is managed, it can prove a viable means for dealing with stress. For example, if your children thoughtlessly turn your just-cleaned family room into a shambles prior to the arrival of guests, and you are forced to do a Wonder Woman clean-up job which cancels out the shower you just took, anger helps you assert your rights and communicate your understandable displeasure. Rather than bottling up these feelings, anger gives them a vent and paves the way for higher levels of understanding and a smoother relationship. It is an opportunity to deal with the situation, then forgive and forget. However, it takes some skill to realize these high-sounding advantages.

Anger must involve communication and change rather than manipulation and punishment. Your basic goal shouldn't be getting even or laying on guilt. Some parents attempt mind control with unspoken threats of hysterics, depression, or rejection. They are experts at making others feel sorry for them.

Communication goes beyond merely "speaking *your* mind." It is a two-way, give-and-take process. The first step is understanding your own feelings. Take the case of Sara Chapin. She finds herself becoming progressively more angry and hurt due to the fact that her husband is paying more attention to their eleven-year-old than to her. He has arrived home from work quite late and Sara has been dying to tell him about her pressing problems at work. His lack of attention makes her feel slighted, and Sara begins to give him the cold shoulder. However, when she stops to think about it for a moment, she realizes that he simply wants to spend time with their child before bedtime. Sara recognizes her anger as juvenile and unjustified. She reasons that there will be time to talk later.

It is usually unwise to react immediately to your own, or to others', anger. Allow some time for thought and consideration. Words uttered in haste rarely reflect knowledge of all the facts, plausible solutions, or true feelings. However, if you do shoot from the hip, and later realize that you have made an error in judgment, don't hesitate to admit it—even to children. Although words uttered in anger cannot be taken back, they can be accepted for exactly what they are—angry words. Realize that during an argument it is quite common to make statements you don't mean at all. Don't allow yourself or your children to fret over an imagined dark side of the personality which causes the awful outbursts. Be willing to offer and accept the real explanation: "I don't know why I said those things. I really didn't mean them."

Anger needs expression. Ideally, it should result in positive suggestions for improving a relationship. If you need a physical release, exercise can help dissipate anger-energy—or try screaming into a pillow or beating it up. If you are carrying the burden of old hurts, they are better forgotten. If forgetting is not possible, talk them out once and for all and then don't allow yourself to mentally rehash dead issues.

Healthy, constructive expression of anger begins with a specific statement of your case and the relief you demand. Fight the tendency to degrade, threaten, or make broad statements such as "You have no regard for my feelings." An attack on another's self-concept is never in order. Make it clear you disapprove of a behavior—not the individual. Don't forget to listen, listen, listen. Listen to your explanation of your anger and feelings. Is it an accurate description, free from unrelated history and accusation? Don't force an immediate response and listen to the reply offered. When others are angry with you, listen objectively to their case without becoming instantly defensive. After you have listened, think. Develop the ability to study the situation from differing points of view by slipping in and out of the other person's shoes.

Parenting Practices That Generate Stress

The way parents deal with children is important for everyone involved. Children are extremely vulnerable, are dependent on their parents, and can be easily influenced under the guise of good intentions. They often have an inflated impression of adults, thinking parents are incapable of mistakes or wrongdoings. Many common parenting practices create a distorted view of the real world and increase children's stress levels. Dr. Thomas Gordon has designed a system called Parent Effectiveness Training, which treats the parent-child relationship. Many of the parenting practices below are covered in his book.[2]

Example 1   Mom and Dad take five-year-old Susan to a funeral in a neighboring city. They had to arise early and drive two hours to arrive on time. During the service Susan begins to get restless. Mother tells her, "Stop turning around and sit quietly!" She complies for a few minutes, but soon Mother notices her "petting" the fur coat worn by the lady in front of them. Mother takes Susan outside. When they return, a teary-eyed Susan is wearing a red slap-mark on her leg.

Demands are made that cannot possibly be fulfilled. When the child fails, punishment follows.

Example 2   Jamie is a poor eater. He plays with his food and often refuses to eat. On one particular occasion, while the family was traveling, Mom was desperate to get him to eat. She knew it would be hours before they would stop again. She told Jamie that if he didn't quickly eat all his food, the restaurant owner would have him arrested. The ploy worked, and Mom continued to use it each time they dined out. Gradually Jamie developed an absolute aversion to restaurants. When forced to eat out, Jamie gobbles his food rapidly but is often sick later.

Bizarre threats are made, and although they are not quite understood, the child is frightened because a trusted adult has predicted the horrible consequences.

Example 3   Ben enters the living room as Dad storms out. Mom is visibly upset. When Ben asks what happened, Mom replies: "Oh, nothing. Dad and I were just having a little discussion. Everything is fine."

Obvious signals which communicate important feelings are denied with words designed to shelter or protect the child from unhappiness or unpleasantness.

Example 4   Mother is rushing to get ready for dinner guests. She is chopping celery when Kristin enters the kitchen. Kristin begins to complain about the outfit Mother has laid out for her to wear. In the middle of her protests Mother accidentally slices her finger. She turns to Kristin and screams: "Now are you happy? See what you made me do?"

Guilt and evil intentions are heaped on the child by a parent who is dealing ineffectively with a stressful situation.

Example 5   Dad has decided that Danny's sloppiness is getting out of hand. On Saturday he really gets on Danny's case, riding him about neatness and insisting he clean his room, straighten the yard, and clean up after himself. By the end of the day Danny is obviously irritated. Dad asks him what the problem is. Danny replies, "Nothing," and starts to leave the room. Dad calls him back and says: "I want to know what's bugging you. Now you tell me." Danny explodes: "I'm sick of you telling me what to do! You're just as big a slob as I am. Just look at the garage." Dad is furious and grounds Danny for a week for being so disrespectful.

A no-win situation has been established in which the child doesn't know which way to turn. If Danny refuses to tell what's "bugging him," Dad will be angry, and if he does tell the truth, he is in trouble.

Example 6   Donald is putting together his new model car. Mother calls him for dinner. He mutters, "Be right there," as he struggles to get a piece in place before the glue dries. Three minutes later Mother calls again. Donald says: "I'll be there in a second. I almost have this piece in." Mother screams, "Get in here now!"

The child, ordered to obey, interprets the situation as a demonstration of the parent's position of power with apparent lack of concern for the child's wants. The child's self-image is threatened.

Example 7   Ellen is entering junior high in a few weeks. She approaches her parents with a problem. She is. afraid the other kids will make fun of her "big" nose. Mom suggests that they go downtown and buy some lovely new school clothes. Dad laughs uproariously as he suggests that Ellen tell her friends she will probably do much better in her studies since she has a "nose for detail."

Refusing to acknowledge and assist with stress by joking about it or sidetracking the child are cheap tricks, particularly when the child is seriously concerned.

Example 8   Mary comes home from an afternoon at play in a state of obvious upset. She tells her mother that the other kids don't want to play with her because she won't take turns with the toys. When Mother asks her if she shares, Mary says, "Well, I was on the swing first." Mother replies: "Oh, never mind those bad children. Let's call Fran to play."

The real stressor is overlooked in favor of sympathy and parental support. Gradually the child loses trust for the parent and thinks, "She is just trying to make me feel better." The child stops coming to the parent for coping assistance.

Example 9   Timmy, aged three, and Marnie, aged seven, accompany their mother to the grocery store. Timmy begins nagging Mother to buy him a small car. Marnie follows suit and asks for a plastic jewelry set. Mother turns to Marnie and says: "Oh, yes, I must buy both my babies a toy. Marnie, are you sure you wouldn't rather have a baby rattle?"

Name calling and ridicule are used to shame the child, rather than coping with the situation by discussing it.

Example 10   Tuesday evening is Dad's bowling night. Under the best of circumstances there is just enough time for him to change clothes, eat, and rush off to meet his team. This evening he arrives home to find dinner still in progress. He asks what caused the delay. Mom replies: "I don't know. Things just kind of got out of control." Twelve-year-old Joseph interjects, "Mom decided to jog before dinner today." Mom and Dad exchange a few harsh words. After Dad leaves, Mom gives Joseph the icy cold shoulder. She withdraws to her room to pout and watch television and refuses to talk to him.

Shunning the child and engaging in emotional warfare is one of the most devastating coping techniques employed by parents. It denies children that which they value most—love and attention.

Example 11   Judy has been having a rough time in fifth grade. She often complains of headaches in the morning. Mother tells her: "Judy, the only reason you have a headache is because you don't want to go to school. Your problem is all in your mind."

Verbally psychoanalyzing your children is interpreted as evidence of your supremacy. If your analysis is correct, children feel vulnerable. However, even if your opinion is accurate, children rarely see it that way and experience indignation and frustration at your attempts to read the mind.

Example 12   Laurie visits her friend, Holly, shortly after the tragic death of Laurie's younger sister. Holly notices that Laurie is acting differently. She even sees her begin to cry. After Laurie leaves, Holly tells her father: "Something is wrong with Laurie. She doesn't act the same. I saw her crying." Dad says: "Don't worry about it. Laurie will be fine. Just forget about it."

Gliding over an obvious problem in order to shelter a child or avoid an explanation makes the child begin to doubt personal observations. The child is offered no assistance in coping or understanding.

Example 13   Jeremy is scheduled to attend camp in several days. He persists in teasing his baby brother, and out of desperation Mother warns, "If I have to speak to you again, you aren't going to camp."

Threats of punishment, pain, or loss of privilege result in a variety of reactions. In some cases the child is fearful and vitally aware of the parents' power position. In other situations the child is challenged to test the threat, which often is made with no intention of enforcement.

Example 14   Dorothy is going through a messy stage. Mother feels as if she must walk behind her with a garbage can. Finally, she sits Dorothy down and tells her: "Our whole family works together to keep our house nice. We all have to do our part." Mentally, Dorothy thinks: "Oh, yeah . . . well, the only people I see picking stuff up are Mom and me. Mom wants me to be neat, but she cleans up after Bobby and Dad."

Encouraging a child to share a camaraderie which, in fact, does not exist can prove perturbing. The child is perplexed at being unable to recognize this compatability, while simultaneously feeling excluded.

Example 15   Vince decides to rebuild one of his old bicycles. After completely dismantling it, he loses interest in the project and dumps all the parts into a large box. That evening at dinner Vince's father delivers one of his long lectures, this one centering around the theme, "Finish whatever you start." Vince rolls his eyes, but manages to nod in agreement at the appropriate times. Silently he says: "Here he goes again, back on the pulpit. I wish I had the guts to remind him of a few of the projects he started and never finished."

Lecturing is an automatic turn-off. If in doubt, stop and recall your own childhood.

Example 16   Four-year-old Margie has been very naughty all day. Late in the afternoon Mom tells her daughter: "I am ashamed of you. You have been bad all day. If you do one more thing wrong, I am going to tell Daddy when he gets home. Daddy doesn't like bad girls."

Mom is coping with Margie's difficult behavior in a number of ineffective ways. She is attacking the child's self-image by calling her bad. Children who are frequently told they are bad soon come to believe it and act accordingly. In addition, Mother is using threats and, worst of all, holding Daddy's love and approval as ransom.

If you commonly use any of these parenting practices, you are undoubtedly generating stress for your child, and probably yourself, as well. Next time you find yourself dealing with your child in any of the ways described, stop to analyze the impact of what you are doing. You will probably be able to pinpoint the stressful result and be motivated to work toward more constructive interaction with your child.

Don't Bother Me, I Can't Cope

Out of desperation Norma telephoned her sister long-distance. "I'm so out of control," she said. "I just don't seem to be able to cope anymore, and I feel the kids are suffering. I always wanted to be the perfect parent, but I'm a flop.''

Norma's dreams of being a perfect mother, of raising perfect children in a perfect home environment, are themselves stress-producing. The numerous parenting books she has read have led her to believe that her dreams can come true—that children are easily molded, and you can raise them by following the easy steps. However, when she tries to follow the experts' advice, things never seem to go the way they are supposed to. She wonders if there is something inherently wrong with her children or with her.

In order to provide the perfect environment, Norma has overprogrammed the entire family. Every minute seems scheduled, and someone is always dashing to violin lessons, soccer practice, or PTA meetings. There isn't even one morning in the week when the family can sleep in. Saturdays Norma has Brownies in her home at nine thirty, and Sundays there is church.

From time to time everyone gets the feeling that life is out of control. Stress is approaching the red-alert level, and something has to be done. Norma's first step is to realize that no parent copes perfectly. Child care experts can provide suggestions, but it is up to the parent to decide whether or not to accept them. Second, Norma must accept her children's individuality. Every child is different, and an approach that helps her cope with her son might be all wrong with her daughter. Then she should take steps to deal with her specific areas of coping difficulty. Once she actively launches an attack on her stressors, she will immediately begin to feel more in control.

Chapter Three

Plot Your Child's Individuality Profile

You Can't Fool Mother Nature

Your child is unique and special—a marvelous composite of physical attributes and personality traits put together only once in eternity. The often-mentioned "average" child does not exist. Each child has a matchless set of individual needs, skills, and traits that are distinctly personal. Individuality is a concept that receives a great deal of lip-service. Ask any parents about variations in children, and they will tell you, "Of course, all children are different." However, in actual practice some adults seem to forget their firm belief in individuality and try to change their children, to make them fit a mold.

When parents fail to identify and accept a child's individuality, stress is generated. Demands may be made that are impossible to meet owing to the child's basic makeup. Parents are sometimes oblivious to the child's special needs, fail to understand the child's distinct learning style, or ignore the child's personal reactions to stress. All of these parent behaviors unnecessarily make life more difficult for the child and can generate stress.

There is no question that when it comes to your child, you are the expert. You know your child better than anyone else and have insights into the youngster's personality that border on extrasensory perception. However, recognizing individuality means more than tolerating an isolated idiosyncrasy, such as putting up with a five-year-old's attachment to a beat-up teddy bear or pretending not to notice a teen-ager's fear of escalators. There are numerous important facts about your child you probably never considered. This information is vital in helping you to help your child develop an effective personal coping system. For example, if your child learns more effectively with visual materials, and you consistently offer verbal explanations which are received auditorily by the child, you are unintentionally placing the child in a situation in which the chances of success are not maximized. Obviously, a different approach is in order. A visual approach to learning will make the job easier, something both you and your child should always bear in mind.

A well-known commercial tells us that "you can't fool Mother Nature." Likewise, a child's individuality is undeniable, but adults sometimes don't like what they see and, therefore, refuse to acknowledge certain aspects. Or else they exert effort to get the child in step with the world or with the parents. Of course, some children are harder to deal with than others, but wishing that Bobby was more like his older brother or like you were as a child rarely serves any useful function. Recognition and acceptance of individuality is basic for coping as a parent and for helping children develop a coping system that really works for them. Knowledge of your child's individuality helps you understand what stresses your child, how he or she reacts, and what works best to keep stress under control. You will be able to deal with your child based on singularity rather than on some "ideal average." The range of normal behavior for children at every age level is wide. Expect variance from child to child, even within the same household. Realize that divergencies in temperament can substantially alter the response to a stressor from one child to the next. For example, Sandy might look forward to performing in the school's spring program, while Sally becomes nauseous at the prospect.

Unfortunately, you can't rely on children to verbally communicate all the details about their emotions and personality. Sometimes they don't know themselves, or their self-expression skills are not sophisticated enough to permit full disclosure. Therefore, you must develop a kind of radar which picks up on subtle clues such as body language, facial expressions, eye movements, mood changes, voice inflections, or posture. In fact, tuning in to these signals often yields more reliable information than that gained from verbalizations. An extremely distressed child is rarely able to communicate the intensity of feeling with words. It is usually the child's actions that vividly cry out, "Help me."

Children are not the only ones who communicate their feelings nonverbally. Adults also send subtle messages. A child's awareness of parental acceptance of his or her individuality is crucial in helping the child toward a positive self-image and better self-understanding. Parents can nonverbally communicate disapproval or disinterest in children by unconsciously casting an annoyed or disgusted look or by inattentively responding to a youngster with a preoccupied "Um-mmmmmm."

If You Seek a Perfect Child, Remain Childless

Universally, children are enchanting, appealing, refreshing, and simply magnificent. They are not perfect. Flawless children exist only in the minds of a few who have no children, but imagine what their children would be like if they did have them.

From the checklists on the following pages an individual profile of your child will emerge which will include both strengths and weaknesses. Mark Twain once wrote that "there is no sadder sight than a young pessimist." Don't contribute to your child's pessimism by overreacting to his or her weaknesses. Avoid the tendency to assign more weight to minor human frailties than is due. Parents and children with good mental hygiene work toward maximizing innate human potential, rather than wasting time lamenting over what might have been.

Individuality and Stress Vulnerability

Some children have better coping skills than others. In general, the child who has a positive self-image and experiences home and school situations that are secure and supportive is better able to handle the routine stresses of childhood than a child growing up with a poor self-concept in an atmosphere marked by insecurity.

The more fortunate child gains confidence from the knowledge that when the going gets really tough, there is always someone to help. Concern, love, and wisdom are available, and unreasonable coping demands are not made. When the child is successful in handling a stressful situation, adults are there to notice and provide a pat on the back. As childhood progresses, the youngster becomes more and more confident in coping with stress.

Individual coping strategies vary among children, and there is usually more than one successful means for dealing with a stressful situation. Vulnerability to stress also differs, even in the same child over a brief period of time. A number of variables help to determine the extent of a child's reaction to a potentially stressful occurrence. Consider the following true anecdote. Dave Schmidt is a bright, alert third-grader. Mr. Marshall, his teacher, is a young man whom Dave greatly admires as being intelligent, fair, and "cool." One day Mr. Marshall announced to the class: "I've got some good news for you, kids. Next Wednesday we are going to hitch a ride to the museum. Be sure you return your permission slip and bring a lunch." As the trip grew closer, Dave became obviously upset. He told his mother he didn't want to go. She told him that was nonsense, that he always looked forward to field trips. The evening before the outing Dave begged his parents to allow him to stay home the following day. His parents were puzzled and asked him repeatedly what the problem was. Dave was tormented but wouldn't tell. He had a terrible night's sleep and tried to feign illness on Wednesday morning. Finally, on his way out the door to catch the school bus, Dave exploded: "Mom, I can't go on that trip! I don't want to get Mr. Marshall in trouble, so promise you won't tell, but we are going to hitchhike to the museum." If Dave hadn't already suffered so much, his mother might have thought the whole matter was comical. She said: "Dave, that is impossible. You *must* be going on a bus. I'll call the school secretary and find out for sure." As it turned out, Mr. Marshall did intend to "hitch a ride"—with another class headed to the museum with a half-filled bus. The teacher's offhand statement to the class was made just a few days after Dave had seen a horror movie in which hitchhiking teen-agers met with disaster. The child's genuine admiration for the teacher prevented him from saying anything that he thought might cause trouble for the teacher.

This anecdote reviews a basic principle introduced in Chapter One—stress is the result of a child's perception of a situation as being personally threatening. I am certain that the other children in Mr. Marshall's third grade experienced little stress associated with the excursion. Dave's stress was the result of his own interpretation of the situation. Parents must appreciate the highly individualized nature of a child's stress reaction. Overlooking or glossing over the child's problem with attitudes such as "It's only a stage the child is going through," or "Don't worry about it, everything will be fine," implies that the parent's lack of concern for the problem can be automatically transferred to the distressed child. A few moments of retrospection in which you recall your own childhood will probably rekindle memories of problems you faced which seemed major to you, but rather minor to your parents. Maybe they thought your worries were silly or cute, or didn't recognize them at all, but to you they were a serious source of anxiety.

Your goal as a parent is certainly not the elimination of all stress from childhood. Stress is an important part of growing up and learning how to survive in the real world. Coping with childhood stress is the best training for handling adult stress. For example, separation anxiety—the fear of being away from parents—is one of childhood's best-recognized stressors. Coping effectively with this source of stress contributes to the child's ultimate sense of independence. Stressful upheavals have an important part to play in your child's development. With a little parental assistance, childhood stress need not result in devastation.

However, when stress is nonstop, or the child is in over his or her head and unable to control anxiety, intervention is necessary for the child's satisfactory adjustment.

Coping is much like traveling on a straight road that suddenly forks, with roads going off to the right and to the left. The road symbolizes the path through childhood. Along the way the child is bombarded by a number of *potentially* stressful stimuli. The forks in the road represent reactions to stimuli that the child has identified as *personally* stressful. The typical stress symptoms are experienced, and the child must somehow cope. The youngster now takes either the right-hand or left-hand road. The right-hand road leads back to the straight road—to adjustment to the stressor and preparation for handling the future. The left-hand road is the bumpy byway of maladjustment, which adds little to the child's coping ability. Luckily, along the left-hand road there are opportunities for the child to stop and ask for help and direction. It is possible to branch back onto the path of adjustment, and to realize that it is just a matter of time before another fork in the road is encountered. Happily, each time the child gets onto the right-hand fork, important gains are made which make the lifetime journey smoother.

An important part of understanding your child is recognizing when the child reaches a fork and which path is typically taken. The stress symptoms presented in Chapter One will help you to identify when your child is experiencing stress. If the child quickly moves onto the course of adjustment, and stress serves as a stimulating force leading to positive problem solving and improved performance, you have little cause for concern. Perhaps your child often recognizes stress and even asks for help, in order to move more rapidly toward adjustment. On the other hand, some children are prone to maladjustive coping techniques. They freeze up during stress. When this type of child avoids as much stress as possible, it is actually a form of maladjusted behavior which contributes nothing to learning about long-term adjustment. Instead of attempting to protect the child from the inevitable, parents should be involved in facilitating adjustment to stress by offering whatever help and support is needed, and in redirecting maladjusted behavior. Initially, your child may hesitate to ask for adult assistance. The child might not recognize that it is needed, that you have something of value to offer, or that inability to cope is not synonymous with failure. It can be difficult to approach a child who has chosen isolation. However, once children recognize that adults are willing and able to offer valuable assistance, they more readily seek it. Optimal results are possible when the child senses the parents' readiness to help and seeks this aid without hesitation—before stress is out of control. The following checklist will help you identify which paths your child typically takes when faced with stress:

READ YOUR CHILD'S COPING ROAD MAP

_____ 1. My child seems energized by a stressful situation and usually jumps right in to start finding effective solutions for adapting to the stress.

_____ 2. My child reacts to stress by trying to avoid the particular problem or to avoid stressful situations altogether.

_____ 3. My child becomes isolated during stress.

_____ 4. My child tries to hide true feelings during stress by faking the appearance of being tough, silly, angry, or happy.

_____ 5. My child builds mountains out of mole hills by magnifying the seriousness of the perceived threat, which in turn amplifies the stress reaction.

_____ 6. My child introduces additional, irrelevant stressors to the stressful situation. When stressed, the child becomes upset about other problems which are totally unrelated and usually not worth worrying about.

_____ 7. My child reacts to stress by trying to control others with temper tantrums or by bullying children.

_____ 8. My child becomes overly dependent on others to handle stressful situations instead of personally coping with them. The child looks to others to "do something," stop fights, or run interference. The child thinks everyone should understand when stress is a problem and render kid-glove treatment.

_____ 9. My child collaborates with others who are suffering from similar maladjustive coping processes, thinking that there is safety in numbers. For example, rather than handling problems at school the child joins with other children who are having similar difficulties, and everyone tells each other that "school is for the birds, anyway."

_____ 10. My child simply gives up the fight. For example, if the child is experiencing stress associated with per-

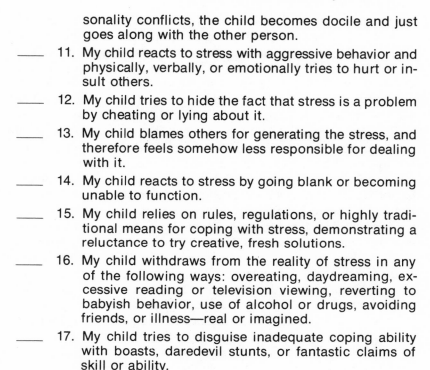

sonality conflicts, the child becomes docile and just goes along with the other person.

_____ 11. My child reacts to stress with aggressive behavior and physically, verbally, or emotionally tries to hurt or insult others.

_____ 12. My child tries to hide the fact that stress is a problem by cheating or lying about it.

_____ 13. My child blames others for generating the stress, and therefore feels somehow less responsible for dealing with it.

_____ 14. My child reacts to stress by going blank or becoming unable to function.

_____ 15. My child relies on rules, regulations, or highly traditional means for coping with stress, demonstrating a reluctance to try creative, fresh solutions.

_____ 16. My child withdraws from the reality of stress in any of the following ways: overeating, daydreaming, excessive reading or television viewing, reverting to babyish behavior, use of alcohol or drugs, avoiding friends, or illness—real or imagined.

_____ 17. My child tries to disguise inadequate coping ability with boasts, daredevil stunts, or fantastic claims of skill or ability.

If you checked statement number 1, you probably checked few, if any, of the others. The remaining sixteen descriptions all indicate that the child is using maladjustive coping strategies. You can help your child adjust more easily and quickly to stress by:

> Reassuring the child that the stressful situation does not signal the end of the world. The problem can be solved.

> Discussing the ineffective coping strategy being used, in light of the child's better perspective on the problem.

> Developing an effective coping strategy. Detailed steps are included in the final chapter.

> Assisting the child in using a relaxation technique to provide relief from stress. These techniques are also found in the final chapter.

An example of maladjustive coping might be the child who is overwhelmed at having fallen desperately behind in homework, finding the enormousness of the job ahead too much to face. The child uses coping strategy number 9—collaborating with others who are suffering with a similar problem. He or she suddenly prefers the company of underachievers and poor students. You can help by working with your child to break the pile of work down into small chunks, so he or she sees a realistic possibility for progress.

Or take coping strategy number 17—disguising inadequate coping ability with boasts, daredevil stunts, or fantastic claims of skill or ability. Children from about three years of age to adolescence use this strategy. A young child might claim to have superpowers, while a preteen will attempt foolish feats. In any case, this strategy can be dangerous. Preschoolers have been seriously injured trying to leap off of buildings, and older children have sustained broken bones doing jumps with their bikes off a ramp. This type of behavior signals that a child is attempting to bolster his or her self-image to counteract feelings of inadequacy and limitation. In younger children fantasizing is a natural part of play, as well as a way of coping with fears and stress. However, after the age of six most children abandon this coping technique. If it persists, it is a sign of lack of self-confidence. Younger children should be encouraged to talk about their fantasies. However, parents should not confuse children by acting as though they actually believe the imaginary story. After a child finishes telling about a superhuman accomplishment, the parent might say: "That was a good story. It sure is fun to pretend." Children of any age need to develop self-confidence by being given opportunities to develop independence, as well as being given recognition for real achievements.

Prolonged exposure to stress or maladjusted behavior which goes unchanged is demoralizing. Under certain long-term stressful circumstances such as a death or divorce, parents need to provide the support necessary for a child to make it through the bad times. Even under these adverse conditions children can learn and grow. However, I disagree with those who believe that suffering somehow makes a better person. The best-adjusted children are the happiest.

Individuality Profile

Terry and Nicky attend the same fifth grade. Both are straight A students, with good attitudes toward school and learning. However, a close look at these two students reveals few similarities beyond those just mentioned. Terry lives a well-organized life and likes to study every day at exactly the same time and place. Nicky is just the opposite, sometimes getting up early to do homework, other days avoiding the job until it is necessary to stay up late. When Terry is concentrating, the entire household tries to keep the noise level down. He would never think of studying with the radio or television blaring. Nicky often plays the stereo while at work and has little difficulty concentrating, even when other children are talking or arguing. When Terry and Nicky study together, they find they can't agree on the temperature of the room or the amount of light. Terry would rather plan study sessions at the library, while Nicky likes to flop on the bed.

One factor they have in common is that both students have parents who recognize their unique learning styles and accept rather than fight them. These two separate sets of parents realize the importance of allowing children to function in terms of their special individuality. This practice minimizes family stress and enables the parents to realistically assist in the coping process.

The pages that follow contain four separate checklists for determining your child's individuality profile. Although the checklists are by no means scientific, they are designed to focus your attention on some areas you might not have previously considered. In many cases you will find that you actually do have knowledge of the traits examined or can easily find out about them. The important question is, Are you using this information to keep stress under control and help your child develop coping ability?

The complete individuality profile contains four areas: (1) temperament, (2) modality preference, (3) learning style, and (4) comparison of individuality.

Assessment 1—TEMPERAMENT

Background Information

How many times have you heard parents describe children with statements such as "She is as neat as a pin," "He is full of the devil," "Those two never stop moving," or "You could set a clock by that kid"? These remarks indicate that parents are aware of children's special characteristics. These basic differences in personality are the foundation upon which individuality is built, and are called temperament.

Temperament is usually thought of as a set of inborn dispositions toward a particular style of behavior. It is the inherited tendency of an individual's nature or makeup to respond to life in a distinctive manner and to attempt to seek out and organize environments that correspond to this temperament. For example, Ellen Henry has two daughters, Barbara and Carol. She often remarks that "Barbara is not happy unless she is in the middle of a three-ring circus. If there is no excitement going on, she will create some.'' On the other hand, when Ellen describes her other daughter she says: "Carol is just the opposite. She can be in the midst of a big group of kids, and she will suddenly just quietly pick up and go off by herself to happily read or draw a picture.'' The difference in temperaments between these two sisters helps to explain their varying behavior. Drs. Stella Chess, Alexander Thomas, and Herbert Birch conducted careful research into the development of temperament and its affect on personality. They studied a number of children and found that as early as the first week of life infants demonstrate differences in temperament. Most of the children continued to exhibit many of the same styles of behavior as they grew older. Problems arise when parents refuse to acknowledge the child's temperament and make impossible demands or try to overhaul the child. In some cases children experience prolonged stress caused by their parents' efforts to fight basic, natural tendencies or temperaments.

The following scale is a way to explore the elements of your child's temperament.[1] Some parents are fortunate to have amiable and good-natured children who make the job of parenting seem easy. Other children are more difficult to raise. They are crabby, unpleasant, and present a real challenge for parents. Recognizing the differences in temperament can rid parents of nagging doubts such as "Johnny is such a handful, I must have done something wrong.'' There is nothing abnormal about any of the behaviors presented. Difficult children don't automatically face a life of doom, especially if parents take their special traits into consideration. Drs. Chess, Thomas, and Birch have suggested that parents accept their children's temperament as a "given,'' and work with it—rather than against it.

Following are the nine categories that Dr. Chess and her fellow researchers have identified in their study of temperament. The following scale is a way to explore the elments of your child's temperament. Accompanying each category are five statements that describe behavior. Read each statement and decide if it applies "almost never" to your child, "sometimes,'' or "almost always.'' Circle your choice, based on the way you think your child compares to other children of the same age.

Interpretation

The nine types of behavior you just rated make up your child's temperament, which is one ingredient in the child's life—not the entire recipe. Happiness and adjustment can be realized if the par-

ACTIVITY LEVEL

	Almost Never	Some- times	Almost Always
My child has difficulty sitting still, even for reasonable periods of time.	0	1	2
My child squirms and wiggles at the dinner table, while I am help- ing with homework, in the car, or at the movies.	0	1	2
At regular intervals my child needs physical activity as an outlet for excess energy.	0	1	2
My child prefers play that involves movement, such as playing ball or running, to quiet play such as coloring.	0	1	2
My child moves rapidly and likes to run rather than walk.	0	1	2

Record your child's total score. ____

Plot your child's score on the line below.

0	5	10
Low activity level	Moderate activity level	High activity level

REGULARITY

	Almost Never	Some- times	Almost Always
My child goes to sleep and awak- ens at the same time each day (within the half hour).	0	1	2
My child gets hungry at about the same time each day.	0	1	2
My child has a bowel movement at about the same time each day.	0	1	2
My child sleeps about the same number of hours each night.	0	1	2
My child eats about the same amount of food each day.	0	1	2

Record your child's total score. ____

Plot your child's score on the line below.

0	5	10
Irregular	Variable	Regular

APPROACH/WITHDRAWAL

	Almost Never	Some-times	Almost Always
My child likes to perform in front of others.	0	1	2
My child is outgoing when it comes to meeting new people.	0	1	2
My child enjoys jumping into new activities and new situations rather than holding back at the sidelines.	0	1	2
My child prefers new toys or clothes to old, familiar ones.	0	1	2
My child enjoys trying new foods or experiencing new surroundings.	0	1	2

Record your child's total score. ____

Plot your child's score on the line below.

0	5	10
Rejects and withdraws	Variable	Accepting and approachable

ADAPTABILITY

	Almost Never	Some-times	Almost Always
My child learns to like food that was once disliked.	0	1	2
My child easily "makes himself/herself at home" in new surroundings by easily adapting to the new life-style or set of rules that apply.	0	1	2
After a break in routine such as a trip or school vacation, my child easily gets back into the routine.	0	1	2
My child gets over attacks of shyness very rapidly.	0	1	2
My child changes the rules or format for games and play.	0	1	2

Record your child's total score. ____

Plot your child's score on the line below.

0	5	10
Slow to adapt	Moderate rate of adapting	Quick to adapt

SENSORY THRESHOLD

	Almost Never	Some-times	Almost Always
My child is conscious of odors and comments on pleasant and un-pleasant smells.	0	1	2
My child is sensitive to temperature and apt to complain that a room is too hot or too cold, or that food is not the right temperature.	0	1	2
My child cries easily when suffer-ing a minor cut or bruise.	0	1	2
My child is sensitive to noise and apt to complain about loud mu-sic, bells, or alarms.	0	1	2
My child complains when clothing is too tight, itchy, ill-fitting, or if it becomes dirty or damp.	0	1	2

Record your child's total score. _____

Plot your child's score on the line below.

0	5	10
High threshold (responds to major changes in environment)	Moderate threshold	Low threshold (responds to slight changes in environment)

POSITIVE/NEGATIVE MOOD

	Almost Never	Some-times	Almost Always
My child laughs, smiles, and seems to be having a good time.	0	1	2
When my child is upset, it is easy to comfort the child.	0	1	2
My child takes losing a game in stride, without upset.	0	1	2
My child avoids arguments or be-coming upset when not given own way.	0	1	2
My child tends to tell me about the good things that happen, avoid-ing complaints and criticism.	0	1	2

Record your child's total score. _____

Plot your child's score on the line below.

0	5	10
Negative mood	Variable mood	Positive mood

INTENSITY OF REACTION

	Almost Never	Some-times	Almost Always
My child shows emotions with facial expressions, body language, or verbal intonations.	0	1	2
It is obvious when my child is under stress.	0	1	2
My child gets enthusiastic and excited when telling a story.	0	1	2
My child reacts immediately and vigorously when the child feels rights have been violated.	0	1	2
My child reacts with enthusiasm and excitement to special events, trips, or visitors—rather than taking things "cooly."	0	1	2

Record your child's total score. ____

Plot your child's score on the line below.

0	5	10
Low-intensity reactions	Moderate-intensity reactions	High-intensity reactions

DISTRACTIBILITY

	Almost Never	Some-times	Almost Always
My child's concentration is easily broken by noises, other children, or whispering.	0	1	2
If my child is set on one particular toy or activity, it is easy to substitute another.	0	1	2
If my child is in a bad mood, it is easy to snap the child out of it.	0	1	2
If someone tries to interrupt while I am explaining something to my child, the child loses attention.	0	1	2
When the child is involved in a task, the child responds quickly when told it is time to stop and drops everything.	0	1	2

Record your child's total score. ____

Plot your child's score on the line below.

0	5	10
Hard to distract	Moderately distractible	Easy to distract

ATTENTION SPAN/PERSISTENCE

	Almost Never	Some- times	Almost Always
When my child is interrupted, the child does not go back to the same activity.	0	1	2
When my child is learning some- thing new, the child is easily frustrated and wants to do some- thing else.	0	1	2
If I am too busy to answer a ques- tion, the child goes away and does not come back later for the answer.	0	1	2
My child dislikes doing the same thing for a long period of time and doesn't finish what is started.	0	1	2
If my child has difficulty with something, the child looks for immediate assistance, rather than trying to figure it out.	0	1	2

Record your child's total score. ____

Plot your child's score on the line below.

0	5	10
Long attention span	Moderate attention span	Short attention span

ent and child work with the raw material they have rather than wishing it were different or trying to alter it.

Contrary to some common beliefs children cannot be molded like clay. They enter life with their basic temperament, and although the process of growth and development will be accompanied by some change, parents are better off adapting to the child's personality, instead of trying to modify it.

The combination of traits makes some children more difficult to raise than others. High activity level, irregularity, rejection, slow adaptability, low sensory threshold, negative mood, high-intensity reactions, distractibility, and short attention span are among the characteristics often associated with the difficult child. These elements of the personality can produce friction between parent and child if the parent does not accept them and work toward helping the child adjust. On the other hand, even parents with children who might be classified as easy to raise aren't satisfied. Take the example of Sharon Rush, who was very adaptable and had a sunny disposition. Her mother was concerned that she was too agreeable and told her she was "easy pickins." Sharon was often stressed by her mother's insistence that she become more assertive and her mother experienced guilt, doubt, and a sense of failure at not raising a better-adjusted child.

Another child, Linda Washington, was extremely active and highly distractible. Her parents were deeply committed to this difficult child's successful adjustment and never expected overnight success. They were patient when she was fidgety or flighty. They didn't blame themselves or some mistake they had made when she was an infant. Little by little they helped Linda understand and adapt to life's rules, routines, and natural consequences—always letting her know they supported, accepted, and loved her.

You can avoid putting yourself and your child under stress by understanding the temperamental tendencies. While you may not be able to change the fact that your child is prone to slow adaptation or is highly irregular, it is possible to help the child acknowledge these characteristics and actively work to form good habits and self-discipline. While a child's personality will always have the predisposition toward certain types of behavior, this behavior can often be controlled.

Assessment 2—MODALITY PREFERENCE

Background Information

Have you ever noticed the different ways people absorb information? For example, when given an important set of directions, one person might say, "Wait a minute, I want to write that down," while another asks: "Would you mind saying that again? I want to be sure I have it straight." In the first case the individual prefers to rely on sight for processing facts. In the second case hearing is the choice. Perhaps you fall apart trying to follow a set of step-by-step directions for assembling a new toy. You just can't "see" how it all goes together unless a visual diagram is provided. Each situation illustrates the importance of modality. Modality refers to the way we process information. There are three basic modalities: (1) Visual (sight), (2) auditory (hearing), and (3) kinesthetic (touch).

Research shows that approximately one third of elementary school students are strongest in the visual modality; about one third have mixed modality, which means they are equally strong in two or more areas; one fourth possess auditory strength; and only fifteen percent are kinesthetic learners. Younger children are generally more auditorily inclined. In the later grades many begin to develop visual and kinesthetic potential, and by adulthood substantial numbers of people have mixed modality.

The implications of modality preference for learning and learning-related stress are clear. Children with mixed modality, or strength in all three areas, have a definite advantage. They can pick up on information no matter how it is presented. For children with strength in only one area the struggle to understand often generates stress. Their difficulties do not stem from lack of intelligence, but from the incongruence between their method for learning and the method of teaching. If you are basically a visual person, chances are you will teach your child in a visual way. That's fine—if your child has visual-modality strength. If not, the child may face an unnecessary stumbling block. When you find yourself saying, "I must have told you that a hundred times," or "I showed you that over and over," it is time to stop and think. If your child hasn't learned after being "told a hundred times," or "shown over and over," maybe it is time to change the technique which has been proven ineffective. The following short questionnaire will provide a very rough indication of your child's modality strengths. Select the choice that best fits your child. In a few cases you may find it necessary to mark more than one. If a statement is not applicable at this time, try to judge how the child reacted in the past or would react in the future. If you are uncertain how to respond, ask your child.

Interpretation

This assessment gives you a crude indication of your child's preference of modality. Perhaps your child's strength is clearly in one area, or scattered almost equally among the three areas. Don't be surprised if you found you checked a large number of kinesthetic responses. Most children enjoy learning by doing and like lots of "hands on" experiences, although it may not be their strongest area. Unfortunately, many parents and teachers do not take advantage of this natural tendency. If your child would prefer to grow a penicillium mold on bread rather than read about it, why not make greater use of the kinesthetic modality?

Modality is another component of your child's total individuality. Stress can be minimized and learning maximized when you take it into account. To get the best indication of your child's modality strength, watch your child in action, discuss the matter with his or her teacher, and experiment by presenting information in the various modalities.

MODALITY STRENGTH

When it is time to play indoors, my child prefers	A. listening to the radio, records, or tapes. K. "doing" something, such as coloring or assembling a model. V. watching television.
My child most likes to see his/her good work noted by	A. hearing himself/herself praised in glowing terms. K. receiving a handshake, slap on the back, or hug and kiss. V. seeing good work on display around the house or stuck on the refrigerator.
My child would probably learn best how to cut a valentine heart if I	A. explained it verbally. K. stood over the child as he/she attempted the first heart and guided the actual cutting. V. showed the child a sample.
If I were selecting a gift to bring home for my child, the gift my child would most enjoy would be	A. a musical toy. K. a coloring book. V. a decorative item to hang in the child's room.
My child would probably best learn a new board game by	A. listening to an explanation of the game. K. jumping right in and learning while playing. V. watching others play the game.
My child would be most excited if the classroom teacher planned	A. a new listening corner with tapes and records. K. a "hands on" experience, such as an experiment. V. a movie.
If my child entered a room filled with debris, and heard a telephone ringing and couldn't find it, my child would try to locate the phone by	A. listening for the ring. K. moving items around and groping for the phone. V. trying to spot the phone.

The most effective way to teach my child a new skill would probably be to	A. buy a set of taped lessons. K. enroll the child in lessons. V. buy a book on the subject.
If my child wanted to learn more about insects, the child would probably	A. ask questions. K. catch some. V. get a book on the subject.
If my child had three social studies assignments, the first one the child would probably do is	A. ask older residents about the history of the community. K. make a model of a building in the community out of a cardboard box. V. read the article about communities in the children's magazine.

Total number of *A.* (auditory) responses: _____
Total number of *K.* (kinesthetic) responses: _____
Total number of *V.* (visual) responses: _____

Assessment 3—LEARNING STYLE

Background Information

Few children learn in exactly the same way. Your child's individuality dictates a particular learning style, which consists of a number of interrelated characteristics. Once you recognize the conditions that promote your child's learning, you can boost effectiveness by providing the environment and materials that fit. I am certain you can recall frustrating times when you were trying to study for an important test and were disturbed by noise, poor lighting, or icy feet. Throughout childhood, you were developing a gradual awareness of your learning style.

The next assessment is designed to help you zero in on your child's learning style, but more importantly, it is intended to help you help your child to understand it. Research studies show that children can discover how they learn, and you can speed the process along.

Following is a learning style survey to conduct with your child.[2] The procedure is informal, and you will probably want to ask your child to elaborate on some of the answers, or even to add questions of your own. Its major purpose is to heighten family sensitivity to learning style. Some questions do not apply to younger children.

LEARNING STYLES

Social

Do you learn better alone, with one friend, or in a group?

When you are studying, do you like to have adults help, be available to help, or leave you alone?

Time Rhythm

Do you learn best early in the morning, right before lunch, after lunch, after school, or right before bedtime?

Does it take you a long time to really feel awake in the morning?

Do you sometimes have trouble staying awake after lunch or dinner?

Do you like to get up early?

If you stay up late, do you feel "foggy" the next day?

Location

Where is the best place for you to study? (Examples—at a desk, in bed, at the library, on the floor.)

Do you like to study in a room with bright or dim lights?

Temperature

Do you think you feel cold or hot more often than other people?

Do you like a room to be a little on the warm side or a little on the cool side?

Auditory Stimuli

Can you study if you hear a radio or television in the background?

Are you distracted if you hear people talking or other children playing?

Do you like to study with music playing? If so, what kind of music?

Would you rather study alone, in a quiet room?

Movement

Do you find it hard to sit still while studying for a long time and need a lot of breaks?

Do you like to leave your studies to go see what is going on, get a drink, or change room or position?

Do you like to keep at your work until it is done?

Eating Habits

Do you like to eat, chew gum, or have a drink while you are learning?

Do you overeat, or chew your fingernails or a pencil when you are nervous?

Do you have trouble eating when you are nervous?

Motivation

Are good grades important to you?

Do you think your grades are really important to your teacher and parents?

Do you think getting a good education is one of the most important things in life?

Do you think reading is important for more things in life than just school?

Is it more important for you to get good grades to please adults or to please yourself?

Do you like school?

Do you let things go to the last minute?

Do you feel responsible for your learning? Does it bother you when you don't do well, are late, or don't finish an assignment?

Do you like solving your own problems or do you prefer being told exactly what is expected and how to do it?

Do you get upset easily when you are learning?

Do you like to learn and find out, even when you aren't in school and don't have to?

Do you have trouble concentrating? Do you find you daydream a lot?

Does it bother you when someone criticizes you?

Do you usually try to do your very best?

Anxiety

Do you think you worry more about school or tests than the other children?

Do you feel "shaky" when the teacher asks you to read aloud, get up in front of the class, or write on the board?

Do you ever have bad dreams about school or learning, such as making the teacher mad because you don't know your lessons or having a "surprise" test?

Interpretation

The implications of your child's responses to the above questions are relatively obvious. For example, if the child indicates a preference for studying alone, it makes little sense to suggest that a friend come over for a study session. Answers dealing with the best time of day to learn, location for study, temperature preference, noise level, movement requirements, and eating habits clearly suggest the ideal setting for your child's learning.

However, many children and parents never consider what the optimal conditions should be. Study is a hit-or-miss proposition. The learning style survey calls attention to these factors. While the home environment can be structured to correspond to the learning style, the school tends to be a more fixed environment. If your child functions best in an atmosphere of little structure, an open classroom, in which a hundred or more students share a large open space with no walls, could be ideal. However, the child who has a short attention span, is distractible, and requires fixed routines and structure as well as a low noise level would probably fall apart in such an environment. Or, if your child learns best in the afternoon, the common practice of teaching reading in the morning may not be the best approach in his or her case.

If you think that there is a wide difference between your child's learning style and the school's style, discuss the matter with the teacher. In some cases adjustments can be made. For example, if your child is distractible, the teacher might be able to arrange to move the child from the open classroom to a traditional classroom, or to provide a quiet corner or ''office'' by surrounding three sides of the student's desk with a large cardboard box. If you find that the conditions cannot be modified, you may want to look into other schools or make whatever adjustments are possible.

There are two other areas of the survey to bear in mind. The first deals with motivation. Your child's answers will provide some insight into the level of motivation. If you found the level low, perhaps the learning experience is not stimulating enough or doesn't offer enough chances for success. Further discussion of this subject occurs in Chapter Seven. The second area examines anxiety. Studies show that most children who perform under low levels of anxiety do better on difficult tasks than highly anxious children. Therefore, it is important to keep this type of stress under control. Take time to discuss the problem with your child and develop a plan, using approaches suggested in Chapter Twelve.

Winston Churchill once said, ''Personally, I'm always ready to learn, although I do not always like being taught.'' Use the results of the survey to maximize learning and you will help provide your child with a precious endowment—the love of learning.

Assessment 4—COMPARISON OF INDIVIDUALITY

Can You Mix Oil and Water?

In the process of analyzing your child's individuality you most likely found yourself examining your own, making comparisons between yourself and your child. Parents' personalities, too, must be taken into account in the parent/child relationship. The noted lawyer Clarence Darrow once observed, ''The first half of our lives is ruined by our parents, and the second half by our children.'' Unfortunately, there can be an element of truth to his statement. Great contrasts between the parent and child in temperament, modality preference, or learning style can be stress-producing for everyone concerned. Therefore, individuality cannot be considered in isolation. Many parents face a real dilemma. Firmly committed to both their own and their child's individuality, they find that each must be provided for within the context of the other. Following are some illustrations of this point.

Case 1   Fran and Mark Blake have one son, Joseph. Mr. and Mrs. Blake love a change. They like to eat supper seated on the floor Japanese-style, camp out in the backyard, or have surprise visitors. Their son feels more comfortable with a fixed routine. He likes to awaken at the same time, eat at the same hour each day, and follow a general pattern. The older Blakes' quest for something different has resulted in three moves in the past eight years. Fran and Mark have enjoyed the experiences of living in Manhattan, Denver, and San Francisco. However, since their last move, Joseph is noticeably more anxious than ever before. This condition is interfering with his schoolwork and social life.

Fran and Mark are highly adaptable and not overly concerned with regularity. Joseph, on the other hand, is not. His parents' frequent adaptation demands may be the source of the child's stress.

Case 2

Edward Rymes is a self-made man. His parents were poor and uneducated, and from the time Ed was seven years old, he worked hard for everything he got. At sixteen he held a full-time job to help support his family and earned top marks in school. He worked his way through college, set records in track, and won tennis championships. He graduated with honors and went on to law school. Edward Rymes believes that anything worth doing is not only worth doing well, but is worth doing better than anyone else. His son Claude has always been a good student, even making the honor roll on a few occasions. The teachers report that he is cooperative and has many friends. Claude enjoys baseball and football. When his father told him that if he didn't make better grades he'd never get into law school, Claude replied "So what?" Lately, Ed has been riding the boy more than ever, and the teachers report that Claude seems to have quit trying.

The root of the problem between Ed and Claude Rymes is a difference in their levels of aspiration. Ed is competitive, while Claude is cooperative. This fact is demonstrated in their respective choices in sports—Ed electing tennis and track, while his son prefers team sports. The conflict between the two has produced a stressful situation, in which Claude has stopped trying in school out of the frustration of never being able to please his father or perhaps merely to rebel.

Case 3

Marta Lyons loves her twelve-year-old daughter Paula, but the two just can't seem to get along. Marta is a widow, and she has managed to work herself up into an excellent job in her company. She never trusts anything to chance, especially when it comes to her daughter. People who know Marta say she is in perfect control of her life. Paula is much like her mother. She is a leader and serves as class president and a teacher's assistant at Sunday school. She usually takes command of games and play activities with her friends. When a counselor recently asked Paula why she had disobeyed her mother and sneaked into a R-rated movie, Paula responded: "I did it because Mom told me not to. I really didn't want to see that dumb picture. I am just sick and tired of her telling me everything to do. She won't even let me pick my own clothes or friends."

Marta and Paula both share an extreme desire to control. This strong personality trait results in constant friction, in which Paula will often buy some item she doesn't even want or do something she doesn't want to do, simply to prove that she is in control.

Case 4   Karen Carmichael is convinced there is something wrong with her three-year-old Amy. The child awakes to the slightest noise, refuses to eat most foods, and cries vigorously when only slightly injured. This child is not her first, and she can't figure out why Amy has been so difficult since birth.

There is nothing wrong with Amy. She merely has a different sensory threshold than Karen's other children. She is more sensitive to sound, taste, and pain. Karen apparently does not share this sensitivity and hasn't been able to recognize it, so far.

These cases reveal that individual differences can be powerful stressors. In some cases, the wide variation in personalities between parent and child is the source of strain, while in others the close similarity creates tension. Admittedly, there are no simple solutions. However, in each situation there is a lack of understanding and tolerance. If the parents recognized and accepted their children's basic temperament, as well as their own, they would take the first big step toward adjusting to the problems. The Blakes, realizing their son is not highly adaptable, might stick to a slightly more fixed routine when the child is involved. When an unusual circumstance or move puts Joseph under stress, they can provide coping assistance by avoiding additional disruption, offering extra warmth and security, and helping the boy develop a coping strategy.

Ed Rymes needs to acknowledge the differences in levels of aspiration and competitiveness between him and his son. Although it might be difficult to accept, Ed should realize that his son will probably never share his drive. While there is no need for Ed to change, neither is it imperative that Claude change. Ed should tolerate and respect his son's individuality. In situations like this one, professional counseling is often useful.

Marta and Paula Lyons should both learn to compromise. Once they identify the components of their personalities that cause the friction between them, they can make progress. This case is another that might best be handled by a family therapist.

Karen Carmichael's problem is the easiest to solve. Hopefully, Amy's pediatrician or a more experienced parent will set her straight.

Following is the final assessment, a comparison of individuality exercise. This scale is designed to compare how you and your child match on twenty individuality factors. Read each pair of traits. Start at the point in the middle of the line, which is the average or neutral position. Decide how close you fall to either extreme of behavior listed. Place a mark on the line. Repeat the procedure for your child, using a different-colored pen. For example, on the first item, if you feel you are about average when it comes to disposition, you would place a mark somewhere near the midline. If you feel your child is very moody, you would place a second mark near the end of the line where it says "Moody disposition." Remember, this assessment tool is designed to compare differences and similarities, rather than to assign a precise value. If you or your child doesn't lean toward either extreme, your mark should be close to the midpoint. The greater the strength of the characteristic listed, the closer the mark should be placed to the extreme or end point.

Interpretation

After you have completed the comparison exercise, look at the range of differences between you and your child for each set of traits. In some cases you might be at the opposite ends of the continuum, while in others you are probably quite close. In either

COMPARISON OF INDIVIDUALITY

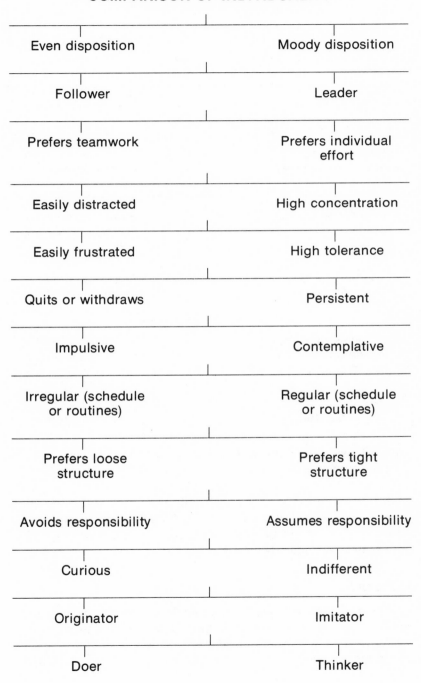

Even disposition	Moody disposition
Follower	Leader
Prefers teamwork	Prefers individual effort
Easily distracted	High concentration
Easily frustrated	High tolerance
Quits or withdraws	Persistent
Impulsive	Contemplative
Irregular (schedule or routines)	Regular (schedule or routines)
Prefers loose structure	Prefers tight structure
Avoids responsibility	Assumes responsibility
Curious	Indifferent
Originator	Imitator
Doer	Thinker

COMPARISON OF INDIVIDUALITY

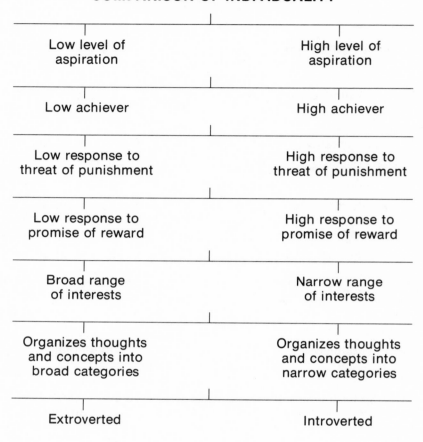

Low level of aspiration	High level of aspiration
Low achiever	High achiever
Low response to threat of punishment	High response to threat of punishment
Low response to promise of reward	High response to promise of reward
Broad range of interests	Narrow range of interests
Organizes thoughts and concepts into broad categories	Organizes thoughts and concepts into narrow categories
Extroverted	Introverted

case ask yourself if the wide variation or close similarity is contributing to family stress.

If the answer is yes, everyone concerned needs to work jointly at developing a coping strategy. Family life is a reciprocal arrangement. Stress is bound to occur when family members continually lock horns. Belief in the uniqueness of each and every individual results in a live-and-let-live attitude.

Conclusion

The ancient Greeks were fond of advising that one should "know thyself." The task is easier said than done. Most of us are continually learning who we are and what makes us tick, perhaps because we are constantly growing and changing. Obviously, if it is difficult to understand ourselves, understanding our children is a real challenge. It is a challenge that must be met, however, if parents are truly interested in preventing, minimizing, and controlling stress.

Since stress is a personal reaction, you first need to know about the person before you can understand the reaction. Information on temperament, modality preference, and learning style can help you understand why your child is stressed. With this knowledge you can prevent yourself from unwittingly contributing to a child's stress by working at odds with the child's individuality. And you will be better prepared to assist your child in developing coping strategies that will work.

PART II

Minimize and Prevent Stress

Chapter Four

Raise a Free Child

The heart of coping ability is freedom. The coping child has a good, strong self-image and doesn't sense subtle pressure to repress true emotions or to conform to molds that don't quite fit. Your child is one of a kind. Stereotypes, firmly anchored in tradition, threaten to diminish and compromise this precious uniqueness. The masculine stereotype, which forces men to be macho and prove it in sports, sex, work, and war, produces stress and anxiety, reflected in a higher male incidence of ulcers, strokes, heart disease, and early death. The feminine stereotype results in undue emphasis on appearance, lack of self-confidence, overdependence, and simultaneous fear of both success and failure.

Unfortunately, while most parents claim to hold freedom sacred, they don't work actively toward raising free children. Freedom is more than the absence of oppression and tyranny. It also means freedom to be oneself. Parents usually display one of two poohpoohing tendencies for avoiding the issue of sexism. First, they dismiss the whole issue on the basis that they are on the right track and already avoid stereotyping. This smugness is generally unjustified, but even in cases where the parents are themselves doing an adequate job, the child is nonetheless being molded by a host of outside influences. The second tendency is for parents to associate this issue with the women's movement and simply react with a "Not interested." Well, no parent serious about childhood stress can afford to be "not interested."

From the time that children are born, parents and society begin to make demands of children which force them to go underground. You wouldn't dream of insisting that your child wear shoes that don't fit, yet you may be unconsciously guiding your child toward a life-style that doesn't quite fit. The implications for generating a stressful condition are obvious. Trying to be something you're not, or working or playing at one thing when you'd rather be doing something else, produces stress.

Coping requires the ability to easily and rapidly adapt to changing situations. In raising a free child you don't limit the child's range. The free youngster grows into an adult who is equally adept at dealing with the stresses of a sick infant or a clogged plumbing pipe.

Sex stereotyping curtails the freedom of both boys and girls. The boy who is made to feel inferior because he didn't "stand up and fight" experiences stress in much the same way as the girl who wants to win but is afraid she will appear unfeminine.

Raising a free child makes historically repressed components of the male or female personality acceptable. It means freeing-up options for your sons and daughters. Perpetuating traditional stereotyping in your home, or permitting it to go unquestioned in school, books, or in the media, not only creates stress by clearly defining limits for your children, but also renders youngsters less versatile when it comes to coping with emotional and practical stresses.

Male or Female—Can You Tell the Difference?

Before a child is born, sex stereotyping begins. Friends and relatives attempt the impossible—predicting the baby's sex based on the activity level of the unborn or the way the mother's stomach is protruding. When the child is born, the very first question parents ask about their baby, even prior to inquiring about health, is "Is it a boy or a girl?" The infant is tagged Baby Boy Smith or Baby Girl Jones and, in many hospitals, wrapped in a pink or blue blanket. The proud papa distributes cigars proclaiming, "It's a boy!" or "It's a girl!" Friends and relatives delay gift selection until the sex of the child is known, although the newborn can hardly differentiate between the masculine or the feminine. Within the very first hours of life parents begin to deal with their new offspring in a sex-typed manner.

In one study the parents of newborns were questioned during the first day of the baby's life. Although the male and female infants did not differ substantially in birth length, weight, or score on the Apgar vital signs rating scale, parental labeling was obvious. Fathers tended to stereotype their newborns more often than mothers. Girls were described as softer, finer, littler, while boys were firmer, more alert, and stronger. What advantage is there for these infant boys or girls in assigning nonexistent traits? Roles, clothes, behaviors, toys, and expectations are assigned on the basis of sex, rather than individuality. Parental failure to acknowledge individual predispositions toward a wide range of behavior is a major cause of childhood stress. Firmly entrenched stereotypes drastically interfere with the child's ability to form positive self-feelings, maximize full potential, and cope with stress using a variety of responses.

Following is a quiz which tests your knowledge of the real differences between girls and boys. See if you are raising your children based on myth or reality.

DO YOU KNOW THE REAL DIFFERENCES?

Read each statement and judge if it is a myth or reality. Mark *M* or *R* on the line.

M or R

_____   1. I can skip this section if my children are all boys.

_____   2. I can skip this section if my consciousness has already been raised.

_____   3. I can skip this section if I firmly believe that this women's movement stuff only complicates an already complicated world.

_____   4. Intellectually outstanding boys tend to be unusually active, competitive, free from anxiety, and independent.

_____   5. Intellectually outstanding girls tend to be timid, not highly aggressive, and anxious.

_____   6. The degree of pressure to be "manly" has been directly related to male childhood anxiety.

_____   7. Girls are more dependent than boys.

_____   8. Boys are more aggressive than girls.

_____   9. Girls have more empathy than boys.

_____ 10. Boys are more intelligent than girls.

_____ 11. Girls are more fearful than boys.

_____ 12. Boys are more competitive than girls.

_____ 13. Girls are more creative than boys.

_____ 14. Boys are less social than girls.

_____ 15. Girls have better reading and verbal skills than boys.

_____ 16. Boys have better math skills than girls.

_____ 17. Girls are more passive than boys.

_____ 18. The brain accounts for a greater percentage of body weight in the male than in the female.

_____ 19. The causes of male aggression, competitiveness and violence are biological in nature.

_____ 20. Stress can cause females to have anxiety about achieving success.

_____ 21. The Christian, Jewish, and Islamic religions have always emphasized equality of the sexes.

_____ 22. Girls mature at a faster and steadier rate than boys.

_____ 23. Pseudohermaphrodites (individuals born with the external genitalia of one sex, but the chromosomes and internal genitalia of the opposite sex) will assume the sex identity associated with the external genitalia.

_____ 24. Sex roles are biologically linked and do not vary greatly from culture to culture.

_____ 25. Trained educators are taught to deal with children in nonsexist terms.

ANSWER KEY:

__M__ 1. Stereotyping is a source of childhood stress that affects both boys and girls. In fact, during the early years sex role demands are even more stringent for boys. Many parents can easily accept their daughter playing with "boys'" toys or dressing in "male" clothing. Similar behavior in their son is harshly criticized. The small boy functions daily in a setting ideal for generating anxiety. Poorly understood demands are rigidly placed on a youngster who cannot comprehend the reasons for these demands. Enforcement is by threats, punishment, and mockery from those most near and dear. Anything feminine is regarded as sissy and inferior. The child is ultimately conditioned to transfer this negativity to females, as well.

__M__ 2. You may be a staunch supporter of ERA, buy trucks for your daughter, and teach your son to knit. You may also believe that sex stereotyping is a dead issue—that the women's movement solved all the really big problems years ago. Parents' influence on children is, of course, primary. However, children are also socialized by schools, teachers, television, advertisements, toys, books, their peers, and other adults. Doing your nonsexist thing as a parent may not be enough to counteract the other stereotyping forces. You cannot afford to jeopardize all your hard work by taking nonsexist child raising for granted. You must recognize stereotyping in all its forms.

__M__ 3. You may be feeling anxious or confused about abandoning traditional sex-role typing. Perhaps you believe that girls should be taught to do "girl" things and vice versa for boys. Maybe you fear that the social order will be affected or homosexuality will increase. The obvious physical differences that exist in females and males have created a bias in which the actual differences have been vastly exaggerated. In most traits and abilities, sexual differences are almost nonexistent.

There is simply no logical reason for attempting to force children into molds. It makes about as much sense as a preschooler trying to pound a puzzle piece into the wrong spot. Ridding our children of sex-role stereotypes will not result in social chaos. The issue of sexuality in a nonstereotyped society has been addressed by experts who point out that physical differences will always exist, and therefore the sexual appeal associated with these differences will certainly persist. In fact, eliminating traditional stereotypes will not increase homosexuality, but might actually result in more interesting, genuine male-female relationships.

M 4. Eleanor Maccoby and Carol Jacklin of Stanford University have found the opposite to be true. They discovered that intellectually outstanding boys were often timid, anxious, not overtly aggressive, and less active. These traits are not generally associated with the masculine stereotype and could easily prove a source of childhood stress in boys.

M 5. The Maccoby–Jacklin study found the opposite to be true in this case as well. Intellectually superior girls were unusually active, independent, competitive, and free from anxiety. Again, these traits are not associated with femininity and could prove stress-provoking.

R 6. The emphasis on manliness is directly related to male childhood stress. Boys who are free from constricting role expectations have a lower anxiety level.

M 7. There is no evidence that girls cling to parents, teachers, or other adults any more than boys of their same age.

R 8. Aggression is one of the few areas in which research does support sex differences. Boys engage in more physical and verbal battling and efforts to dominate. Although male aggression is encouraged by our culture, it is also exhibited by other primates, leading experts to believe it is linked to the hormone testosterone. Aggression is a highly inefficient way of coping with stress.

M   9. No evidence exists to prove that girls are more empathetic than boys.

M   10. There is no significant difference in overall intelligence test scores between the sexes.

M   11. Girls are not more fearful. They are simply more open about admitting their fears. Boys have been conditioned to hide fears, which often leads to a bottling up of stress.

R   12. Studies have shown that when girls and boys are given a task to perform, girls do better under neutral conditions. However, when competition is introduced, boys are more motivated and catch up to the girls' performance.

M   13. Research findings indicate no difference in verbal or nonverbal creativity between males and females.

M   14. There is no evidence that during infancy or childhood girls are any more social than boys. The old wives' tale about girls responding to people while boys respond to objects is unjustified. However, patterns of friendship vary. Girls tend to have fewer, more intense friendships. Boys feel secure when interacting with a group or gang.

R   15. Boys are definitely the majority in remedial reading classes.

R   16. It is uncertain whether male superiority in math is a cultural phenomenon or the result of better visual-spatial aptitude. Some experts believe that the visual-spatial ability is related to a recessive gene. There is sex crossover, and approximately one half of all males—as compared to only one fourth of all females—possess this special aptitude.

M   17. No evidence exists to support the supposition that girls are more passive. They are just as active as boys—but in different ways. Female play is sometimes more peaceful and imaginative, while male play is more vigorous.

M   18. Although the male brain weighs an average of four ounces more than the female brain, the female brain is actually 2.5 percent of total body weight, as compared to 2 percent for the male. However, these facts are irrelevant. Brain size is not an indicator of intelligence.

More M
than R 19. Differences between men and women are almost entirely limited to sex and reproduction. Although there might be a link between hormones and aggressive behavior, the majority of researchers believe this behavior is more closely tied to societal expectations.

R 20. Some experts feel that females are motivated to avoid success because it is not acceptable with the stereotype of femininity. Females are placed in an approach-avoidance conflict. They are attracted by success but threatened by the negative consequences that they perceive will follow. Consider the statement by Martin Luther, "No gown worse becomes a woman than the desire to be wise."

M 21. In a book entitled, *Sexism and Youth,* Diane Gersoni-Stavn points out that religious ideology contains numerous examples of nonegalitarian sentiment:

ISLAMIC   Men are superior to women on account of the qualities in which God has given them preeminence.
                                        —The Koran, sacred text of Islam

JEWISH   Blessed art Thou, oh Lord our God, King of the Universe, that I was not born a woman.
                                        —Morning Prayer of the Orthodox Jew

CHRISTIAN   For a man . . . is the image and glory of God; but the woman is the glory of the man.
                For the man is not of the woman; but the woman of the man.
                Neither was the man created for the woman; but the woman for the man.
                                        —I Cor. 11:7–9.

R 22. Girls usually reach puberty one to two years ahead of boys.

M 23. Pseudohermaphrodites will gain their sexual identity from the socializing influence of their parents. They will be taught to assume the male or the female role, establishing the significance of socialization on sex role formation.

M 24. In 1935 noted anthropologist Margaret Mead studied three New Guinea tribes. Each culture demonstrates sex roles strikingly different from our own.

The Arapesh are mountain people whose male and female children develop traits our society would consider feminine. Boys and girls are socialized to be passive, peaceful, and gentle. At birth both parents are said to have "born the child." Authority figures are offensive to the Arapesh. Therefore, leaders must be selected during childhood and specially trained. If not, there might be no leadership.

The Mundugumor live a mere eighty miles from the Arapesh. In their culture both the males and females are trained to be aggressive, violent, and competitive. Jealousy and combat abound, and the mother spends as little time as possible nurturing her child.

The last tribe is the exact opposite of our culture. The Tchambuli females provide the sustenance, are the sexual aggressors, and dominate the society. The males dress in finery, are dependent, are expected to be sensitive and artistic.

After considering these three widely varying sets of sex roles, all of which vary drastically from ours, Margaret Mead wrote:

> . . . many, if not all, of the personality traits which we have called masculine or feminine are as lightly linked to sex as are the clothing, the manners, and the form of headdress that a society at a given period assigns to either sex . . . the evidence is overwhelming in favor of social conditioning.[1]

__M__   25. Few teachers have had training in recognizing sexist practices, books, or materials. Your child's education is probably loaded with stereotypical indoctrination. This fact is alarming when you consider the blind faith and trust children place in their school, teacher, and books. Could poor teacher training be related to the boys' unexplained lower reading scores referred to in question 15?

How did you do? If you are like most parents, you probably missed several questions. The quiz was designed to present an overview of the large volume of information and research findings directly related to raising a free child. As you can see, most of the differences that exist between the sexes are created by the socialization process. For example, if your daughter is more dependent than your son, it might be a learned, rather than an inherited biological trait. Any questions missed should signal a source of misinformation, and you should ask yourself if this misinformation has influenced your child-raising practices. For example, if you were not aware that pressures to be manly are a cause of a male childhood anxiety, have you unwittingly placed such pressures on your son?

Child-raising decisions must be based on fact rather than folklore. Creating differences that do not actually exist between boys and girls creates a stressful situation in which children must subordinate their true selves in favor of perceived selves. In addition, it results in a loss of potential, potential that could be used for effectively managing a wider range stress.

Is Your Spouse a Feminist or Your Child Androgynous?

Every new social movement tends to produce a litter of new terms. Many of the words are vague, awkward, and confusing. The free-child movement has led to the realization that assignment of rigid male-female roles in a contemporary society can be a source of stress from childhood through adulthood, for both males and females. Before we go any further, we must define the most often encountered terms born of this movement. Read the definitions and then answer the question, Is your spouse a feminist or your child androgynous?

Sexism

The attitudes, beliefs, behaviors, or practices of individuals, institutions, or society which assume that one sex is superior to another.

Example:

Sara is scheduled for a haircut. Her friend has recommended Terry as the top hairdresser in the area. Sara calls for an appointment. When the receptionist says, "He can take you at three o'clock," Sara hangs up. When her husband gets home, she tells him: "There is *no way* I'd let a man cut my hair. What does a man know about women's hair?"

Sex Discrimination

The denying of opportunity, privilege, right or reward on the basis of sex.

Example:

Ms. Stewart teaches kindergarten. Every Friday she changes the jobs on her "Helping Hands" chart. Billy approaches her desk and asks if he can be the "duster." Ms. Stewart replies: "Of course not. The girls do that job—but you may hold the doors."

Sex Role Stereotyping

The biased assumption that all females share a set of common interests, abilities, values, and roles. And that males, on the other hand, share a separate set of characteristics. The result of stereotyping is the assignment of "appropriate" roles and occupations based on gender rather than on individuality.

Example: Billy and Sue are playing a precarious version of tag—running along the top of the fence. Mom enters the scene just as Billy takes a tumble and begins to shriek. Sue springs down from the fence. Mom determines that Billy is not seriously injured and admonishes, "Billy, big boys don't cry," and "Sue, act like a lady and stop hopping along that fence like a squirrel."

Social-ization The manner in which children are prepared to function in the various physical, social, psychological, economic, and political roles that make up society. Families, schools, and society provide children with experiences and models that teach the children attitudes, knowledge, and skills deemed necessary for survival.

Example: Every Saturday morning the DiCantro family perform weekly chores. Mom and Delores vacuum, dust, and change beds. Dad, Bob, and Louis work on the car or in the yard. Dad is fond of telling the boys, "Someday you will be supporting a family." Mother tells Delores, "A good mother keeps a happy home."

Sex Equality The belief that men and women have equal ability and an equal role to play in the intellectual, political, athletic, and artistic spheres of life.

Example: Carolyn Laird is recognized in her company as an expert in computer programming. She is respected, jealously sought after for many projects, and paid on a level equal to her male counterparts.

Androgyny The original Greek word comprised of *andr* (referring to male) and *gynē* (referring to female), which described the presence of both male and female characteristics in a single organism. The ancient Greeks called this organism hermaphrodite. The modern meaning of the word is not physical-sexual, but rather psychological-sociocultural. It connotes flexibility of sex role. The androgynous individual is capable of behaving in both masculine and feminine ways. I prefer to use this confusing term only as an attention getter.

Example: Roy Manning is an aggressive salesman. He thrives on competition and actively plots a program of ''attack'' when trying to land a new account. Today he beat out the competition's top man. He feels a sense of achievement when he arrives home. He is met at the door by his son Jerry. Jerry presents him with a letter he wrote in first grade that day. It says, ''I love the loviest Dad in the world.'' Bob is touched. He tenderly holds his son, hugs and kisses him, and sheds a few tears of joy. Bob is androgynous. His personality is a union of characteristics traditionally considered male, as well as female.

Feminists The group of individuals who advocate legal and social changes that produce social, economic, and political equality of the sexes. Being a feminist does not necessarily mean endorsing abortion on demand, drafting women, or other extreme positions often associated with the women's movement.

Example: Fran and Dave are a working couple with two children under three years of age. Fran hates grocery shopping, making the bed, and changing dirty diapers. Dave usually performs these jobs. Dave hates taking the car in for repairs, cooking, and lawn work. Fran takes care of these chores. Fran and Dave both demonstrate feminist beliefs. They have worked out arrangements that support self-determination and family intimacy.

Nonsexist child raising The method for rearing children that results in freedom to be individuals. Nonsexist children are free to make their own decisions about their lives without being limited by sex. Nonsexist child raising does *not* mean nonsexual. Some parents imagine it means ignoring all differences. Others think that nonsexist means consciously giving a boy a doll, while giving a girl a truck. Nonsexist child raising recognizes the differences in girls and boys. It does not attempt to create confusion by giving children an overabundance of playthings usually associated with the opposite sex. If your daughter prefers a doll to a truck, that's fine—but if she prefers a truck to a doll, that's okay too. Nonsexist parents accept the uniqueness and differences of every child without establishing parameters based on sex.

Example: Mark enters Montessori school at age three. He has never played with housekeeping toys before. Mark loves the play iron that actually generates heat. Dad is delighted at Mark's pleasure with the new toy and buys one for Mark's fourth birthday. Mark also likes to dress in football gear and play tackle. Mom and Dad regularly play backyard football with him. Mark's seven-year-old brother, Frank, wants to learn to crochet. Mom teaches him and Dad to crochet. The teacher comments that crocheting improves eye-hand coordination. When Mark cries, he is treated no differently than his twin, Mary. Mark is being raised in a nonsexist home.

Is Your Head on Straight?

In building any structure a good solid foundation is required. In raising a free child you—the parent—are the foundation. You must free yourself from stress-producing parenting practices inherited from your parents and learned through socialization. Your commitment to raising a free child must be reflected daily. Sex roles are largely learned, and parents are the most effective teachers. Consider the tragic, but true, story of identical male twins.[2] One of the babies lost his penis during electrocautery circumcision. Plastic surgery was performed to construct female genitalia, and hormone treatment was planned for adolescence. Prior to any latter treatment the mother reported that the twins, genetically identical, at the age of ten were amazingly different. The boy was described as "masculine"—messy, athletic, and prone to imitate his father. The girl was "feminine"—tidy, fussy about pretty dresses, fond of dolls, and prone to imitate her mother. Born male, the twins had learned quite different sex roles.

After reading a report like this one, it is easy to go overboard, but the study does spotlight the highly significant role of parents in the ultimate development of their children. In the case reported, the learned behavior was more significant than the inherited sex. Anatomical differences do obviously exist, and it makes no sense to attempt to deny gender identity. In order to be well-adjusted a child must be aware of his or her sex. Some overzealous parents have dressed their children in unisex clothing and bombarded them with toys and experiences traditionally associated with the opposite sex. This practice can result in a child who is sexually confused, a prime source of stress. Nonsexist child raising means that the child is free to choose—free to choose ballet over baseball, *regardless* of sex. It does *not* mean insisting that your daughter go to baseball practice while forcing your son to take ballet. I am reminded of a skit I once enjoyed. The feminist parents decided to ignore the letters to Santa their son and daughter had written. Jack requested a truck—Jill, a doll. On Christmas morning they heard the children excitedly unwrapping the packages. They tiptoed in to see Jill cradling her truck, while Jack slid the doll across the floor, yelling, *"Rrrrrroooooooooom."*

There are feminist coloring and picture books that show only women driving a truck, building a house, or installing a telephone. A child might get the impression from these materials that men don't work and women no longer care for children. Obviously, these extremes can create confusion and over the long run contribute to stress.

There have been millions of words written by psychologists, sociologists, educators, pediatricians, and others regarding the best way to raise children. Books are available in libraries, book shops, bus depots, grocery stores, and newsstands everywhere. Each year they make their way into thousands of American homes. You probably have several on your bookshelf. Unfortunately, the vast majority of these books—particularly those with early copyright dates—assume that the mother will almost solely raise the children. About one half of them fail to mention sex role development. The other half range from those books which urge parents to delineate those stress-producing specific male and female sex roles to a few more modern volumes that do discuss raising a free child.

It seems that everywhere you turn, you face stereotyping in progress. In order to raise a truly free child you must be willing to reevaluate many of the values you assimilated from parents and experts and from our culture to alter your sexist thinking. We all learn by example. Many of our child-raising techniques are identical to those our parents used. In simpler times many of these practices might have been appropriate, but today you must be on the alert for outdated stereotypes. The majority of books on rearing children have taught you to socialize your boys to be masculine, while training your daughters to be feminine. The resultant stress, experienced relatively early in the lives of males, can eventually result in double stress in females who may worry not only about failure, but about success, as well.

A number of significant influences, including parents, recognized experts, and society as a whole, encourage differential treatment for boys and girls, the most stress-producing examples of which are listed below.

The Double Standard

When it comes to sons and daughters, many parents deal with identical behaviors in very different ways. Do you accept your daughter playing with boys' toys or acting like a tomboy, but put your foot down when it comes to your son acting girlish? Small boys, particularly, are placed in a high-anxiety situation when they are threatened, punished, or mocked for behavior no one ever directly told them to avoid. They learn more about what not to do than what to do. They are confused when anything feminine is regarded as sissylike and experience stress when they genuinely feel a natural attraction to a doll, makeup kit, or female playmate.

Many parents habitually offer more assistance to daughters than to sons. The boys are told to solve problems on their own. This practice obviously creates the stress of rivalry between siblings, and can both slow down boys' progress in being able to solve problems and create overdependence in girls.

In some households acts of aggression and assertiveness are more readily tolerated in boys than in girls. Boys are thereby encouraged to deal with stress in more aggressive terms, while girls are puzzled when they are disciplined for dealing with stressful situations in a manner which was acceptable in their brothers. In fact, the very act of repressing anger and aggression can create a stressful situation. Children need the freedom to express emotions, for maintaining a keyed-up condition can ultimately produce emotional and physical problems. So often, parents discourage their sons from releasing tension with tears while reinforcing such behavior by providing comforting words to daughters when they cry. While the venting of anger through aggression might be an important release, it is a highly inefficient coping mechanism. Boys who are socialized to adopt aggressive techniques are handicapped in developing a workable method for coping with childhood—and later adult—stress.

The importance of stimulating early verbal development is well recorded in research findings. That boys do not do as well as girls in reading and verbal skills might, in part, be due to the fact that many parents talk to and give more physical contact to infant daughters than to sons.

The constant growth toward independence should be equal for both sons and daughters. Is independence encouraged more in your son than in your daughter? Do you tolerate clinging, dependent behavior in your daughter? Is your daughter more reliant on the opinions of others? Decisions regarding your child's level of independence must be based on individuality, rather than sex. Moving a child ahead too rapidly, or sheltering a child needlessly, can create undue stress and render the child less capable of adjusting to the adult world.

Every human being wants and needs love, affection, and physical warmth and contact. Children deprived of these basics will develop serious behavioral problems and become insecure or experience difficulty with interpersonal relationships. Some parents, fathers in particular, have a tendency to shower more demonstrable affection on girls than boys. Sibling rivalry (a great source of childhood stress) and various forms of deprivation are potential dangers.

The options for play and playthings should be no different for boys than for girls. A wide variety of toys and activities should be available, without regard to sex. Fathers should guard against spending more time roughhousing with boys and teaching them sports than they do with girls. Mothers should be careful not to discourage boys from imitating them as they encourage girls to do. Play and imitation are important sources of information, helping children develop cognitive, perceptual, and physical abilities. In addition, children role-play solutions to many of life's stressful situations. With so much to learn, no activity should be excluded simply on the basis of sex.

Last, there is the matter of appearance. The same standards of grooming should be applied to all children. Many young boys are stressed when their sister is always the object of large clothing expenditures and much attention at family gatherings. Also, don't be upset if your preschool son wants a skirt. He is simply fascinated by the beauty of the swirling fabric and shouldn't be put to shame for his request, whether or not you fulfill it.

A clear understanding of the individuality of your child, as well as of the stress potential of stereotyping, will help you set realistic goals in nonsexist parenting. Common sense will create the balance. The groundwork has been laid. You are aware of the most prevailing sexist misconceptions which not only affect the parent-child relationship, but also permeate a multitude of daily outside interactions. As a parent you must work around the stereotyping ingrained in society. Once you are convinced that raising a free child is an important way to reduce stress and help your child develop the adaptability necessary for managing the inevitable pressures of life, you can begin to rid yourself of the menacing stereotyping of the past. Don't be surprised if a few die-hard practices linger on. Despite any slight holdovers, you will find that your modified parenting attitudes will help you to be more relaxed, less vulnerable to parental stress.

If you are successful in raising a free child, you can expect your son or daughter to view parenthood as a shared experience, to believe that both husband and wife should nurture children. Your child will express a full range of often opposite emotions. The free child may be tough one minute and tender the next; independent in some areas and dependent in others. Your child will engage in both active and passive activities. Both sexes will develop a keen interest in physical fitness, an important stress-preventer, and will be challenged to maximize physical potential. Your free child will consider a wide range of options for leisure, as well as occupational, choices. Decisions will be based on interests, values, and abilities—rather than on sex. Last, your child will avoid unnecessary stress resulting from confining sex roles which impinge on emotional, occupational, and leisure-time freedom.

The remainder of this chapter will deal with societal influences beyond the family. But first, let's see how you rate on a scale of one to ten. Wait one month and evaluate yourself again to see if you are closer to becoming a perfect "ten."

ARE YOU A PERFECT "TEN"?

Give yourself one point each for: **Score**

1. Providing your child with a variety of nonsexist role models, by not limiting your activities. Both mothers and fathers should engage in nurturing and domestic roles as well as repairs and maintenance.   ____

2. Aiding your child in developing a wide range of coping competencies such as nurturing, sewing, cleaning, cooking, fixing, working with tools, and so on.   ____

3. Taking the stress out of exercising nontraditional options in toys, career interests, personality development, emotional expression, and play. ____

4. Recognizing stress-provoking stereotypes in schools and books and doing something about it by speaking up, writing letters—but most importantly, discussing it critically with your child. ____

5. Promoting physical and athletic development in both boys and girls. Physical fitness is effective in stress prevention. ____

6. Limiting and regulating television viewing. Discussing stereotypes in programming and advertisements. ____

7. Ridding your language of sexism, such as telling your son that big boys don't cry. ____

8. Dressing your son or daughter appropriately for play and realizing that play dirt is healthy dirt. ____

9. Making children aware of their own stress-provoking behavior. For example, children should be counseled when they make up such rules as, "This club is for girls only," or "Only boys can play in our baseball games." ____

10. Loving your son or daughter and showing it in words, physical contact, deeds, and a determination to protect their freedom to be individuals. ____

Total (first time) ____

Total (second time) ____

Education and the Free Child

Despite the fact that parents play the most influential role in raising free children, a host of outside factors also affect the child's development. These influences have the potential to greatly mitigate the progress being made in the home if the parent fails to acknowledge their power.

The biggest thrust for personal freedom is found on college campuses, in the world of work, and in other adult-centered settings. However, it is extremely difficult to reverse the results of stereotyping eighteen or more years later. The promotion of equality and freedom should begin in early childhood. Unfortunately, it rarely does. Sex role stereotyping is part and parcel of the entire educational experience. Yet, I feel certain that if you asked your child's teacher what the goals were for the year, the answer would reflect a commitment to developing each child's full potential. That goal is difficult when stereotyping forces children to subordinate their true selves to a learned "ideal."

Research studies show that sexist practices do exist in schools, and most of our teacher-training programs are doing little, if anything, to prevent it.

Schools often reflect sexist staffing. Although figures vary, the number of female teachers is estimated by most researchers to be 85 percent at the elementary level with approximately 79 percent of the elementary-school principals being male. Women are also underrepresented on school boards and in the leadership of their local unions and professional organizations.

What are the effects of education on raising a free child? The evidence indicates that there is consistent sex bias in the schools which favors girls in some situations and boys in others. Such practices create confusion and anxiety in both sexes, ultimately demeaning the talents of girls and placing conflicting demands on boys. Girls are given a double dose of femininity training, being socialized at both home and school to be docile, dependent, and obedient. Boys are expected to demonstrate the masculine traits of independence, activity, and achievement, while simultaneously reflecting the good student traits of conformity, quiet, and passivity. Teachers interact more often with boys than with girls in all major categories of interpersonal relations, including approval, disapproval, instruction, and listening attention. Girls have been socialized to behave and are, therefore, ignored—the squeaky wheel gets the oil. Boys are the greatest source of discipline problems for the teacher and are disciplined more harshly than girls. Certain courses, such as sewing or wood shop, have traditionally been sex-segregated. Many classrooms separate boys and girls for seating, lineup, or locker assignment. Girls more often receive disapproval for lack of skill, knowledge, or wrong answers than boys, yet when teachers criticize boys, they use an angrier tone; girls are more often reprimanded in a normal voice. Girls have a lower self-concept than boys of the same age and IQ. Girls receive higher grades than boys for equal achievement. Both boys and girls view common classroom objects, such as the blackboard, desks, or textbooks, as feminine. As both boys and girls progress through the grades, their general assessment of male ability increases while their assessment of female ability begins to decline.

What conclusions can we draw? Apparently, a child's sex can have a bearing on the discipline, interaction, grading, and overall education provided by our schools. Teachers are teaching boys and girls instead of children.

Boys Against the Girls

Assuming that you manage to avoid stereotypical child-raising practices and are conscientiously working to raise a free child, it would be a shame for the school to frustrate your efforts. Forewarned is forearmed. Get your pencil and grade your school's report card. You may have to ask an expert to help you on some of the points—so keep your child nearby.

REPORT CARD

	PASS	FAIL
Achieves a balance of male and female teachers and administrators.	——	——
Mixes boys and girls for seating and line arrangements.	——	——
Equally assigns girls and boys as hall guards, crossing guards, office assistants, teacher assistants, and audiovisual aides.	——	——
Maintains standard disciplinary policy for boys and girls. The same person handles both male and female discipline problems.	——	——
Opens clubs and extracurricular activities to both boys and girls. There is equal representation of the sexes in club leadership.	——	——
Maintains no designation of books, toys, and equipment for boys and girls. They are actually used by both sexes.	——	——
Enrolls girls in drafting, wood shop, auto mechanics, and industrial arts.	——	——
Enrolls boys in secretarial courses, home economics, and music electives.	——	——
Counselor suggests course offerings and career opportunities based on individuality rather than on sex.	——	——
Displays pictures showing an equal number of males and females.	——	——
Involves fathers as much as mothers in conferences, field trips, communications, and programs.	——	——
Gives boys and girls equal instructional time.	——	——

Avoids verbal reinforcement of sex-typed behavior in statements such as, "Big boys don't _____." "Nice girls shouldn't _____." "It's a spelling bee. Boys against the girls."   ___   ___

Involves classroom resource people representing men and women in nontraditional roles.   ___   ___

Intervenes when children discriminate against each other. ("Girls are not allowed to play in our soccer game.")   ___   ___

ASSIGNING A GRADE

13 to 15 pass grades	Give your school an A	Your school is doing well and helping to make free children.
9 to 12 pass grades	Give your school a B	Your school has begun to make progress toward educating free children, but more needs to be done.
5 to 8 pass grades	Give your school a C	Your school needs to review its materials, policies, and practices. Change is needed.
1 to 4 pass grades	Give your school a D	Your school is behind the times. A thorough evaluation should be conducted—with substantial change.
0	Give your school an F	Your school is in trouble. Get help!!!!

If you are not happy with your school's grade, your first move should be to discuss the matter with the classroom teacher. The teacher might, in turn, suggest additional meetings with the principal, superintendent, or school board. Someone in the district is familiar with Title IX (1972 Educational Amendments) services in your area and might be able to arrange for a consultant to assist the district in making changes. In some cases parents have joined with other parents and with educators to form a task force to study the problem.

By all means, when you detect a practice or assignment that is detrimental to the development of free children, point it out to your child.

Books and the Free Child

Books are an important source of children's information. From them they learn about the world and acquire sex roles. However, throughout history children's books have taught traditional stereotypes. Consider the very first nursery rhymes and fairy tales we teach our small children. You remember Little Miss Muffett—she left her meal because she was frightened by a spider. Little Red Riding Hood was quite foolish—but luckily the Woodsman saved her. Jack was nimble; he was quick.

A number of experts have completed exhaustive analyses of children's reading materials and found that the ratio of male to female central characters is at least two to one; in biographies the ratio climbs to six to one. Boys are more often portrayed as resourceful, competitive, adventurous, and courageous. They are shown in positions of authority, and are excellent in sports and at solving problems. Girls are portrayed as passive homebodies, docile and dependent, preparing for future domestic roles; they lack skill, bravery, and initiative. They are mothers, little old ladies, witches, and other stereotypical figures. Friends are usually portrayed as being of the same sex. Neither boys nor girls are often shown as expressing any real feelings or emotions. The fantasy worlds of such notables as Dr. Seuss, Richard Scarry, or Maurice Sendak have been almost entirely male or male-dominated. Men are shown in three times as many occupational roles. The majority of early Caldecott award-winning books do not portray women in any occupation, and illustrations are overloaded with males. Lions, tigers, and bears are usually male. Cows, hens, and hippopotamuses are female. In children's books females are often invisible, or depicted in dull or degrading situations. If a female is riding with a male in a car, on a bike, or by horseback, she will almost always be the passenger.

Stereotyping is encountered in all forms of literature for children. Many new books attempt to avoid it, but usually the older the copyright date, the more blatant the violations. Stereotypical roles in children's literature reinforce obstacles to raising free children found throughout society. Real life is not reflected when the contributions, responsibilities, or careers of women and men are presented in tunnel vision rather than the Cinerama of the actual world. Children are taught limits which narrow their range of emotional expression and options for life. To want to be different can result in stress and anxiety, since to many the printed word is viewed as sacred.

Look, Jane, Look! See Dick Run!

Ask your child to get four leisure reading books and two textbooks. Using the checklist below, work together to spot stress-producing stereotypes.

CHECKLIST FOR SPOTTING SEXISM IN BOOKS

_____ Do males display a narrow range of emotions?

_____ Are females pictured less often than males?

_____ Are females pictured smaller than males?

_____ Are females illustrated in overshadowed or background positions?

_____ Are females in passive, rather than active, positions?

_____ Are females dependent?

_____ Are females vain, overly concerned about clothes or appearance, or silly?

_____ Is the language sexist? For example, is "he" used to subsume women?

_____ Are the roles, occupations, and problems of males given more coverage?

_____ Is the male portrayed as strong, unemotional, and stable, while females are portrayed as flighty, insecure, emotional, or fearful?

_____ Are interests portrayed using the traditional masculine-feminine dichotomy? (Boys like sports—girls like cooking.)

_____ Are strong, bold colors used when illustrating males, while pastels and fuzzy lines are used for females?

Raising an Androgynous Bookworm

Now that you and your child can recognize the printed influences that ultimately affect freedom, what can you do about them?

If you are reading aloud to your child, change the "he" or "she" and substitute the child's name. Develop critical thinking by discussing stereotypical literature. When you encounter stereotypes, ask your child to be a textbook editor. The editor must make changes. In the following examples, work on spotting the stereotypical thinking and changing it.

1. Tom bit his bottom lip and refused to cry.

2. Women should be more actively involved in politics because of their interest in preserving homelife and maintaining peace.

3. Racial discrimination prevented the black man from gaining his right to equality.

4. The settler made a home for his wife on the prairie.

5. Young Daniel Boone was a fine lad—full of spunk and the dickens.

As a parent you should realize the influential position of school and public librarians. The librarians not only select books for purchase, but also recommend books to children. Many librarians place primary emphasis on the literary value of the book, overlooking obvious stereotypes. Since you and your child depend on your librarian, make it clear that you hope the library is making a conscious effort to add books to their collection that reinforce individual freedom and to refer young readers to these books. Apply pressure to publishers by writing to them as a concerned parent. Express your displeasure at the general failure of publishers to print appropriate books.

Bring examples of stereotypes in textbooks to the teacher's attention. Suggest that the teacher might point them out to the class. Textbook selection occurs at regular intervals in every district. If the educators realize that parents are displeased by the books, they will seek fair-minded materials. Strive for a balance in your own home library. Select books for purchase with care and avoid books that don't further your goal of raising a free child. Be careful of books with a copyright dating earlier than 1970. Attempt to achieve a fifty-fifty representation of males and females, with occasional books depicting boys and girls in nontraditional roles. (For example, an emotional boy or a mischievous girl.) Be careful not to overload your library with too many books that show women engaged solely in household or child care duties. A woman's place is no longer in the home. The majority of women work outside the home, and they do so out of necessity—not merely to earn pin money. Children can become confused or even develop feelings of inferiority when the literary stereotype of a mother does not match the image at home. The child experiences stress because "Mom" isn't quite what she should be.

Play and the Free Child

Childhood is a time to play. Play can be a reliable source of information about the world, as well as of stereotypical information about sex roles. Young preschoolers usually play with the friend or relative living closest. However, as the children enter school, many begin to limit their play to same-sex friends. The older the children become, the more sex-segregated the playmates. Boys engage in more competitive team sports. Girls get involved in simple games, such as hopscotch, or practice domestic roles. Toy catalogs reveal that so-called masculine toys are wider-ranging, more expensive, more complex, and involve more activity. Toys classified as feminine involve less activity, are simpler, and often relate to household or nurturing roles. Toy packaging is notoriously stereotypical. Boys are pictured on the boxtops of chemistry sets, girls on tea sets. Catalogs show boys dressed in cowboy suits, girls in nurses' uniforms. Boys adorn doctors' kits, girls, housekeeping sets. Up to the age of two, children receive the same toys. Blocks, stuffed animals, stacking and nesting sets, and educational toys are the usual. As children grow, toy selection is more and more sex-controlled. Most toy buyers consider certain toys male-oriented and others female-oriented, although there are some toys or play activities that are considered sex-neutral. Lincoln Logs, Tinkertoys, hide-and-seek, or tag have long been acceptable for either sex. Other play activities, such as making snow sculptures, playing in the sand, or baking mud pies are called natural play. When children play or share toys with friends or siblings of the opposite sex, crossover rarely occurs. Sex-neutral or natural play and playthings are the rule, rather than experimentation with play activities usually associated with the opposite sex.

I have observed a group of six-year-old boys and girls play with stuffed animals. They dress them, cuddle them, and tow them in wagons made of plastic laundry baskets and rope. These young children have been conditioned to avoid the natural inclination to play dolls. Instead, they substitute the more acceptable stuffed toys. I have also watched as both boys and girls enthusiastically make up as clowns. That is acceptable, but it is a disgrace if a boy experiments on his own with makeup. How sad it is that our children feel it necessary to redesign their play in order to avoid stress. Play can be an important source of growth, learning, and creativity for your child. Below are the "Ten Commandments for Free Play." Follow them in your program to raise a free child.

TEN COMMANDMENTS FOR FREE PLAY

1. Don't give children toys that are sexist-packaged. (If you cannot find a tool set with both sexes pictured, you might (a) make your own tool set of real, inexpensive tools in a metal tool chest or (b) buy a set and re-package it in a plain box.)
2. Don't give a child a toy with sex or age labeled. Tear off the label that says, "Girl, age 6."

3. Don't fail to consider the purchase of any toy simply because it is a boy's toy or a girl's toy. (If your five-year-old wants a play stove and refrigerator, sex of the child should not influence the decision to purchase.)
4. Do realize that all children need to play with dolls, just as they need to play with trucks. (One expert has commented that children play with dolls more hours in their lifetime than they subsequently play with their real children.)
5. Don't encourage passivity by dressing children inappropriately for play or warning them not to get dirty.
6. Do provide a nonsexist role model for your children by readily joining in playing football or dolls, regardless of your sex or the sex of your child.
7. Do guide your children toward more natural and unstructured play.
8. Do look beyond the toy department for playthings. Check out art supply stores, office supply stores, notions departments, hardware stores, housewares departments, and even that box of clothes you're donating to charity.
9. Do encourage your children to engage in physical activity and contact sports.
10. Do encourage your children to participate in play traditionally reserved for the opposite sex.

Television, Advertising, and the Free Child

Television and advertising influence children daily. The average child under five spends two thirds of the waking hours in front of the set. By the end of high school the child will have viewed 350,000 commercials. Television and advertising not only waste valuable time that could be spent in play and learning, they also distort children's perceptions of reality, suggest hackneyed sex roles, and encourage passive behavior.

Television is dominated by male narrators, actors, and athletes. Women are depicted as economically dependent and usually appear as housewives, nurses, secretaries, or glamour girls. Children are taught sex roles that can threaten self-esteem. Even the otherwise beneficial *Sesame Street* has been cited as stereotyped. Past studies have noted that the number of males on the show was double the number of females. I trust that by this time the situation has changed. The "strong, silent" male or the "rough and tough" male provides boys with a model that suggests emotions should be stifled and aggression should be used in coping with stress.

If you are worried about television and commercials, do something about it. Start by limiting the amount of viewing time. Even as moderate viewers, youngsters watch almost four hours of commercials per week, not to mention the many stereotyped programs. Sit down with your child and work out an agreement. Then stick to it. Next, teach your child to be a television critic. When stereotyping occurs (almost constantly), point it out. Watch television with your child and use it as a point of departure for discussions, additional reading or follow-up family trips. Be on the alert for negative behavior children might imitate. Pay close attention to the commercials. Compare the television characters and situations to real life.

Assist your child in becoming a wise consumer. Discuss the reasoning behind naming of products and the scheduling of Saturday or after-school commercials. Note the similarity of the people in ads to real people. Ask your child to get out several toys you have purchased under the pressure of television advertising. Discuss their quality, price, durability, and long-term interest value. Recognize the power you—as a consumer—actually enjoy. Join together with your local parent organization and write letters to sponsors, the Federal Trade Commission, Bureau of Consumer Protection, and the Federal Communications Commission. Tell them what you think of program quality, stereotyping, and advertising.

Some alarming statistics exist that deal with the quantity and quality of time parents devote to their children. In many situations the quantity of time children spend with the television is significantly greater than the time spent with their father—and maybe even their mother. Consider your own family. Rank the influence of television with that of the parents.

Language and the Free Child

Language is instrumental in shaping the stereotypes learned early in life and reinforced throughout childhood. Written and spoken language are a reflection of our thoughts. Therefore, it is not surprising that there are so many instances of sexism in our daily communication. One dictionary examined by a researcher had 68 percent masculine-gender words, 23 percent feminine, and 9 percent neutral.

Removing sexism from language requires an active effort on the part of speakers, writers, and publishers. It also involves the invention of new words and a conscious effort to use existing nonsexist words and phrasing. However, our language will never be completely free from sexism until society's basic attitudes about sex roles change. Test your ability to provide alternatives for everyday words and phrases that subtly reinforce the stress of sexism. Cover the possible answers on the right.

SEXIST SEVENTEEN

Sexist	Alternative
1. Mankind	Humanity
2. Brotherhood	Unity
3. Manpower	Human energy
4. Everyone did his work.	Everyone did their work.
5. Housewife	Homemaker
6. Man on the street	Average person
7. Farmer and his wife	Farmers or farm couple
8. She is a pretty good golfer for a girl.	She is a good golfer.
9. Woman doctor	Doctor
10. Old maid	Woman; unmarried woman
11. Man-made	Synthetic; manufactured
12. Mailman	Mail carrier
13. Forefathers	Ancestors
14. Right-hand man	Assistant
15. After man invented the wheel	After the wheel was invented
16. Housewives are feeling the pinch of inflation.	Consumers are feeling the pinch of inflation.
17. Weaker sex	Forget this one—it doesn't exist

KICK THE HABIT OF:

Omitting women from humanity by using the generic *man* or *he*
(example—early man, black men, founding fathers).

Referring to occupations as if only men held the job
(example—policeman, fireman, congressman).

Putting women down by patronizing, poking fun, or referring to appearance, unless a male parallel exists
(example—broad, sexy blonde, libber, fairer sex, goddess on a pedestal).

Stereotyping with common labels
(example—scatterbrained female, henpecked male, catty
female, nagging mother-in-law).

Insulting by using sexual innuendo
(example—hot little number, frustrated broad).

Promoting the myth of men's dependence on women
(example—he's like a child when he's sick; can't find the
washing machine).

Making women possessions by using expressions such as "man
and his wife."

The Tyranny of Should

By the time they are three years old, children learn their sex. Between the ages of three and four they also begin to sense flexible sex-role expectations of parents and society. However, by five years old the rigor mortis of sex role has already begun to set in. Interview your child and determine if personal freedom has been affected. The older the child, the greater the potential for stereotyping. After you have been actively working to raise a free child for several months, re-administer the questionnaire.

THE TYRANNY OF SHOULD

Should boys be big and strong?	Yes	No
Should girls be big and strong?	Yes	No
Should girls wear dresses because they look better in dresses?	Yes	No
Should you ever call a boy a sissy?	Yes	No
Should girls do the indoor work and boys do the outdoor work?	Yes	No
Should girls act like tomboys?	Yes	No
Should girls and boys play sports together?	Yes	No
Should boys play the harp?	Yes	No
Should boys have long hair?	Yes	No
Should women be firefighters?	Yes	No
Should Father take care of a new baby?	Yes	No

Should Mother fix a leaky pipe?	Yes	No
Should boys play with dolls?	Yes	No
Should boys get in fistfights?	Yes	No
Should girls get in fistfights?	Yes	No

I hope your child answered in an honest, free, and healthy manner. Sometimes children ''psych out'' the questionnaire and give the answer they think is correct. If you were disappointed, don't despair. It's not too late. Grandmothers and grandfathers have had their consciousness raised. Get to work today to raise a free child.

Boxes, Little Boxes

Sex role identity is only slightly governed by biology, genes, and hormones. The influences of parents, adults, and culture far outweigh the chromosomes, anatomy, and hormones. Growing up isn't easy. Raising your child to incorporate those masculine and feminine traits that the child perceives as best, most useful, and most comfortable will result in a free child. Stress will be reduced and the child will be better able to cope with life's many diverse demands and changing situations when not forced into boxes.

Admittedly, your child may find that pursuing interests, regardless of sex, freely expressing emotions, or dealing with people as individuals, can have repercussions from adults and peers who still follow the traditional stereotypes. However, I think you will discover that children who dare to be free have developed a strong self-image that withstands the battering by those less free.

Chapter Five

Accentuate the Positive

A favorable self-image is absolutely indispensable in coping with stress. Children are not born with a self-image, but one begins to form early in life. The people with whom children interact serve as a mirror. They reflect back their impressions of the children. These impressions tell the children who they are and what they do well. Opinions don't have to be spoken. Children can sense someone's reaction. If the image reflected back is favorable, children feel confident and good about themselves. If the image is unfavorable, children learn to dislike themselves and doubt their ability to cope. Children who don't think much of themselves obviously aren't very happy with life.

Let's consider two children. Beverly is confident in her ability to succeed and welcomes the challenge of a new experience. She is sure enough about herself to accept criticism or to take an occasional failure in stride. Beverly is a leader. She gets involved and isn't afraid to speak her mind to teachers, parents, or friends. Everyone likes and respects Beverly, and she returns their feelings. Beverly is a positive person. When faced with stress, she is self-assured and immediately takes hold of the situation to work the problem out.

Ben, on the other hand, is a "sad sack." He is a chronic complainer and tenses up at the prospect of a challenging new experience. He doesn't have much faith in his own ability and usually approaches a situation saying, "I can't do that!" His defeatist attitude makes him wonder, "Why even try?" so he doesn't—which means he usually does fail, reinforcing his poor self-image. Ben is a follower. He spends a lot of time worrying about doing the right thing. His pessimistic approach to life causes most of his friends to eventually drop him, striking another blow to his already injured self-concept. When faced with stress, Ben just falls apart.

Putting the Pieces Together

Self-image is a composite of impressions the child receives from family, teachers, friends, and others. The first component to emerge is usually the physical image. The child learns about the different parts of the body and develops a sex identity. Sometimes a particular physical characteristic gets blown out of proportion, as when the child is given a nickname such as Fat Fred or Shorty. Constant taunting provides unfavorable input and can negatively affect the second component of self-image, the psychological image, which includes the feelings and emotions concerning oneself. Ultimately, such taunting influences the child's coping ability and overall adjustment to life.

Children use different types of information to form their self-image.[1] Through their relationships with other people, particularly parents, they make judgments regarding their own importance. They also assess their level of competence by noting successes and failures. Children learn whether they are "good" or "bad" by comparing their behavior to the standards set by their teachers, parents, or church, and by seeing how much power they have in influencing their own lives and the lives of others. In addition, adults often tell children what they think of them.

Many times children get a distorted image of themselves. They misinterpret a reaction or assign it more importance than is justified. For example, if a child is often referred to as a "little devil," the child may incorporate that perception into an unfavorable self-image. Or, if one child in the family is handicapped and receives more of the parents' attention, brothers and sisters may mistakenly think that their parents love that child more. When it comes to the behavior of others, children are not always able to make fine distinctions and interpretations. I am reminded of a brief period in our daughter's life when she thought she had been given a stolen ski jacket. It had been brought to her by her father as a gift following a ski trip. When someone asked him where he got it, he said, "Oh, I hit some little kid over the head at the airport." Another case of a casual joke made innocently by an adult. Our daughter had no reason to disbelieve the story and viewed the jacket as demeaning to her self-image. Not only was she indirectly responsible for the theft but her father was a "bad guy," and she avoided wearing the jacket whenever possible.

Children with a strong self-image come from homes in which the parents love their children unconditionally and provide a secure atmosphere. However, parents must help children set and work toward realistic goals. Building a positive self-image should not be confused with permissiveness or lack of discipline, which many children actually read as a sign that their parents don't really care enough about them to see that they do the right thing. You really can't give your child too much love. Some parents fear that it might make them overly dependent, but actually the opposite is true. Children who embark on life's adventures from a secure home base will be more self-reliant and independent.

In addition to the actual self-image, children also have an ideal image—of the person they'd most like to be. The ideal image is a conglomeration from many sources. Often it is unrealistic and may even be contradictory in nature. Ideal images can be stress-producing. Children seek to have the appearance or capability of others which leads to dissatisfaction with themselves. Threats to self-image are as real as physical threats. While it is true that an ideal image can provide the child with hope for improvement and a model worth emulating, if the image is unrealistic the child will soon become discouraged, and the real self-image will suffer. Common sources for ideal images are parents, brothers or sisters, relatives, friends, teachers, coaches, school leaders, television or movie stars, singers, sports heroes, "superheroes" such as Superman or Batman, heroes in the news, or literary characters.

A second source of stress associated with self-image is the inconsistent impressions a child receives. Adults who react unpredictably to a child play a large part in contributing to the child's ambivalence. The youngster is confused when a dirty face brings warm smiles and an "Isn't she cute" one day but prompts parents to disapprove and call the child a "little animal" the next. Helping your child form a positive self-image means providing the child with congruent impressions.

Does Your Child Have an Identity Crisis?

It is important to recognize when your child is suffering from low self-esteem and then to analyze the cause. Only by getting to the root of the problem can steps be taken to enhance the self-image. The following checklist will help you spot the typical symptoms of declining self-worth, but only through close observation and discussions with your child will you be able to isolate the precipitating factors. If you suspect your child is troubled, administer the checklist. If the child responds, "yes" to any of the items, perhaps you will want to follow-up by asking "why".

I often disappoint people.	Yes	No
I don't like my looks.	Yes	No
I am often ashamed of myself.	Yes	No

When I try to do something, it seems that usually everything goes all wrong.	Yes	No
I often feel nervous or afraid.	Yes	No
I wish I could completely change myself.	Yes	No
I am a quitter.	Yes	No
I often make up stories to make others think more of me.	Yes	No
I am usually afraid to try a new or strange activity.	Yes	No
I need a lot of praise and encouragement to keep me going.	Yes	No
I don't like my size.	Yes	No
I would rather have someone else take charge than be in charge myself.	Yes	No
I often feel confused.	Yes	No
I know I could do better in school.	Yes	No
I like to play with children who are in lower grades than I am in.	Yes	No
I wish people would pay more attention to me.	Yes	No
I get very upset if I fail at anything.	Yes	No
Most people don't like me.	Yes	No
I sometimes pick on others to make myself feel better.	Yes	No
I don't many people.	Yes	No
I'd rather watch television than play with friends.	Yes	No
I wish I were a boy/girl (opposite sex).	Yes	No

Every ''yes'' answer is a clue to a possibly serious threat to your child's self-image and an indication of stress. You can take some general, positive steps to improve that image by using some of the following suggestions. Some of the ideas are elaborated upon in the following pages.

1. Provide an environment that is steady, reliable, predictable, and responsive to the needs of the child.
2. Encourage the child to make decisions, express opinions, and practice independence.
3. Spend more time encouraging good behavior and less time punishing bad behavior.
4. Provide a clear-cut model of values and ethics.

5. Support the child when the child fails, letting the child know that there is much to be learned from failure, and it is an unavoidable, normal part of life.

6. State your expectancies, rules, regulations, and disciplinary measures in a positive way.

7. Allow time for unstructured play and exploration.

8. Be sure your child has opportunities to play with other children of the same age level and of differing age levels—both younger and older.

9. Demand that children treat adults and other children with good manners, courtesy, and kindness. Serve as a model for this type of behavior.

10. Listen when the child talks to you.

11. Encourage the child's curiosity and structure opportunities for the child to find answers through firsthand experiences.

12. Help the child develop a sense of competence with good basic reading, writing, arithmetic, and survival skills.

13. Prove adults can be trusted.

14. Let the child know that you value compassion, caring, sharing, generosity, and helping.

15. Don't embarrass or correct the child in front of others.

16. Don't act as if the child's concerns, fears or worries are silly.

17. Don't forget to apologize if you make a mistake, are rude, or feel crabby.

18. Don't overprotect or fail to allow the child to realize the natural consequence of a behavior. Sometimes discipline truly does hurt the parent more than the child.

19. Don't compare the child to others.

20. Let the child have some personal space in the house where he or she can store belongings and escape to for some privacy.

21. Don't allow the child to downgrade himself or herself.

22. Plan a time each day to interact one-to-one with the child.

23. Don't make unrealistic demands or expect perfection.

24. Don't live vicariously through your child. When you find yourself becoming unreasonably demanding ask yourself, "Am I doing this for the child or for myself or to please others?"

25. Show the child how important you think he or she is by including the child in your vacation or social plans.

26. Give the child some important family responsibilities.
27. Don't link self-image entirely to performance or achievement, while overlooking the importance of kindness, sincerity, and perseverance.
28. Show the child you accept the child's individuality by providing warmth and physical signs of your love. Offer liberal, genuine praise.

You will be able to tell that you are making progress when you note an increase in the child's vigor, self-initiative, self-confidence, and sense of pride in accomplishments. In addition, the child will probably show improvement in work habits and face an occasional failure with less frustration and greater optimism for the future.

To Praise or Not to Praise

It has been pointed out that care must be exercised in our verbal exchanges with children. Unkind comparisons, such as "You always look like such a pig;" unflattering nicknames, such as Fireplug; or dire predictions, such as "You'll never amount to a hill of beans;" can seriously injure the emerging self-image. In addition, unless your child is totally deaf, you should consider the effect of remarks made to other adults in the child's presence, such as "I don't know what's the matter with that kid. I was never like that at his age."

Before you decide that more praise is the answer to promoting your child's self-image, remember one thing—a sense of accomplishment is earned. You cannot give your child this feeling with words, a pat on the back, or a candy bar. Praise and reward are important, because they let the child know you recognize his or her worth. However, if the praise or reward are given mechanically, with a lack of sincerity, or when unearned, they become meaningless. You lose credibility, and then when recognition is in order, your praise seems less genuine. In addition, some experts believe that constant praise can cause a child to work for the praise itself, rather than for a sense of personal accomplishment. As soon as the praise or reward is received, the child mentally closes up shop.

Stop for a moment and analyze your use of praise. The following questions will help you:

1. Do you use the same words or phrases over and over again? (Example: "Great," "Good job," "Excellent," or "Nice work.")

2. Do you use praise when a probing question would serve as a more effective motivator? (Example: "Nice going!" instead of "That's right, but what if we carried things one step further?")

3. Is your praise vague or does it have substance and speak to the actual accomplishment? (Example: "Fine work!" instead of "You really did a thorough report on that book.")

4. Do you sometimes use praise to try to encourage your child to do something? (Example: "You look so pretty, why don't you sing for our guests?")

5. Do children sometimes mock or imitate your praise?

6. Do you use praise for ulterior motives—such as distracting or, worse yet, coercing your child? (Example: "I realize the truck belongs to you, Mary, but you're such a good girl that I know you will let Mark play with it.")

7. Do you always precede your criticism with a compliment? Children psych out that routine in short order and become apprehensive every time they receive certain types of praise. (Example: "You did a good job in the yard, *but* I can't understand why you didn't trim around the trees.")

8. Do you use praise in an effort to get a compliment in return? (Example: Mom says, "You looked better than any kid on that stage!" Child responds, "That's because you made my dress.")

9. Do you offer distracted praise as you pretend to examine corrected homework papers or hurriedly sign your child's report card before the bus leaves or while watching television?

10. Do you use praise as an indirect insult? (Example: "This is really good work! Are you sure you did this?")

Don't get me wrong! I am in favor of praise, encouragement, and rewards to motivate and build self-image. However, it is important to strive for meaning and sincerity. Make your praise as specific as possible, and don't forget to recognize effort, even if it didn't result in success. Now and then it is nice to make the reward a logical outcome of the achievement; rewarding outstanding artwork with a set of charcoals, for example, is appropriate.

Every Day Is Independence Day!

Positive self-image and a sense of independence go hand in hand. It's difficult to have one without the other, and they are mutually enhancing. A child with a strong self-image is self-reliant and doesn't fear independent activities which build the child's self-image further. Independence is a demonstration of competence, while simultaneously contributing to it.

The urge for independence is evident in the two-year-old child who demands "I do! I do!" and constantly challenges the parents' authority. Overprotective parents can thwart a child's natural desire by restricting freedom or unconsciously limiting the environment so that independence is impossible. Help your child celebrate his or her independence—each and every day.

INDEPENDENCE, EVERY DAY!

Provide your child with plenty of attention. Children who don't get enough attention will spend their time hovering around adults, trying to get more—instead of trying out their independence.

Provide a secure home base from which the child can venture out into independent activities, knowing there is always a safe place to which to return.

Provide time for independence. If you are always in a rush to get your child off to school, there probably isn't adequate opportunity for the child to select clothing or pack a lunch.

Provide an environment that is conducive to independence. Install clothes racks at the child's level, get a stool for the sink, teach the child to use the microwave—whatever suits your lifestyle and the child's level.

Provide opportunities for your child to share in planning for activities that contribute to independence.

Use discipline and problem-solving techniques based on self-control and voluntary participation, rather than commands and orders.

Provide explanations whenever possible.

Let younger children wander a little under controlled circumstances, such as at a party or in a store.

Let the child organize his or her own bedroom.

When driving in the car or traveling, pretend you don't know what to do or where to go and have your child direct you.

Give your child hypothetical situations to cope with. (Example—losing parents in a store, calling an ambulance for an injured parent.)

Don't overorganize your child's life so that there is no time for independent activity. Lessons, clubs, and athletics are important—but so is time for oneself.

Show that you value independent behavior by serving as a model for your child. Don't get hung up on sex roles that make you dependent on your wife to wash a shirt or on your husband to change a fuse.

Who's Responsible?

Ask any parents about their goals in child raising and the word "responsible" is bound to crop up amidst the adjectives "happy" and "healthy." The big question is how to foster responsibility? Booker T. Washington had the right answer. He said, "Few things help an individual more than to place responsibility upon him, and to let him know that you trust him." Simple, right? Wrong—actually it is quite complex. It is true that children develop responsibility by being responsible. However, they must get a sense of fulfillment if the lesson is to be meaningful. If a child fails to meet a responsibility or views it as a menial chore—rather than a challenge—self-esteem declines. Therefore, it is crucial that responsibilities be tailored to the competence of the child.

It is impossible to force your child to be more responsible. Responsibility comes from within the child and involves a sense of duty and accountability. Responsibility develops as the direct result of performing successfully in demanding situations, rather than from parents demanding that the child act responsibly. Practice may not always make perfect, but in the case of responsibility it does help children see that certain behaviors are desirable, beneficial, and expected. It also gives children the opportunity to build self-image. The following plan can help your child toward responsible adjustment:

NEVER UNDERESTIMATE THE POWER OF A CHILD

1. Begin early to allow your child to make choices. The child can select food, clothing, or a toy to take to Grandma and Grandpa's.
2. Don't ask your child to make a choice if your mind is already made up. If you don't accept the child's choice, you end up making the child feel less responsible.
3. Don't present your child with a choice that is overwhelming. Help the child narrow the field of confusing alternatives.
4. Don't place your child in a position in which you think there

is a likelihood the child will make a disappointing or frustrating choice. The child will feel irresponsible and less prone to accept his or her own judgment the next time.

5. Involve your child in plans to assign responsibilities, and provide some choice. Don't give the child all the dirty work.
6. Make a chart and schedule. Your child will probably plan to accomplish more than is reasonable and will need your guidance in establishing a more realistic program.
7. Use the chart as a means to remind your child, and avoid nagging and prodding.
8. Don't give your child responsibilities beyond his or her level.
9. Select activities that can be quickly accomplished.
10. Plan for variety.
11. Rotate the tedious, dull jobs among family members.
12. Allow enough time for your child to complete a task. Granted, dinner may be delayed while you wait for the child to finish peeling the potatoes or setting the table. However, the long-term benefits justify the inconvenience.
13. If your child expresses an interest in assuming a certain responsibility, accept the help graciously, rather than saying, "Well, okay, I guess I'll let you try it."
14. Don't breathe down the child's back. After providing a clear set of instructions or expectations, leave the child alone unless your assistance is requested.
15. Judge your child's performance according to the child's level, rather than by a fixed standard.
16. Don't compare children.
17. Follow up. Provide praise, reward, or thanks. If the child did not fulfill the responsibility, find out why. Discuss the matter. Perhaps the responsibility was unrealistic.
18. If you decide to discipline your child for failure to meet a responsibility, involve the child *in advance* in establishing a fair disciplinary measure so the child knows what to expect.
19. Program some flexibility into meeting responsibilities.
20. Be a responsible model for your child. If the child sees you littering, thoughtlessly messing up store displays, or trying to pull a fast one on a store clerk, expect the child to follow in your footsteps.
21. Don't underestimate your child's capability. In doing so, you are demeaning their self-image.

Parents, Can You Spare a Dime?

How many times have you heard parents complain, "Kids today don't know the value of a dollar''? If that is true, parents have only themselves to blame. One of the most important components of responsibility involves handling money. Norman Lobsenz has addressed this issue, and many of his ideas follow.[2]

The parents of today grew up in less affluent times. It feels good to be able to give your children what they want, whether they need it or not. It provides the parent with a sense of competence, success, and security—to say nothing of the joy of hearing, "Oh, thanks! I love it!" and seeing that smiling face.

There are a number of theories regarding allowances. Some advocate that children receive a fixed amount each week, with no strings attached. Others say children should work around the house to earn money. A predetermined deduction is made each time the child fails to meet a responsibility. The problem with this approach is that some children begin to think they should be paid every time they share in family chores. A child may even decide to quit. Some parents don't believe in allowances at all. The child just asks the parent for money when it is needed, and the parent decides whether or not to provide it. Critics of this method say it doesn't give the child an opportunity to budget, plan, or save. In addition, the child may resent continually asking for a handout.

Using money for reward or punishment has also come under attack. Children may learn to associate love and approval with money. In addition, if the child is trying to budget, losing his allowance for a week or two can be a disaster.

Your economic level, as well as your attitudes about spending, will no doubt influence your child no matter what you decide about allowances. Personally, I prefer a rather loosely structured system in which the child understands that he or she shares in the family income so is expected to contribute to the smooth functioning of the household by sharing in the work. I would not fine a child for nonperformance and would consider requests for funds to cover extraordinary expenditures. Children of all ages sometimes fail to understand where money comes from. Therefore, it is important to emphasize that parents work to earn money which they share, but children have a responsibility to share in work. Since they can't do it at the parents' place of business, they assume responsibilities at home. Extra income for out-of-the-ordinary chores helps reinforce this cause and effect relationship. You don't get something for nothing, and money is tangible proof that a responsibility has been fulfilled. The next step is learning to handle it.

Money can be a source of stress for parent and child. Don't be surprised if your child:

Makes mistakes. Mistakes are an important source of information. However, you should encourage your child to seek financial advice. (After all, adults do it!)

Takes money less seriously than you do. Come on—do you really want your child to worry about interest rates, taxes, or the mortgage payment?

Fluctuates erratically from one extreme to another—changing from a spendthrift to a miser, and back again.

Adopts your values. If you enjoy spending on clothes or gifts, your child may follow suit.

Shares your compulsion to "get the most for each dollar."

Family money matters should involve the entire family. Young children can understand the necessity for economizing and learn from watching parents deal with financial matters. Handle transactions with your child in a businesslike fashion and be practical in what you expect allowance money to cover. Don't criticize the child for poor judgment. (Just look in your closet for evidence of your poor choices!) If you threaten your child's self-image, expect the child to become secretive. Lastly, watch for signs that your child has contracted the gimme-gimmes. Television commercials are a common carrier of this ailment, which is discussed more fully in Chapter Eight.

A Sense of Values

Values are defined as those aspects of life and behavior which an individual deems as most important and worthy, such as freedom, eternal salvation, or hard work. However, the most basic value of all is the belief in your own self-worth. This value ultimately serves as the "enforcer," since the individual internalizes and lives by all other values in order to maintain self-esteem. The value system is tied integrally to the self-image. If you are true to your values, self-image is enhanced. However, a decline in self-image is usually accompanied by crumbling in values.

The emergence of your child's value system coincides with the formation of self-image. Children internalize values from many of the same people who provide them with impressions regarding their worth. In an effort to gain approval by being like these people, children are apt to adopt their values. The young child is most heavily influenced by parents, although ideal images—such as sports heroes or rock stars—can play a minor role. However, the situation often changes when the child reaches preadolescence or teen years. Parents are dismayed to find their children abandoning family values in favor of values parents find less acceptable. Alice Sawyer was shocked when her daughter's seventh grade teacher called her to school. "You can be *sure* she didn't learn that at home!" explained Mrs. Sawyer. "Rhonda has always been taught the dignity of each and every human being. I can't imagine her making racist slurs!" The fact is that Rhonda did make insulting remarks about minority students. Some children reject parental values during preadolescence or teens in order to rebel or demonstrate independence. In other cases they are internalizing the values of their peers. A New York consulting firm conducted a recent study, published in the *Chicago Tribune,* which indicated that in 1960 the top three influences on a teen's values were, in order: parents, teachers, and friends. Twenty years later, in 1980, the order of the three had changed to friends, parents, and media. Teachers had dropped to fourth place.

Any person who significantly touches your child's life is portraying the values most important to him or her. However, the family is the most instrumental in the formation of that first set of values. If the child has learned to cherish these values, they won't erode in later life. Children need a clear-cut model. Parents themselves must have a well-defined value system and play by the rules. Children are quick to note inconsistencies. For example, what does your child think if you insist he or she tell the truth, and then you telephone your office to say you're sick when you're not in order to finish Christmas shopping. The child may question or reject the value of truth, without critically examining its worth.

Some educators have stated that children should be guided in clarifying their own value systems, rather than being indoctrinated by adults. That word "indoctrination" is a turn-off for many people, but whatever you call it, children need to know where their parents stand. Television, movies, advertisements, and song lyrics all project values with which parents may not be in accord. The peer group also suggests values.

It is important to know about your own child's values. Following are two identical questionnaires. You take the first and then have your child take the second. Indicate whether you agree or disagree with each statement by placing an "A" or "D" in the first column. Then record how you think your child would respond in the second column. Your child just reverses the procedure. When completed, check your answer sheets to see how your values compare and how familiar you are with each other's values. You may want to substitute more appropriate statements for some of those listed, depending on the level of your child, or add some statements of special interest to you.

VALUES VERIFICATION—PARENTS' VERSION

Read each statement and mark "A" for agree or "D" for disagree.

	Parent	**Child**
(How I feel.) (How I think my child feels.)		
1. It's okay to tell a lie if it doesn't hurt anyone.	___	___
2. The major reason for work is to earn money to provide pleasure.	___	___
3. War is sometimes necessary.	___	___
4. A woman has the right to choose to have an abortion.	___	___
5. I could have a best friend of another race.	___	___
6. Parents should take their children to church, even if children don't want to go.	___	___
7. I would be happier if I had more money.	___	___
8. If a friend committed a serious crime, it would be my duty to inform the police.	___	___
9. Mothers are more loving than fathers.	___	___
10. Boys should play with dolls if they feel like it.	___	___
11. Women should be firefighters.	___	___
12. Children should have to work around the house in order to get an allowance.	___	___
13. I would be willing to die for a cause.	___	___
14. Teachers should be tougher.	___	___
15. I would rather be rich than famous.	___	___

VALUES VERIFICATION—CHILD'S VERSION

Read each statement and mark "A" for agree or "D" for disagree.

	Parent	Child
(How I think my parent feels.) (How I feel.)		
1. It's okay to tell a lie if it doesn't hurt anyone.	___	___
2. The major reason for work is to earn money to provide pleasure.	___	___
3. War is sometimes necessary.	___	___
4. A woman has the right to choose to have an abortion.	___	___
5. I could have a best friend of another race.	___	___
6. Parents should take their children to church, even if their children don't want to go.	___	___
7. I would be happier if I had more money.	___	___
8. If a friend committed a serious crime, it would be my duty to inform the police.	___	___
9. Mothers are more loving than fathers.	___	___
10. Boys should play with dolls if they feel like it.	___	___
11. Women should be firefighters.	___	___
12. Children should have to work around the house in order to get an allowance.	___	___
13. I would be willing to die for a cause.	___	___
14. Teachers should be tougher.	___	___
15. I would rather be rich than famous.	___	___

Interpretation:

You probably found some differences between parent and child, as well as some surprises regarding how your child views your values. These variations are to be expected. You and your spouse probably don't agree on all values (but note that if you differ widely, your child can experience confusion and stress). Issues involving morals and values have long been a source of friction between parent and child, and few children turn out to be carbon copies of their parents. Children can be forced to follow your rules, but they cannot be compelled to internalize your values. The value system, although initially modeled after the parents', derives its strength from a positive self-image.

Love Demands Infinitely Less Than Friendship

Every human being needs contact with others. Early in life the infant cries for companionship. By the age of one the baby wants to play. The baby's first friends are usually family members, since children of the same age are similarly self-involved and unable to play cooperatively. However, when the child is about two years old, the need for outside friendships emerges. Friendships are an important part of social adjustment. Safe and secure in the shelter of the family, children are egocentric—concerned primarily with personal needs and wants. Friendships help a child develop a sensitivity to others and competence in social interactions.

Children need an opportunity to practice friendship. Only-children, particularly, experience occasional difficulty in social interactions. If you have a preschooler, arrange for friends to visit, or consider enrolling the child in a play group or part-time preschool. If your child is school-aged and friendless, there is a problem. Don't let the child fool you by insisting: "I don't want to play with the other kids. I'd rather be by myself." While it is true that everyone enjoys being alone at times, a friendless child is an unhappy child. Friendships are a natural, healthy part of life. However, some children lack the self-confidence to make friends or have such a poor self-image that they are sure no one will like them. Patterns of friendship may vary among children, with some children preferring a large number of friends, and others having fewer, more intense relationships. Either way is fine—as long as the child does have some friends.

Childhood relationships teach some of life's most brutal lessons. Children can be cruel, insensitive, and stress-provoking. They will taunt a physically unattractive or handicapped child. They ridicule the slow learner and laugh at failure. Damage is done to the budding self-images of everyone concerned. It is impossible to insulate your child from inevitable peer pressure and stress. However, the stronger a child's self-image, the greater the child's resiliency. Encourage your child to discuss hurt feelings. In some cases you can provide a new slant to the situation which the child hadn't considered. My daughter arrived home from school one day obviously crushed. I inquired about the day's events, and soon the problem came spilling out, "We have this club at school, and Laurie said I was thrown out because I was absent. She just made that up. No one ever said anything about being absent before." It hurt to see my daughter rejected—her self-image bruised—but I realized that in spite of my indignation the club was still attractive to Carly. I told her: "You know, I don't understand what kind of club you have. I am in a few clubs, and when one of our members is sick we send a card or flowers. We'd never throw them out." So obvious—yet Carly hadn't considered the possibility that maybe the club wasn't so desirable. A smile filled her face, and she said, "Thanks, Mom," with genuine sincerity. The following day when I asked about the club she told me, "Oh, they wanted to let me back in, but I told them I didn't want to be in a club that treats people so bad." Score one victory for self-image.

Unkind behavior usually signals that a child's self-image is weak. Inflicting hurt gives a temporary feeling of power. As your child's self-image grows stronger, and the child becomes more independent and responsible, you will find he or she is less open for giving or receiving injury.

To Have a Friend, Be a Friend

Children have to learn how to be a good friend. They sense it has something to do with being kind and loyal and having fun together. Beginning in the preschool years and continuing throughout childhood, you can give your child a deeper understanding by explaining the following points:

Your friends have a self-image, which is growing, just like yours. You are like a mirror. Your reactions to your friends let them know if they are good or bad, important or unimportant, skilled or unskilled. Help them form a strong self-image by telling them the things you like about them and the things they do well. They will want to be your friend, and that's good for your self-image.

Don't say bad things about people just to make yourself feel big or better. It shows that your self-image is still weak. Even if the person you are talking about isn't your friend, the friend you are gossiping with may think you'd do the same to him or her. Try to say only good things. You never hurt anyone that way, and that's good for your self-image too.

Remember how much you like it when someone listens to you. It makes you feel important. Listen to your friends and make them feel important.

Don't make promises. They are too easy to break, and that hurts everyone's self-image.

If you aren't sure you can keep a secret, tell your friend not to tell you. If you tell just one person, and that person tells just one person, and so on, and so on . . . just think of how many people will know.

Remember that almost no one can keep a secret. If you tell your friend an important secret, lots of people will probably end up knowing your business.

Share with your friends and treat them with courtesy.

Don't exclude certain children from your play. Everyone can have fun together.

If your friends hurt your feelings or are mean to you, it is bad for their self-image and yours. Stand up for your rights or don't play with them, but don't let it bother you for long. Your self-image is strong, and no one can hurt your feelings unless you let them.

When you are angry or crabby, you aren't having any fun. Get happy again, fast. Smile and laugh a lot.

Argument Etiquette

A child's self-image is still tender and it doesn't take much to threaten it, with stress as the result. Children are easily insulted or wronged. Childhood fights and squabbles are a way of showing independence and power, besides providing an immediate vent for tension. In a few cases fighting can be fun and making up is even better! Try to impress the following points on your child:

The very best way to handle an argument is to avoid it, if possible.

Tell your friend exactly what is bothering you. *Be calm* and don't call names or bring up old fights.

Give your friend a chance to speak his or her mind. Listen carefully to what is being said. If your friend brings up something that happened long ago, reply that that isn't part of this argument.

If you see that you were wrong, admit it right away.

Try to think of a solution to the problem that makes everyone happy.

If your friend says, "I'm sorry," accept the apology quickly and go on with your play.

If you part angry, try smiling and saying, "Hi!" the next time you see your friend. He or she probably wants to forget the whole thing too.

If your friend won't speak to you, play with someone else. Don't waste time moping around.

A Star Is Born

Your child's self-concept is vital in the coping process. A strong self-image helps the child resist stress or cope with it confidently In addition, self-image is closely related to the nature and permanence of your child's value system. You can help promote a positive self-image by providing your child with security, treating your child with respect, and showing concern. Further the development of independence and responsibility by giving your child freedom commensurate with his or her level. Don't expect perfection or make unreasonable demands that doom a child to failure. Notice and comment on your child's many small achievements, such as getting through a whole Saturday without once fighting with a sibling. Be on the alert for feelings of inadequacy which are revealed, for example, when a child says, "I can't!" before even attempting an activity or, after completing a project, complains, "Mine's no good!" Don't overdo competition or unfairly compare children. A boost to the morale of one child can come at the expense of another child's self-image. Above all, provide unconditional love. Although you may disapprove of some behavior, your objection should not be confused with a withdrawal of love.

Chapter Six

Eliminate the Negative

Kevin was the terror of the neighborhood. His mother was over-indulgent and spoiled him hopelessly. The day he entered kindergarten, she dressed him in knickers and knee socks, sent him off, and waited all morning for his return. When he finally arrived home, Mom rushed to the door, hugged him, and asked: "How was your very first day of school? I hope you didn't cry!" "No," sneered Kevin, "I didn't cry, but the teacher did!" As this joke illustrates, special problems not only generate stress for the child, but can also affect those with whom the child daily interacts.

The previous chapter discussed the importance of building a positive self-image in order to accentuate your child's positive qualities. This chapter will suggest techniques for eliminating, or at least minimizing, some of the common childhood problems that create stress and strain for everyone involved. The topics are presented in alphabetical order.

Aggression and Hostility

Aggression and hostility are the fight response in the fight-or-flight reaction to stress. Hostility is characterized by a state of unfriendliness or opposition. Sometimes the hostile state is prolonged, affecting innocent bystanders—including family and friends with whom the child is not directly angry. Hostility can ultimately lead to aggression, whereby a child attempts to do damage to a person or thing. The assault may be physical or verbal. Young children are more likely to engage in physically aggressive behavior to retrieve a possession, get their turn, or avenge an affront. In some cases the urge is so overwhelming that a child will beat a stuffed toy, kick a piece of furniture, or even bite him or herself. As children mature, the nature of stressors changes, and children are more apt to resort to verbal expression—with decreasing physical aggression.

Let's take a closer look at hostility, as reflected in moodiness, petulance, or rebelliousness. It is important to recognize your child's lows and assist the child in coping with them. Your child transmits many clues, both verbal and nonverbal, which give some indication of the child's emotional state. Consider the following example. Dad is standing near the window when Grant gets off the bus after a long day in eighth grade. The boy's body language communicates that it has been a hard day. Grant's shoulders are slumped; he lets himself drop down the bus steps; as he walks, he angrily kicks a stone that gets in his way. He enters the house, letting the door slam. Slamming doors is one of Dad's pet peeves. Dad calls to him, "Do you want a snack before dinner?" Grant's only response is a gruff "No." He goes to his room, slamming the door again. Dad thinks: "Well, it's going to be one of those days. Looks like we are headed for trouble." Fifteen minutes later Dad goes to his son's room and reminds him that he forgot to take care of the garbage. Grant gives him a dirty look and goes to do his chores, slamming the garage door on his way out. Dad follows him outside and tells him: "Listen, young man. I have had enough of your moodiness and door slamming. Just who do you think you are, anyway? No one in this house did anything to you." Grant blows up, and the entire situation turns into a near brawl.

Swings in mood are not limited to adults and adolescents. Children of any age can experience moodiness stemming from the stressors of a bad day. Yet, a child's rude behavior, sarcasm, or silence can be exasperating or even frightening to a parent. There's an urge to set the child straight with a slap, shaking, or command to "snap out of it!" Actually, confrontation is the worst possible alternative. Generally, children want either to be left alone or to be allowed to blow up. In both cases it is important that the child realize that someone understands, but children struggling to assert their independence may initially reject parents' offers to help. They don't want to discuss problems and may subsequently remain in a prolonged state of stress. If your child does not accept the invitation to talk it out, try to stay out of the way until the emotional storm has subsided. However, rude or violent behavior affects the entire family and cannot be tolerated simply because the child is in a bad mood. In this case the child must be firmly told: "I can see you are troubled. I'd like to help. If you want to be left alone until you feel better, that's okay, too. However, your behavior is upsetting everyone. I don't want to make your problems worse by becoming angry, so please control yourself." The best way to encourage children to seek your assistance is to establish credibility when you *are* consulted. Show you understand the problem and guide the child in working out a personal solution rather than offering a pat answer, becoming judgmental, or blaming the child. The stress-management techniques discussed in the final chapter can help your child control hostility. Remember, in these situations it is often necessary for you to control your own hostility and instead react by patiently waiting for the child's cloud to lift.

When hostility leads to aggression, temporarily ignoring the problem is not the answer. However, it is not easy to deal directly with this type of behavior. Even the word *aggression* is confusing. For example, a mother would certainly be alarmed if the preschool teacher identified her child as aggressive after the child whacked a playmate in the head with a truck. However, the same parent might glow with pride when her husband's employer refers to him as being aggressive in the business world. We live in a society that glorifies aggression, particularly as a "manly" trait. Television programs, movies, and news are filled with acts of physical violence, and the crowd goes wild when it witnesses brutality in football or hockey. Boxing fans love to watch as grown men get in a ring and try to knock each other out. Why shouldn't children be confused when they are disciplined for imitating the aggressive acts of a peer or television character? Why is it okay to retaliate against a playmate in anger but not an adult? Parents are also in a quandary, wondering how to raise a child to be assertive but not brutal. They question why one child is so much more aggressive than another, even though both have been raised in the same environment.

Although aggressive behavior is learned, understanding the temperamental differences among children can help to explain why some children are more prone to aggression than others. Consider the following example. Angry Andrew was the nickname his mother gave Andy almost as soon as he was born, and he certainly was often angry. Andy didn't enter a room—he charged into it, in a way that reminded you of the police breaking down a door in pursuit of a criminal. Andy was a handful from birth. He seemed to cry constantly and had a low frustration level. In fact, his mother used to say: "When Andy was newborn everyone told me that infants are lovable bundles that sleep most of the time. Well, he must not have read the baby books, because Andy was fussy, demanding, and hardly ever slept." During the preschool years he was prone to temper tantrums and acts of aggression. He banged his head against his crib if his parents didn't immediately respond to his cries. On one occasion his mother had to take a visiting playmate to the emergency room after Andy bit the youngster so hard he punctured the skin. Now six years old, Andy, according to his teacher, ineffectively handles stress and frequently lashes out at his classmates. Although his IQ is high, the child is doing poorly in school.

Unfortunately, many children with problems similar to Andy's earn the "bad child" reputation. As they grow older and do not improve in their ability to cope with stress, these problems get worse.

In addition to differences in temperament which affect a child's ability to cope, in recent years a number of investigators have begun to explore the relationship of nutrition, allergies, biochemical differences, genetic weakness, and stress. One of the leaders in this field is Dr. Lendon Smith, and I recommend that parents with an interest in learning more about this subject read his book *Improving Your Child's Behavior Chemistry*. Dr. Smith says that everyone has a different tolerance level for stress. His basic premise is that individuals are chemically different. These differences can be caused genetically; by conditions in utero, such as the mother's nutrition; as the result of illness or accident; or from diet. Just as individuals have different anatomies, they also demonstrate varying levels of enzyme and endocrine activity, as well as differences in the composition of the blood and other body fluids. They have distinct responses to drugs, chemicals, illnesses, and disease. Therefore, some experts believe that there can be no single concept of a "balanced diet," or "minimum daily requirement" for nutrients. In some cases adequate nutrition might mean vitamin or mineral quantities far exceeding the average.

Dr. Smith believes that there is a delicate balance of chemistry that involves hormones such as adrenaline; the cortex and limbic system of the brain; and blood sugar. He further states that we can alter the reaction to stress by treating the body's imbalance and strengthening the enzyme systems that are involved in the stress reaction.

Dr. Smith theorizes that children act rotten because they feel rotten. He writes that "people who have allergies, nervous symptoms, insomnia, obesity, alcoholism, migraine, and hyperactivity are suffering from enzyme-chemical dysfunctions and you must add the nutrients to activate the enzymes, or supply the missing chemicals."[1] It is important to recognize which children have difficulty with stress as early as possible, so that aggressive behavior doesn't become an unalterable habit. A complete analysis of diet, physical condition, and environment is in order. We are just beginning to scratch the surface of biochemical individuality, stress, and diet as they affect behavior. Nevertheless, parents who sense their child has a problem are encouraged to locate professionals in their area who can help. Following are a few general guidelines which can provide a more healthy diet for your entire family:

1. Reduce the amount of sugar and salt added to food.
2. Keep calorie consumption in balance with energy expenditure.
3. Increase the consumption of fresh fruits, vegetables, and whole grains.
4. Reduce fat consumption by substituting meat and dairy products with poultry and fish.
5. Serve a nourishing, high-protein breakfast.
6. Attempt to eliminate sweets from the diet. Replace them with nuts or fruit.
7. Avoid foods with artificial colors, preservatives, and flavorings.

Once you recognize how temperament, hyperactivity, and biochemical imbalance and diet can be related to aggression, the next step is to ask yourself if you are encouraging aggressive behavior.

During my tenure as an elementary school teacher I encountered many parents who told their children, "If somebody bothers you, you just let 'em have it." Teachers are placed in a difficult position when they remind a child that aggressive behavior is forbidden at school, only to be told, "Oh, yeah, well my daddy said that if someone messes with me, I should stand up for my rights." Somehow I always managed to handle the situation diplomatically, telling the child that Daddy didn't mean you should fight when the teacher was present to help mediate the problem. But believe me, many a time I bit my lip to keep from saying: "I don't care what your daddy told you! School is too special a place for fighting, and I don't allow it!"

In addition to directly sanctioning aggressive responses to stress, we encourage aggression in a number of other ways. When we allow aggression to prove a satisfying method for dealing with stress, the child is inclined to continue its use. For example, if Amy experiences satisfaction at her power to strike a playmate and make her cry, Amy is apt to continue hitting. If Jack learns that when he grabs a toy from his older brother, his parents will probably say: "Oh, let Jack have it! He's younger than you," Jack will frequently rely on this technique. When a vicious verbal attack stuns her opponent and wins an argument for Sandy, she is likely to resort to this battle plan in the future. Aggressive behavior is reinforced because it works. Letting children get away with aggression, ignoring acts of aggression, or fondly referring to your child as a "bruiser" or "little toughy" are interpreted by the child as approval and make aggressive acts more likely.

In some cases children engage in aggressive acts because they crave attention so much they will settle for any kind they can get—even if it is negative. Obviously, these children need more attention for desirable behavior and minimal attention for the undesirable. If you suspect that your child is after attention, consider the possibility that the child is experiencing the stress of rejection. Become more involved with your child, but respond to aggression swiftly and briefly. You might tell the child to go to his or her room until the child feels better and can behave properly. In this way your disapproval is communicated without providing undue attention, which reinforces this pattern of behavior.

Children find models for aggressive behavior wherever they turn. Not only is violence found in entertainment and news accounts, it is also demonstrated by the peer group, teachers, and parents. As one puzzled parent put it: "I can't understand why Jamie keeps hitting her sister. She must have gotten spanked a hundred times for doing that." While it's true that a slap is effective in immediately bringing a situation under control, the control is being imposed from outside. Children must learn self-control, and the child who is physically punished is more apt to engage in aggressive behavior. Physical punishment provides a model for the aggressive behavior you are telling the child is unacceptable. In effect, you are telling the child, "Do as I say, not as I do." The child perceives that aggression is actually acceptable if you are in authority and bigger and stronger than your victim. In addition, physical punishment increases the child's level of stress and animosity. Frustration is increased—and frustration is one of the big stressors prompting aggression in the first place.

Frustration is the disappointment or defeat experienced by a child who doesn't get what he or she wants, which can range from a plaything to the love and attention of a parent. Extremely harsh or severe punishment increases frustration levels. Not only does the punishment impede progress toward a satisfying response to stress, but it can be interpreted by the child as a withdrawal of parental love or respect. Obviously, it is neither possible nor desirable to remove all sources of childhood frustration. Learning to cope is an important part of growing, but the nature of modern-day existence is so filled with frustrations that controlling a few when possible certainly will not deprive your child of the opportunity to practice adjustment. In our interactions with children we can minimize frustration by refraining from discipline that insults, humiliates, or otherwise attacks the child's self-image. We can occasionally look the other way when the child is experiencing extraordinary stress, such as problems at school, illness, or defeat. We can also avoid making conflicting or petty demands that are difficult—if not impossible—to meet. For example, six-year-old Randy can't understand why it is permissible for Uncle Ken to tease him about being a "fatso belly", when he teases Uncle Ken about being obviously overweight, Randy is accused of being a smart aleck. It is also frustrating for twelve-year-old Judy to attempt to follow her parents' set of unreasonable, yet strictly enforced rules, most of which begin with "Don't" and control daily activities ranging from how to load the dishwasher to how to select her friends. However, in school Judy has no trouble at all following the reasonable set of positively stated rules and regulations, the reasons for which she clearly understands. Frustration can also be reduced by moving into some situations before they get out of hand. For example, wild, rough-and tumble play almost always results in accidental, minor injury which can prompt an aggressive reaction in the victim. Allow children to work through their own problems, but when you see they've reached the point where they simply can't cope, help settle the matter before a fight erupts. In other words, frustration can be minimized by establishing an environment that is not overdirected, and yet not underdirected. Overpermissiveness is just as frustrating to the child who wants and needs limits that show love and concern, as is overcontrol. If your child is in the process of hurting a person or thing, direct parental intervention and control is required. The child cannot be permitted to continue this aggression. However, following the incident, your child should be guided in developing more socially appropriate means for coping with stress. In addition, we must guard against paradox parenting, in which we approve of or ignore an act of aggression one day, only to jump all over the child for the same behavior at a future time. This situation often arises because we feel too tired or too busy to deal with a child's misbehavior at the moment, vowing to set the child straight the next time.

The following model is designed to help you control your child's aggressive behavior:

EDGING OUT AGGRESSION

Step 1   Specifically identify the behaviors you feel are aggressive and wish to control.

Step 2   Note the frequency of these behaviors. Our goal is gradual improvement, and you will not see a total elimination of aggressiveness. However, a decline in frequency can signal progress.

Step 3   Note the situations that most often prompt aggressive acts, as well as the outcomes. Is the child receiving some sort of satisfaction from aggressive behavior? If so, what can you do to change this situation? Do you step in to control aggression quickly, so that the child does not have the opportunity for satisfaction?

Step 4   Determine whether or not you communicate your disapproval of aggressive behavior in a calm, nonviolent manner. Does your child know where you stand? Do you discuss behavior problems and punish by restricting privileges or making discipline a logical outgrowth of misbehavior, rather than resorting to explosive verbal abuse or physical punishment? Do you apply the same standards to boys and girls?

Step 5   Consciously attempt to reinforce positive behavior by providing attention and meaningful praise for your child, as well as other children, when your child is observing. Remember, if your child is highly aggressive, the child might have learned that aggression is the most effective way to gain attention, since adults and other children likely have learned to avoid the child because of his or her frequent acts of violence.

Step 6   Provide your child with opportunities to experience independence and decision-making so the child does not feel smothered by authority and compelled to rebel.

Step 7   Clearly define a realistic, reasonable set of rules and expectations. Let your child know in advance what will and will not be tolerated, as well as the reasons why. Let the child know that aggressive feelings are a natural response to stress, and that control doesn't mean supressing them, but instead learning more acceptable means for expression.

Step 8   Following an incident of aggression, discuss the matter with your child. Tell the child you know how he or she feels with remarks such as "I know how important it was to you to get a turn on the swing," or "I can understand why Jim was bugging you." Encourage the child to suggest alternative, satisfying approaches to aggression. Talk about how the child might respond the next time, perhaps even role-playing the situation.

Step 9   Provide activities that help the child vent aggression. For example:

Physical activity—such as running, jumping, climbing, or riding

Water play or activity—such as swimming, washing the car or some toys, playing in the sink or bathtub, blowing soap bubbles, or making mudpies

Art activities—such as finger painting, clay modeling, or drawing

Cooking or baking a special treat

Role-playing or dramatic play with dolls

Singing, dancing, or playing a musical instrument

Letting it out on inanimate objects—such as smashing milk cartons; ripping old newspapers, magazines, or sheets; punching inflatable toys; or pounding with a hammer (Note: Opinions differ regarding the advisability of expressing aggression on objects, so do what you think is best.)

Having a snowball fight with crumbled newspapers or pieces of foam rubber for snowballs

Step 10   Teach your child some of the stress-management techniques presented in the final chapter.

Step 11   Involve your child in the progress being made. Comment on the improvement you have noticed or on how well the child handled a particular situation that might have provoked aggression.

Anxiety

The only time twelve-year-old Nicole seems happy and relaxed is when she is planted in front of the television set, lost in the fantasy worlds created by TV producers. Nicole seems to have lost the joy of childhood. She awakens for school on Mondays with some of the worst cases of the blue Mondays her parents have ever seen. She is obviously tense, and the slightest change in routine throws her into a panic. A temporarily mislaid homework paper, spot on her jeans, or delay getting into the bathroom devastate her to the point where she may develop a headache, backache, or chest pains. In an effort to put some fun back into her life, Nicole's parents have tried enrolling her in a variety of extracurricular activities, all of which have been short-lived. Whether it was ballet, softball, tumbling, or piano lessons, Nicole's adverse, tense reaction every time it was scheduled made it seem hardly worth the effort. However, when questioned, Nicole genuinely can't identify what's bothering her. She does well in whatever she attempts and doesn't appear to have any major problems, although she often complains that her nervousness impairs her performance in school. She seems to dread just about anything that puts her in the public eye.

Nicole is the victim of anxiety, of the "flight" response in the fight-or-flight reaction to stress. Anxiety is the first cousin to fear, the major difference being that fear has a specific, known cause, while anxiety is reflected in a nonspecific sense of uneasiness. It is much easier to deal with fear than with anxiety. Remove or control the threat, and fear vanishes. However, anxiety is another matter. It causes the child's thought processes to become disorganized and reduces concentration. Anxiety has a spiral effect. Once the child begins to worry, the worry seems to feed on itself. One troublesome thought leads to another, and the child becomes convinced he or she can't cope, thinking things like, "I knew I was going to have trouble!" or "Why does this always happen to me?"

Anxiety signals that stress is out of control. The child doesn't feel competent to cope, although the culprit stressors usually go unidentified, and the child doesn't know what it is she or he can't cope with. The following stressors may be to blame, either singularly or in combination:

Conflict   The constant undertone of conflict can be found in home, school, or social settings. It might take the form of constant overt confrontation or covert attempts at manipulation, often accompanied by a struggle to keep up the appearance of peace and harmony. Your child might be in conflict with peers, teachers, or family members, causing the child to dread the possibilities for conflict accompanying each new day.

Pushing   The highly competitive nature of our society influences children at a tender age. By preadolescence a few have developed the habit of near-compulsive overdoing. They just keep push-push-pushing. Relief never seems to be in sight, since two new projects take the place of each one completed. The child feels compelled to achieve.

Role   Children today receive conflicting, confusing role messages. In many ways they are urged to hurry and grow up, and they develop a maturity far in advance of that possessed by their parents at the same age. The entrance of large numbers of mothers into the work force has made it necessary for some children to fend for themselves. Yet many of these children do not feel that their parents give them the authority, support, and information they need and deserve in their more responsible roles. They face questions that range from whether or not to steal third base to how to wash a white shirt with navy blue collar so the colors don't bleed.

Burnout   Few adults think about burnout in terms of children. Executives, air traffic controllers, or teachers burn out—not youngsters. The overprogrammed life led by many children makes the possibility of burnout not entirely remote. Children who move from one activity to another in a state of chronic, uncontrolled stress can suffer physical or emotional illness or feelings of exhaustion and depression.

Loneliness   Children can be lonely not only when they are alone but when they are integrally involved with family, classmates, or friends. Loneliness stems from a sense of isolation or a feeling that no one really cares about you. It can also arise from rejection, especially if you are overly dependent on one person in particular, or on others in general. Many children of busy, self-centered me-generation parents experience profound loneliness and rejection.

Inferiority

Feelings of inferiority result from the agony of real or imagined human limitations or disadvantages. The victim feels inferior to others in terms of background, appearance, intelligence, coping ability, or success.

Life Change

Major life changes occur with regularity. Births, deaths, parents' divorce, moving, or serious illness are but a few examples of upheavals that require major life adjustments. Until the adjustment is made, the child functions in a state of general uneasiness.

Self-image

The protection of one's own self-image is a natural, healthy drive. Some children become anxious because parents, peers, teachers, or they themselves have set standards and expectations that are unrealistic and unattainable. The goal is to "go out there and knock 'em dead" each and every day. After a few failures are experienced, children lose confidence and are tense about life in general.

Worry

Once the pattern of constant worry begins, it becomes a habit used for defense. Forewarned is forearmed, so they say, and worry is perceived by the worrier as a state of alert.

Children can be helped if you encourage them to discuss their feelings and discover the origin of the stressor. Once they are aware of their overreaction, they can pull the reigns on their runaway worrying and regain control. The stress-management techniques presented in the final chapter can help.

Bed-wetting

Mom and Dad are having coffee in the kitchen when the telephone rings. The call is for their eight-year-old, Janice. They can't help but overhear as she says: "I'm really sorry, Patti, I'd love to come, but I have to do something with my parents. Thanks for asking!" As she comes from the phone, Dad says, "What is it that you are doing with us?" Janice nervously replies, "Oh, nothing," and tries to make a hasty retreat, but Mom catches her arm on the way by. "What was that conversation all about, Janice?" Embarrassed, the child barely whispers, "Patti wanted me to come to her slumber party." Mom drops her daughter's arm, sorry to have pressed the issue. Janice goes to her room and cries. She suffers from enuresis, or bed-wetting. Every night the child's sleep is interrupted. She used to wake her parents, who tried to be patient. But Janice could see that they disliked the annoyance, and she began curling up on the floor, rather than hear them say: "Oh, no! Not again, Janice." The youngster wouldn't think of accepting an overnight invitation. When the family goes on vacation, she feels as if the hotel maids have told everyone about her problem. Worst of all, she lives with the fear that her brother will tell the other kids at school, as he has threatened during several arguments.

Bed-wetting is a common source of childhood stress. After toilet training it might take some time before the child develops the control necessary to stay dry all night. Experts believe that the cause for bedwetting may be physical, emotional, or chemical. The child's nervous system may not have control of the muscles that hold the bladder closed or enable the bladder to stretch to hold urine during the night. The bladder might be too small or obstructed. In a few cases the child might be suffering from an infection, diabetes, or stones in the urinary tract. What the stresses, fears, and anxieties are that can contribute to bed-wetting are difficult to pinpoint. Parents should carefully study their child to identify the nature of tensions. Deep sleep is also recognized as a cause for enuresis. Dr. Lendon Smith believes that this deep sleep, which prevents the child from noticing that the bladder is full, may be caused by low blood sugar.[2] He has found that some children will stay dry if they eat a protein snack at bedtime, but wet if given sweets. A highly stressful day can also make the blood sugar fall so low that the nervous system does not have enough spark left to signal to the cerebral cortex that it's time to get up and go to the bathroom.

With all these possible explanations it is difficult to know which one fits your particular situation. Bed-wetting is usually not considered abnormal until after five years of age. At that point your first move should be to consult your pediatrician to determine if there is any physical basis for the problem. Next, you must understand that making your child feel guilty or ashamed only compounds the problem by generating stress which actually contributes to bed-wetting. In addition, you are seriously threatening the child's self-concept.

Tell your child you know how frustrated, angry, and powerless bed-wetting makes someone feel. Involve your child in positive approaches for solving the problem. Some doctors recommend an apparatus with a buzzer that sounds and a light that flashes whenever a bed pad gets even slightly wet. The child then goes into the bathroom. Although some good results have been reported with this device, I am against it. I have the feeling it may generate stress and create more problems than it solves. In some instances the doctor may prescribe a drug to relax the bladder so it will hold more fluid. Other drugs may be used to lighten sleep or to tighten the sphincter muscles of the bladder. My suggestions are to:

1. Eliminate sweets before bedtime.
2. Make the hours before bedtime as relaxing and unstressed as possible.
3. Gradually increase bladder capacity by encouraging the child to drink fluids.
4. Get your child to practice holding the urine as long as possible so as to stretch the bladder, and of course have the child urinate before bedtime.
5. Involve the child in all plans for solving the bed-wetting problem.
6. Provide support and understanding, rather than increasing stress levels with guilt and shame. Ignore occasional failures.

Finally, remember that although bed-wetting can be an important sign that your child is under stress, it doesn't automatically mean this. There are other causes for the problem. Try to get to the root of your child's bed-wetting, bearing in mind that occasional accidents are a normal part of growing up. Also, many children wet for a short period after experiencing some unusual stress, such as the birth of a sibling, parents' divorce, or illness. The problem will usually disappear *if* parents don't give it more emphasis than it deserves. Many experts believe that some children develop enuresis because their parents, during toilet training or treatment of the bed-wetting problem, pay more attention to their being wet than being dry. Under any circumstances bed-wetting is a great source of stress for the child.

Depression and Suicide

The term *depression* is often used synonymously with the familiar expression "[being] down in the dumps." Actually, the term is not that simple to define, and psychiatrists and psychologists have been debating if children can even suffer from depression. A recent article in *The New York Times* supports the position that they can.[3] It is estimated that two percent of all children are probably depressed. Dr. Maria Kovacs of Pittsburgh's Western Psychiatric Institute and Clinic is quoted in the article as detailing the following symptoms:

Mood changes, such as sadness and irritability

Sleep disturbances

Loss of appetite or increased appetite

Feelings of worthlessness

Withdrawal from other people

Researchers report that depression is widespread among teenagers and has been reported in children as young as six years old. It can be caused by a traumatic experience, poor nutrition, or chemical imbalance. You will notice that the symptoms closely parallel those for stress. Watch for evidence that your child is depressed, particularly if the child demonstrates a feeling of worthlessness. Seek professional help. Left untreated, depression can ultimately lead to suicide.

Childhood suicide is a reality, and as the child approaches adolescence, its likelihood increases dramatically. If your child has been depressed, be on the alert for signs of contemplated suicide. A child will spend hours making the decision and often appeals to others for help. The child who says, "I wish I were dead," may not necessarily mean it, but under any circumstances it is a plea for aid. Immediately take time to discuss the intense emotional difficulties that prompted this shocking statement. Usually, you will find that the child simply regards the situation as so desperate that nothing short of a death wish seems to adequately communicate the sense of despondency. In effect, the child is actually say-ing, "I can't cope, and I want you to take me seriously." Once the child feels supported and understood, the problem begins to subside.

In more severe cases you may notice an obvious personality change in a child who has recently experienced a tremendous sense of failure or drastic diminishing of self-worth. The child may be-come withdrawn or begin disposing of the most valued of personal possessions. If the child has experimented with drugs, is impul-sive, or has made a previous, unsuccessful suicide attempt, watch out. Four out of five suicide victims have made at least one prior attempt. Occasionally a child may have a subconscious wish to die. Drug abuse or reckless behavior may be a sign the child can no longer cope.

Whatever the symptoms, don't ignore them or provide tempo-rary distraction. Treat the causes by insisting your child get expert help, by referring the child to local crisis centers, but most impor-tantly, by rebuilding the badly damaged self-image and assisting the child to cope without making him or her feel guilty.

Discipline

Optimally, discipline should help children gain in self-control. It should not be an attempt by the parent to control or punish. Therefore, discipline should follow as a logical outcome of the behavior in question. For example, the child who runs through the flower garden, destroying the plants, might be asked to pay for their replacement and help in the planting or be assigned some other yard work. The exception would be in the case of a small child who is incapable of understanding and must be conditioned, such as a toddler who bolts for the street and gets a whack on the bottom.

In dealing with discipline matters, you should attempt to deter-mine the cause for the problem. It might be that demands were made beyond the child's level or capacity, which would justify a change in adult behavior—rather than the child's.

Many parents have found that they get better results by encour-aging and reinforcing good behavior, rather than focusing on bad. Although at times misbehavior can't be ignored, the approach re-ferred to involves an overall positive philosophy.

Following are some suggestions for discipline that have worked wonders for other parents:

DISCIPLINE THAT WORKS WONDERS

Avoid confrontations by sensing when your child is under stress or approaching the frustration level.

If you sense a squabble is about to turn into a brawl, step in and guide the children in working through their problem (but wait until the last minute, in order to give them a chance at problem solving).

If you elect to use punishment, dispense it as soon after the misbehavior as possible—no waiting "till your father gets home!"

Help young children, in particular, interpret the impact of their actions on others. Since they are basically self-centered, young children rarely deal with the full implications of a behavior.

Remove temptations from the child's environment.

Let children know what is expected of them, when, and why.

Be prepared for unusual situations where discipline might be a problem—such as a trip to the doctor's office or plane flight. Carry entertaining items with you.

Keep an eye on what is happening. Don't leave children entirely on their own for long periods of time.

Distract young children from the problem that you see brewing.

Occasionally ignore a mistake or remark that "just slipped out." Never ignore the child.

Give children the option for a "time-out." If a child is visibly upset, tell the child you are happy to discuss it or the child can think about the problem in privacy and rejoin the group whenever she or he chooses. However, hostility, tantrums, disruptions, or disrespect will not be accepted.

Don't let a child do something self-destructive. Step in and offer some coping suggestions.

Provide a cool-down period right before bed. Limit stimulation and activity.

Don't expect children to immediately stop when an adult is tired of a rowdy game and says, "That's enough."

Involve the whole family in understanding and setting rules. Ask for discipline suggestions from children. Enforce the rules once they are set.

Don't ignore a source of misbehavior one day and discipline the child for the same action the next.

Don't make threats unless you fully intend to carry them through. Your discipline will become meaningless or invite testing.

Don't be afraid to apologize if you are wrong, lose your temper, or are unduly brutal with a tongue-lashing.

Never force a child to read or learn as a punishment. The potential damage to learning motivation is obvious.

Fear

All children have fears. In fact, we often use fear to teach safety precautions. In addition to those learned by experience, others—such as fear of heights—are instinctive and natural. However, some children develop fears that are beyond the normal range and that create stress whenever the specific fear-producing situation arises. Children's fears are diverse and numerous and can range from a fear of dogs to a fear of a crack in the wall.

The causes for these fears vary. Take the case of thirty-year-old Wendy Miller, for example. She was terrified of birds. One day a small wren got into the house through the chimney. Wendy reacted with hysteria, locking herself and her two small children in the bathroom until the bird was caught and released. A few weeks later the incident was repeated while Wendy happened to be out shopping. The baby-sitter didn't know what to do when the children ran screaming into the bathroom, insisting she accompany them. Fears are often transmitted to children via adults or peers. They learn to regard a specific situation as threatening. A previous bad experience can evoke fear. A child who was bitten by a dog will probably tend to fear dogs, and maybe even furry animals in general, unless remedial action was taken after the incident. A terrifying sight on television or in the movies which was not fully understood can be a source for fear, as can an ominous warning made by an adult or a threat, such as "If you stare into the sun, your eyes will fall out." Even well-meaning reassurances, such as "There's nothing to be afraid of at school," instill fear in a child who never thought about being afraid but wonders what you're really driving at with your remark. In addition, a parent can contribute to the problem by being overprotective or inconsistent, by making unreasonable demands or failing to provide the child with the love or attention necessary for the formation of a strong self-image. A fear is a perceived threat, and the best way to handle it is to deal with it specifically. The following program can assist you:

FIGHT FEAR

Step 1   Determine exactly what is fearful to the child. Encourage the child to talk about and explore the cause and nature of the problem. Don't take the fear lightly, ridicule, attempt coercion ("Don't be afraid, touch the birdie"), or ignore the problem. Logical explanations can help, but don't expect to explain away the fear.

Step 2   If possible, arrange for your child to see others happy and safe in the situation he or she fears.

Step 3   Arrange for carefully supervised contact with the fear, during which you provide positive support and understanding. This procedure is called desensitization and might work as follows:

1. Look at pictures of birds. Discuss whether or not a bird could actually harm you.
2. Have the child hold a toy bird of some type, a plastic model, for example, or a stuffed animal.
3. Let the child watch a friend caring for and holding a pet parrakeet.
4. Have the child watch the parrakeet in its cage.
5. Tell the child to touch the parrakeet briefly as the friend holds it.
6. Have the child hold the parrakeet for five seconds with a pair of gloves on.
7. Have the child hold the parrakeet for ten seconds with a pair of gloves on.
8. Have the child hold the parrakeet for five seconds with bare hands.
9. Have the child hold the parrakeet for ten seconds with bare hands.
10. Have the child hold the parrakeet in lap and pet it.

Step 4   Be leery of flooding therapy, in which the child is suddenly thrust into the situation he or she fears.

Step 5   In the case of irrational fears, such as fear of the dark, acknowledge the child's feelings but guard against adding fuel to the fire by giving credibility to the fears. For example, if the child is afraid of a monster hiding in the bedroom, ringing a bell to chase the monster out would reinforce the fear. Instead, talking about the fear, conducting a reassuring search, and leaving on a nightlight can ease the child's tension. Also, it is important to provide comfort without overdoing it. Overcomforting the child with too much attention or too many hugs and kisses can lead to the belief that there is actually something to fear. Some children enjoy the comforting so much they begin responding with fear for the attention they get.

Step 6   Provide opportunities for success, and build self-image, independence, and responsibility which will make the child more self-assured. (See Chapter Five.) Remember, many fears have their roots in childhood. For example, agoraphobia, or the fear of public places, is one of the most crippling and difficult fears to cope with. Researchers have found that agoraphobia victims were often severely criticized as children and subject to rigid rules. As a result, their self-image suffered and they came to expect a great deal from themselves while simultaneously feeling submissive and unable to control their own lives.

Step 7   Teach your child some of the stress-management techniques in the final chapter. Learn to manage your own fears as well, since your child can learn fear from your words, actions, tone of voice, or body language.

Impulsiveness

The dictionary tells us that an impulse is a sudden action, thought, or compelling force causing momentum. If your child is impulsive, it comes as no news to you that the child can be extremely difficult. He or she rushes into things, often imprudently, and has decreased efficiency. Impulsive behavior can be a source of stress for child and parent. Although the child may be bright, effectiveness is often reduced, contributing to failure and a lowered self-image. The child is frustrated, while the parent becomes impatient. You can help your impulsive child gain control by the following:

1. Maintain a family life-style that is low-key and relatively stress-free. Avoid, especially, any situations that might upset the child immediately before departure for school.

2. Act as a model of organization and try to control your own impulsive behavior, if applicable.

3. Provide a system of fixed routines for the impulsive child. Studying, in particular, should be done in a quiet, private setting at the same time each day.

4. Break activities down into small chunks that guarantee a sense of progress and success. Don't allow the child to hop ahead, but instead insist that each step be completed correctly, in sequence.

5. Be sure your child understands what is expected. In some cases you can't be certain unless the child repeats directions back to you.

6. Your child may learn better via the visual or tactile modalities, rather than the auditory. If so, use them.

7. Encourage your child to take "time-outs" when overstimulated. Be certain these breaks are not associated with punishment.

8. Don't overwhelm your child with choice. Present no more options than the child can effectively handle.

9. Avoid games or teaching techniques that create tension, such as a family spelling bee.

10. Teach your child some of the stress management techniques presented in the last chapter for use when the child identifies that she or he is "out of control."

Jealousy

Jealousy takes many forms, ranging from sibling rivalry to competing for the teacher's attention. It is a stress reaction prompted by the real or imagined threat of a loss of affection. Very young children react overtly, with physical aggression, that has even resulted in bite marks on the arm of a newborn sibling.

The very root of jealousy is insecurity, manifested in a fear that love will be lost or diminished. In some cases jealousy is quite understandable, as when there is obvious differential treatment of children in the same family. A gifted child, for example, often receives more than his or her share of the parents' attention, creating jealousy in siblings. As the child matures, jealousy can be experienced in situations away from home. The cause is still basically the same—security and self-image are threatened by loss of attention or affection.

The best protection against jealousy is to provide your child with a sense of love and security that is unconditional. However, even the child who has received all the parents' love and attention may still have difficulty sharing even a part of it. If you are expecting a new baby, there are a number of children's books on the market that can help prepare your child and create a sense of anticipation. Involve your child in caring for the newborn and attempt to minimize the love and attention shown in front of the jealous child, initially, at least. Expect temporary regression to infantile behavior.

Be alert for the signs of jealousy, and be ready to move in with a reaffirmation of love and affection. Talking about the problem may help the child understand it better. Finally, find time each day to interact one-to-one with each of your children.

JEALOUS REACTIONS TO STRESS

Overt hostility, such as hitting, kicking, or biting

Regression to behavior common at an earlier stage of development, for example—bed-wetting, thumb-sucking, or attachment to a security object

Appearance of rejecting that which the child fears losing most—a parent's love, for example

Cheating, lying, or stealing

Attention seeking, such as misbehaving, feigning illness, or refusing to eat

Taunting or name calling directed at the source of the jealousy

Reflection of anger in play or artwork

Lying

Every child tells a lie at some time or another. Nonetheless, parents are usually quite upset when they discover a child is lying, and with good reason. When a child lies, it is often a test to see if she or he can get away with it or to learn the consequences of lying. Parents' handling of the situation is extremely important in the formation of the child's emerging value system.

Children tell lies for a variety of reasons. When a young child lies, it is rarely to deceive others. Instead the child is involved in fantasizing or exaggerating personal achievements. In some cases what might appear to be a lie is actually wishful thinking, a mistake in judgment, or confusion of fact with reality. I am reminded of the joke in which a small boy rushes into the kitchen and tells Dad, "I just saw a big dinosaur in the yard!" Dad scolds the child saying: "Now, Frankie, you know you didn't see a dinosaur. It must have been a big dog. I want you to go to your room and ask God to forgive you for telling a lie." The child returned a short time later, and Dad asked, "Well, did you pray to God for forgiveness?" "Yes," said Frankie, "but God said not to worry. He thought it was a dinosaur when he first saw it, too."

As the child matures, lies may be a stress reaction, used when the child fears punishment or an effort to appear "good" and please parents. In some cases adults even force the child into lying. For example, when children are angry and temporarily filled with hatred, we force them to lie when we insist they express their true feelings. They know that saying, "I can't stand you, Mom!" will certainly result in punishment. Or, parents might unconsciously invite a lie. If your child has been warned to brush his or her teeth twice a day and you ask: "Did you brush your teeth? If you didn't, no cake for snack!" how do you think any child might respond to that question?

Parents often provide children with a model that includes frequent lying. While the parent might say it is just teasing, or "little white lies," or even good manners, the child is usually not able to make these fine value-distinctions. A lie is lie, whether you say you didn't break the vase when you did or whether you tell a friend she looks lovely and later exclaim at how awful she looked.

Studies show that lying usually hits a peak at approximately six years of age, tapers down a bit at seven, goes back up slightly at eight, and then continues a steady decrease through the teen years as children learn more effective ways of coping. The following suggestions may help you cope with the problem:

1. Set a model of truthfulness.
2. Make it clear that you disapprove of lying.
3. Clearly define the punishment or consequences of misbehavior. Don't make the punishment so severe that lying is preferable to facing the consequences.
4. Demonstrate that if your child does something wrong and lies about it, the consequences will be much more severe than if the truth were told.
5. Don't try to trap a child in a lie. Give the child an opportunity to tell the truth and discuss the matter.
6. Don't invite a lie with facial expression, body language, or phrasing of a question. For example, "Johnny, you did wash your hands before coming to the table, didn't you?"
7. Help your child develop coping techniques that can be used as an alternative to lying (for example, admitting a wrong and asking how it can be rectified).
8. Remember that the better the child's self-image, the less likelihood there will be of lying, since lies diminish a self-image.
9. Discipline your child in ways that don't attack the self-image, or the child might feel compelled to lie in self defense.
10. Express your approval when the child tells the truth, even if it follows a lie. You might say, "I am proud of you for telling the truth. I know how difficult it was to do."

Negativism

Your child may have been classified as negative on the temperament portion of the "Individuality Profile" discussed in Chapter Three. Negativism is another one of those difficult traits and can cause stress for both child and those with whom the child comes in contact. Often the negative child is basically antagonistic and prompts a defensive or hostile reaction in others. The child may be moody, crabby, a whiner, or a pouter. The negative child is prone to perceive others as picking on him or her; often blows minor problems, setbacks, or inconveniences out of proportion; and complains bitterly or withdraws entirely from the situation. Negative children are no barrel of laughs! However you can help the child cope more effectively by:

Encouraging the child to discuss his or her feelings.

Helping the child get a better handle on reality (for example, asking whether everyone is *really* out to get him or her?).

Assisting the child in understanding negativism as a personality trait and coping with it.

Reassuring the child that everyone receives occasional slights or unfair treatment.

Providing opportunities for success and the growth of a favorable self-image.

Reinforcing and extending areas of behavior in which the child tends to excel and have a more positive attitude.

Avoiding situations in which the child gains attention for negativism. (Sometimes the child uses this approach as a sure-fire attention getter, since attention for a negative reason is better than no attention at all.)

Avoiding situations in which the child is placed under stress. In some cases negativism is an ineffective coping technique, used to protect the self-image by attacking the credibility or correctness of the stressor. In other words, the world's all wrong, but I'm all right.

Letting the child take his or her time. Negative children are sometimes responding to a feeling of being constantly pressured.

Using positive forms of discipline, rather than punishment.

Structuring situations in which the child experiences satisfaction from cooperating.

Allowing the child to be herself or himself rather than threatening the self-image by insisting the child be more like someone else.

Obesity and Eating Disorders

When Allen was an infant, he was thin and scrawny. His mother assumed that being thin was unhealthy, so she constantly cajoled and rewarded him for eating. Gradually he began to put on weight, and his mother beamed with pride. The family doctor never expressed concern about Allen being too thin, but he did worry about the boy becoming overweight. Allen's mother dismissed his warnings and continued to make mealtimes lavish, festive occasions. She always had cake and ice cream available for snacks. By the time Allen entered kindergarten, he was obviously overweight. The other children poked fun at him, and Allen's weight interfered with his motor development, coordination, and energy level. He found he couldn't keep up with the other children. His early years in schools were unhappy and stressful. While the other children played outside after school, Allen sat friendless in front of the television set, finding comfort in food. His weight problem seemed to work in a vicious circle—the fatter he got, and the more miserable he became, the more he turned to food for solace. Allen feigned an I-don't-care attitude and occasionally gained attention by consuming large portions of food in a single gulp. Finally, in junior high a counselor referred him to a weight-reduction program for preteens. Slowly he began to understand his problem and learned techniques for weight reduction and control. However, he remained basically withdrawn, insecure, and shy.

Fat children undeniably suffer stress related to obesity. Their peers poke fun at them, parents may disapprove, and studies indicate that teachers may even assign a fat child a lower grade than a thin child. Society discriminates against fat people, and fat children experience blows to the ego that scar for a lifetime. The child becomes dependent on food for comfort or relief in times of stress. If the problem is severe, it can even impair gross motor development. Fat children suffer from a higher incidence of respiratory disease, high blood pressure, and cholesterol and triglycerides in the blood. They are more accident-prone and have more orthopedic ailments. Even the parent-child relationship can suffer if the fat child is constantly nagged and urged to stick to a diet.

Obesity is linked to a number of differing factors. Most parents hope the problem is caused by a metabolic disorder, which is rarely the case. Some weight problems are hereditary in nature and involve the efficiency with which the body uses food and stores fat, although an inherited stocky body frame should not be confused with obesity. Temperament can also affect weight. Easygoing, relaxed individuals burn less calories than people with active personalities. However, of all these influences it appears that environmental conditioning is the most significant.

Eating is a family affair. Researchers have even found that the pets of fat people have double the chance of being fat than the pets of thin people. Obesity is linked to attitudes and habits children begin to form in infancy. As a nation we have learned to crave sugar, salt, and spices. Estimates vary, but experts say that the average American consumes as much as 134 pounds of sugar per year. In fact, you can purchase candy in more places in this coun-

try than you can bread. Some experts feel that since sugar consumption has risen so drastically in recent years, it is taking the
place of other vital and less fattening nutrients in our diet. They
link sugar to heart disease, diabetes, allergies, tooth decay, and
obesity. Salt is another potentially dangerous food product. Few
young children will request it, but just watch parents automatically
reach for the shaker and liberally sprinkle the child's entire plate.
After a time the child learns to season food.

You have probably heard the saying, Fat baby, fat adult. Research tends to support this statement: over eighty-five percent of
all overweight children grow up fighting a weight problem. It appears that the development of excessive fat cells may doom the
child to a lifetime of weight gain from the slightest overeating. Fat
cells formed in childhood remain throughout life and quickly absorb fatty end products. Some medical practitioners estimate that
cell development is most rapid in the first two years of life and
between the ages of nine and sixteen.

The treatment of obese children must involve the entire family.
Following are some suggestions for helping your child:

Monitor your child's weight. Check with the doctor to determine if the child is actually overweight.

Analyze when and why your child overeats. If the child eats
when stressed, attempt to control the stressors and teach
your child some of the stress-management techniques given
in the final chapter. Above all, the child should be able to
identify when food is being used as a pacifier. If the child
eats out of loneliness, help the child to arrange some outside social activities or recreational programs. If anger
prompts overeating, the child should be made to realize
that she or he is the only person being punished. Some
children eat when fatigued. Their resistance is down, as is
blood sugar. Insisting that the child eat regular, balanced
meals can help prevent this situation.

Don't assume that a fat baby is more healthy or more appealing. The fat cells that are developing will plague your child
for a lifetime.

Don't constantly feed an infant or use food to calm or appease
a child.

Don't begin a diet of varied, solid foods too early in the child's
life. Consult your pediatrician.

Don't use food as a reward.

Don't urge your child to eat when the child is not hungry. Don't insist that the child clean the plate.

Don't associate eating with achievement, by overreacting when a child eats well, eats a lot, or completely finishes a serving.

Don't allow your child to deal with stress by overindulging. A tasty treat might be effective for relaxation, but you should draw the line at overeating.

Don't serve high-calorie meals or snacks. Serve fruit for dessert.

Don't make eating and mealtime the focal part of family life.

Don't celebrate with food.

Don't try to bolster your child's spirits with food.

Establish firm eating habits and try to stick to them, even on special days, at special events, in restaurants, or on vacation.

If the child expresses a fierce craving for something fattening, suggest that your child have a tiny portion—just to satisfy the taste buds.

Avoid high-calorie school lunches by packing a nutritious, low-calorie lunch.

Serve smaller portions.

If you sense your child is about to overindulge, try to direct him or her to some physical activity.

Involve the child in any weight-reduction program. Since the child is growing, maintaining existing weight may solve the problem if the child is not extremely overweight. Older children sometimes benefit from the accountability provided by enrolling in organized weight-reduction programs.

Younger children probably won't understand the concept of calorie reduction and can interpret being deprived of food as a withdrawal of love. Instead, provide low-calorie meals and snacks. Remember, any diet must begin in the grocery store.

Remember that many healthy foods, such as natural nut mixes, are also fattening. There isn't much difference in calorie intake between consuming a large banana or a Hostess Ho Ho. Check your calorie book when planning your shopping list to identify healthy, low-calorie foods.

Eating disorders, including compulsive eating, anorexia nervosa, and bulimia, have recently attracted widespread public attention. Compulsive eaters often eat in a frenzied fashion, with obesity the end result. Victims of anorexia nervosa, on the other hand, starve themselves to the point of skeletal thinness, which disrupts many normal body functions and can even result in death. Bulimia has only recently been officially recognized as a mental disorder, and research into the problem is new. The bulimic is preoccupied with both food and remaining thin and regularly engages in binge eating, when huge amounts of food are rapidly consumed. One bulimic admitted consuming as much as seventy dollars worth of food in one day, followed by the second phase of the syndrome, purging, when vomiting is self-induced or laxatives and/or diuretics are taken. One woman reported that she took three hundred laxatives per week for a period of five to six years. Some bulimics follow binging with fasting, strenuous exercise, or amphetamine use. Bulimics maintain near normal weight, and unlike anorectics, their appetites and biological functions remain intact.

Ninety percent of the cases of anorexia nervosa are women, and the problem can begin during prepubescence. Bulimia has been diagnosed in individuals from twelve- to forty-five years old, although it is most common during the twenties and thirties. It is predominantly a female disorder, with ninety-eight percent of the victims women and girls. A study conducted at the Anorexia Nervosa Center at Chicago's Michael Reese Hospital revealed that there are many more cases of bulimia than anorexia nervosa. In fact, researcher Craig Johnson estimates that fifteen to twenty percent of the female college population has "some involvement" with the binge/purge syndrome.

All three eating disorders previously mentioned signal an inability to effectively cope with stress and, possibly, have roots in childhood. The compulsive eater uses food for relief from stress and may even get fat in an effort to reject the feminine stereotype, to rebel, to escape from competition among women to be physically attractive, or to avoid sexual relationships. The bulimic also eats to find comfort, or perhaps to recreate a sense of security associated with the nurturing and care provided earlier in life.

However, parental and/or societal pressure to be feminine and attractive cause her to rid her body of the excess calories by purging. Anorectics may stop eating to gain a feeling of control at a time when they are actually unable to cope with life's stresses. The resulting emaciated thinness has also been interpreted as an avoidance of femininity or an attempt to appear frail and to need care.

There is no simple cure for eating disorders. However, the child who learns techniques for coping with stress and develops outlets for healthy expression of anger and anxiety will surely reduce the risk of such problems occurring later in life. In addition, parents can try to teach children to eat properly when hungry, rather than relying on dieting for weight control. Parents can also guard against encouraging children to make food the center of their lives or contributing to the use of food for stress-relief. They can assist their children to develop a strong, nonstereotypical self-image that allows a realistic acceptance of a healthy body weight.

Procrastination

Procrastination is a means for avoiding a threatening or unappealing task. While it is effective in temporarily sidestepping the unpleasant, the satisfaction gained is far outweighed by the considerable amount of resulting stress generated.

Procrastination is often caused by a poor self-image. The child believes that the task is too difficult or that chances for success are minimal. There is a basic lack of confidence or competence. In other situations the child might procrastinate in order to rebel or show independence. Perhaps the activity is genuinely repelling to the child. In addition, many children begin an activity but end up procrastinating as soon as they hit a snag. Their level of persistence is low (see "Individuality Profile"). Passive children are often in this category.

Procrastinators can become experts in making up excuses. Excuses are not unlike lies—they are used to avoid punishment or disapproval. In fact, very young children might even lie and say they've accomplished something that, in fact, they haven't. This coping technique is soon proven ineffective, and children begin blaming circumstances beyond their control or other individuals for their failure. As children mature, they find that one of the most effective methods for explaining procrastination is to accept responsibility. Once a child says: "I'm sorry. I didn't do what I was supposed to. I'm just a big goof-off," the matter is closed. What can the adult say? The child admitted the problem.

Occasionally, the child may genuinely have forgotten a responsibility, rather than procrastinated. It is a good idea to ask a child to repeat an important set of directions. If your child seems to be forgetful, help the child remember by encouraging him or her to make written notes; to place important papers in a predetermined, fixed spot; or to set aside a few times during each day when the mental question "Now what do I have to remember?" is answered. A bulletin board or blackboard, calendar, and note pad should be available in the child's room. The technique of making a daily list might also prove helpful.

The procrastinator can be assisted in facing the problem. The first step is to stop accepting excuses that only avoid the problem. In fact, many parents encourage excuses by anticipating the child's explanation for nonperformance, when there really isn't any. Stop asking, "Why?" if you know the reason is simply procrastination. Lecturing the child is also ineffective. It only promotes guilt and attacks the child's self-image. The child may come to believe he or she really isn't capable. Instead, the child should be guided in examining the cause and ultimate outcome of the behavior. Procrastination is often a bad habit which can be corrected once the child realizes it generates stress. Reconstruct situations and make a plan for the future. Once the child is aware that procrastination creates more problems than it solves, a more effective means for coping is logical.

Shyness

Most children experience a temporary fear of strangers at approximately six months of age, and throughout childhood sporadic stretches of shyness are normal. Physical changes, stress, or factors connected with the stage of development can contribute to it, but children soon return to their old selves. However, if the condition persists, it can limit a child's social life, cause the child to be overlooked, or inhibit creativity. People often underestimate the intelligence of a shy child.

Studies show that, unfortunately, many shy children grow into shy adults. They are anxious in social settings and introverted. In some relationships they may seek constant attention, which usually grates on the nerves of the adults they continuously "bug." The shy-passive child seeks reassurance, acceptance, and approval. Instead of speaking up when angry or insulted, he or she may instead resort to indirect expressions, such as dawdling or simply not doing as told. The problem can result from a lack of security, poor self-image, or overprotection. Children who have suffered chronic illnesses can develop the trait. In some cases shyness is a reaction to stress. The child does not know how to cope or has been punished, criticized, and ridiculed so often that he or she simply withdraws from social situations. In a few cases shyness is the result of a lack of practice in meeting and interacting with others. Sometimes, the shy child has similarly shy parents.

Some experts believe that we attach too much importance to competition. The child who suffers from a poor self-image and lack of confidence, rather than facing failure, withdraws. Acknowledge your child's individuality. Children differ in the way they approach life. If your child is not outgoing, it doesn't signal a fault. Accept the child as is, rather than pressuring him or her to be more friendly or talkative. Trying to force your child to make personality changes can create a problem. You are in effect telling the child there is something wrong with the way he or she is. This knowledge will only cause the child to become more shy and fearful of his or her ability to cope with social situations.

The following suggestions can help the shy child.

1. Keep punishment and criticism to an absolute minimum.

2. Use some of the suggestions in the previous chapter for building a sense of independence and a strong self-image.

3. Avoid situations in which the shy child is directly interacting with a particularly aggressive child, who may either totally ignore or harass the shy child.

4. Enroll the child in courses or recreational programs where success can be experienced, such as an arts and crafts class, team sport, or choral group. Be careful of placing demands on the child to perform solo or to get into the limelight.

5. Ask the teacher to seat your child next to another child with a similar problem.

6. Ask the teacher to provide opportunities for your child to be noticed by the class without experiencing a lot of pressure: for example, passing papers, delivering notes, or holding the door.

7. Encourage and reinforce social interaction. Let the child give a party.

8. Help the child develop alternative means for coping with stress. Use some of the stress-management techniques suggested in the final chapter.

9. Discourage the child from downgrading himself or herself.

10. Tell the child not to call himself or herself shy and try to change that mental image.

11. Point out the child's many strengths and help to eliminate or improve weaknesses.

Speech

If your child has a speech problem, get expert help immediately. Voice disorders, lack of fluency, and poor articulation deserve prompt attention. Stuttering affects approximately one percent of the population, and boy stutterers outnumber girls four to one. Although no one knows precisely what causes the problem, many experts believe that anxiety is a factor. Therefore, it is important for the stutterer to keep stress under control.

The following suggestions may help parents who have children with speech problems:

Don't allow other children to tease or mimic the child.

Don't ask the child to stop, take a deep breath, and start over. This practice is annoying and only adds to feelings of inadequacy.

Allow the child to finish speaking. Don't become impatient, interrupt, or finish the sentence for her or him.

Don't constantly correct the child's speech. Nagging will ultimately cause the child to just keep quiet.

Don't attempt to work on all speech errors at once. Take things one step at a time.

Don't assume that the child can correct speech problems simply by putting a mind to it. Stuttering or poor speech habits require great effort for improvement.

Build the child's self-image by structuring opportunities for success.

Encourage the child to practice speech by engaging in daily conversations.

Provide your child with a good speech model.

Try to prevent the child from feeling guilty about the problem. No one is to blame.

Try to prevent the child from becoming self-conscious about speech. Don't discuss the child's problem or progress with other adults while in the child's presence.

Encourage the child to keep trying. Speech problems are not hopeless.

Tantrums

Tantrums are, perhaps, the most easily identified sign that stress is out of control. Fits of temper are usually associated with the nonverbal preschooler who is unable to cope, cannot express feelings, and engages in screaming, pounding, or head banging. However, older children, and even adults, may respond to frustration by storming, shouting, or swearing.

Nearly every child will try a tantrum at some point, sometimes after seeing it work for another child. Your reaction will determine if this form of behavior persists. Take the case of three-year-old Eddie Avery. His mother had a standing policy regarding candy at the grocery check-out counter, which was simply stated as "No!" One day they stopped to pick up a few items on the way home from the pediatrician's office. Eddie had a slight fever associated with an ear infection. In the check-out line, he watched as another child asked for and was given a bag of M & M's. He asked his mother for a bag and began to cry when she refused. Then she suddenly changed her mind, saying: "Oh, okay. I know you're not feeling well today." The next time they were shopping, Eddie asked again for candy. This time the child was in perfect health, and Mrs. Avery firmly told him, "No!" Much to her surprise, he began screaming, crying, and pounding his legs. She was mortified by his behavior and the attention they were attracting and quickly gave him the candy he requested. Predictably, on the third trip to the grocery store, Eddie again demanded candy. Mrs. Avery was exhausted that particular day and, although she initially said, "No!" swiftly gave in at the first sign of the tantrum brewing, telling Eddie, "Okay, but you can only have one piece before dinner." Lately, Mrs. Avery has found that Eddie refuses to accept "No!" for an answer, and his tantrums are becoming more violent and frightening. On several occasions he has even resorted to head banging and holding his breath.

It is easy to see how Mrs. Avery reinforced Eddie's temper tantrums. Temperamentally, Eddie has a very low frustration level. He has learned to cope by throwing fits, which ultimately satisfy his want, or at least gain him a lot of attention. His violent behavior embarrasses and terrifies his mother, who is afraid he will seriously injure himself.

Children learn coping strategies through trial and error, and many remain with them into adulthood. When children find that fits of rage result in satisfaction, they are apt to rely on tantrums in times of stress. While physical violence usually disappears between the ages of three and five, older children continue to react with unrestraint. They are persistent and overbearing beyond the point of healthy adjustment. Take the following self-test, and see if you unconsciously promote tantrums in your child:

YOU CAN RUN FROM A TANTRUM!

Check each statement that applies.

_____ My child is being raised in a restrictive environment, controlled by many "don'ts" and "mustn'ts."

_____ I am inclined to be inconsistent, forbidding a behavior on one occasion and tolerating it on the next.

_____ If my child does throw a tantrum, I immediately attempt to stop the tantrum and be consoling.

_____ I try to reason and talk sense to my child when he or she is in a rage.

_____ I sometimes give in to fits of bad temper because I am exhausted or my child is sick.

_____ I often lose my temper and engage in explosive behavior.

_____ When my child has a tantrum, I usually lose my composure, particularly if we are in a public place or in the presence of friends or relatives.

_____ I have permitted a tantrum to work by meeting my child's demands.

_____ I have permitted a tantrum to work by reducing my demands on the child.

_____ When my child has a tantrum, I feel guilty and fear the child may become seriously injured.

If you checked even one of the ten statements above, you could be encouraging tantrums. In dealing with a tantrum, don't automatically assume your child is seriously maladjusted or a demon with a Dr. Jekyll–Mr. Hyde personality. Tantrums are effective, logical coping strategies. Your biggest concern in dealing with them is to prevent their recurrence. The first step is to determine the situations that typically stimulate the outbreak. If you recognize your child has a temperament that includes a low frustration level, perhaps you can avoid some of the troublesome situations by removing the frustration or intervening when the child is overtired. In the event a tantrum does occur, keep cool and don't compromise your original stand. Your child's behavior might terrify you, but children rarely hurt themselves. In fact, tantrums usually subside when there is no audience. If you are afraid to leave your child alone during an outburst for fear of injury, remain in the same room but pay no attention. Even glancing at the child can intensify or sustain the tantrum. After the child is calm, discuss the causes for the tantrum. Ask the child what he or she would do if you behaved similarly. Establish some consequences for the next time a tantrum occurs and develop some alternative coping techniques. When the child does exercise self-control, be sure to reinforce the behavior with praise and encouragement.

My daughter had one tantrum during her early years. Not surprisingly, it occurred the day after a young guest had exhibited similar behavior when demanding more cola. "It worked for him, so why not for me?" she must have reasoned. We had had a slight difference of opinion regarding which outfit was most appropriate for preschool that day. Carly went into the new routine. Like any parent, I was taken aback but slightly amused. She really looked quite foolish pounding her feet and screaming just as she had seen the boy do the evening before. The tub was filled for her bath. With barely a thought, I picked her up, carried her to the tub, and put her in—still dressed in her nightgown. She was so stunned she immediately stopped crying and asked indignantly: "What are you doing? I have my nightgown on!" I replied: "Carly, I am so surprised at you I don't know what to do. We'll talk more when you have settled down." In a few minutes she emerged from the bathroom, wrapped in a towel. She ultimately wore the clothes I had suggested and never had another tantrum. Even today she still remembers the incident, and we both laugh.

Testing . . . One, Two, Three . . . Testing

You remember the story of Kevin and his first day of school at the beginning of this chapter. Kevin had the problem, but it affected those around him. The areas covered in this chapter are difficult to cope with for children and parents alike, and the suggestions are designed to relieve stress for both. But when it comes right down to it, you will of course adapt and tailor your solution to your specific situation.

Remember that one of your jobs as a parent is to be a kind of tryout audience for your child, who is testing behavior on you before taking it on the road. Many negative childhood behaviors are attempted on an experimental basis. Swift, definitive parent reaction can nip them in the bud and help your child discover the realities of interacting appropriately in today's world.

In some situations a troublesome pattern of behavior might be a subtle plea for help, for proof of your love, or for the imposing of limits. Children cry out in pain by rebelling, becoming ill, reacting aggressively, or acting sullen. They show off or misbehave to gain attention; withdraw or give up when they feel inept at coping; and become hostile, insulting, defiant, or overbearing in an effort to prove their independence or to retaliate. Whatever the cause, bear in mind that your child's positive self-image is the best defense. Give your child consistent acceptance, respect, concern, and freedom within carefully defined limits.

Chapter Seven

Join the Teaching Team

The basic goal of education is not the transmittal of a body of facts and information. Instead, education is a means for assisting the child in maximizing innate human potential and coping effectively with life. A good education teaches children how to teach themselves. It generates a love and enthusiasm for learning which lasts a lifetime. The self-fulfillment that results enables a child to face life's inevitable stressors with a sense of control and competency. As a parent you must be involved in providing this education for your child, and you must begin the process at birth. You cannot leave the job to the schools. A team approach is vital.

But Can I Really Make a Difference?

Earlier, we talked about the necessity for parents to identify and accept their children's individuality. Such acceptance, however, does not mean that parents cannot have an influence on their children's development. Quite the contrary. Children are born with a set of traits and a level of intelligence that are the child's innate potential. Think of potential as a cup, capable of being filled to the top. However, we can choose to fill it only half, or three-quarters full. That is where you, the parent, comes in. You help create an environment that determines just how full the cup will actually be filled. If the environment is rich and stimulating, the cup is filled to capacity. The child's innate potential is maximized.

For years psychologists argued over whether intelligence was determined by heredity (nature) or environment (nurture). In recent years the nature/nurture controversy has been somewhat resolved. In view of the well-documented inadequacies of intelligence testing, a statement which defines intelligence in terms of such testing has little utility. However, David Wechsler developed a definition which states that "intelligence is the global capacity of the individual to act purposefully, to think rationally, and to deal effectively with his environment."[1] I like this definition because I think it suggests that coping is a part of intelligence. When I talk about intelligence, I am using the term with this definition in mind.

The nature/nurture controversy began years ago. In 1859 Darwin's evolution theory supported the position that intelligence is fixed by nature. According to Darwin, intelligence is inherited from one's parents as part of the genetic package. Other scientists following in Darwin's footsteps also accepted the notion of intelligence fixed by nature, and a definite relationship between heredity and intelligence was established through the research of C. L. Burt. Since identical twins exhibit the closest genetic similarity possible between any two human beings, Burt compared the intelligence of identical twins, nontwin siblings, and unrelated children. Identical twins raised together showed a very high correlation in intelligence, while nontwin siblings were somewhat lower, and unrelated children raised together were lower yet. Burt reasoned that if the correlation of intelligence between identical twins reared apart was higher than the correlation of intelligence between nontwin siblings or unrelated children raised together, heredity was clearly isolated as the key factor of intelligence. Burt's investigation yielded a correlation that *was* higher but *not* as high as it was when the identical twins were raised together. If heredity was the sole determiner of intelligence, it should have been the same whether the twins were raised together or apart.[2]

Researchers H. H. Newman, F. N. Freeman, and J. K. Holzinger conducted a study quite similar to that undertaken by Burt.[3] They found that identical twins correlated most closely in intelligence, followed in order by fraternal twins, and nontwin siblings. At first glance this data appears to corroborate Burt's findings regarding intelligence by heredity. Actually, this study strongly suggests the existence of factors in addition to heredity. It is a biological fact that identical twins are monozygotic, indicating that they have developed from one fertilized egg. After fertilization the zygote splits into two separate cells which will produce two separate babies. However, since both children have been produced from a single zygote and sperm, they will possess identical sex and heredity. The high correlation in intelligence between identical twins is, therefore, quite understandable. In the Newman, Freeman, and Holzinger study the correlation in intelligence between fraternal twins was higher than that between nontwin siblings. There can be no genetic explanation for this phenomenon. Fraternal twins are dizygotic—they develop as a result of fertilization of two separate eggs by separate sperm cells. Fraternal twins inherit no greater genetic similarity to one another than nontwin siblings. In fact, fraternal twins may even be of different sexes. The closer correlation in intelligence discovered between the fraternal twins suggests the importance of environment. Each fraternal twin grows and develops in an environment that closely resembles and corresponds to the environment surrounding the other twin. The early environments of nontwin siblings born some years apart does not usually produce such marked similarities.

Another researcher, Anne Anastasi, reported that the intelligence quotients of twins reared apart during their first three years of life vary in proportion to the educational advantage in the distinct environments.[4] If identical twins are separated, but placed in similar environments, their compared intelligence quotients will differ only slightly. However, if the conditions prevailing in the separate environments differ widely, the compared intelligence quotients will show an even greater difference. Further research conducted by Lester Sontag revealed that environment can affect intelligence by as many as twenty intelligence points.[5] Although the validity of the concept of intelligence quotients might be debated, research proves that intelligence tests do provide a valid predictor of later academic success.[6] A loss as substantial as twenty points certainly merits concern. The estimates of the percentage of intelligence fixed by nature range from 60 percent to 88 percent.

However, the crucial point is that environment does play a part in intellectual development. An environment that provides nothing, or very little, in the way of support for intellectual growth, can be devastating in terms of a child's realization of fullest innate capabilities. It is during a child's first eight years of life that a stimulating environment is most important, and during the first four years the most important of all.

Abraham Maslow has stated: "The needs to know and to understand are seen in late infancy and childhood, perhaps even more strongly than in adulthood. Furthermore, this seems to be a spontaneous product of maturation, rather than of learning, however defined. Children do not have to be taught to be curious. But they *may* be taught, as by institutionalization, *not* to be curious."[7] Many children living within a family unit suffer a comparable loss of curiosity because of the lack of stimulation at home or at school, or both, and as a result are unable to fully realize their potential. These children do not choose to live a life of reduced effectiveness. The choice is unwittingly made for them by parents who do not provide for their total development by joining the teaching team from the day the child is born.

I Know How to Bake a Cake, but How Do You Stimulate?

What does the word *stimulate* mean to you? Do you think of exciting or animating your child, increasing keenness and vitality? A stimulating environment does all these things and simultaneously provides support and fosters growth, learning, and development. As you approach the job of providing a stimulating environment for your child, there are five points to remember. First, you should never force your child. Learning should be smooth and easy. If you find you are placing your child under stress because you are making demands that are too difficult, stop and reevaluate. Second, learning should be fun. If your child does not like a particular activity, try presenting it in a different manner. Third, if your child gets tired, you are no longer stimulating the child. The younger the child, the shorter the attention span. Resist the temptation to plan extended sessions with your child. Two shorter time periods usually work better than one long one. Don't forget to use those precious minutes while riding in the car, preparing a meal, or doing the dishes. Fourth, don't get angry or lose your temper when your child has trouble or makes mistakes. Children do not make mistakes on purpose, and they do not enjoy having trouble. If you become upset, you are generating stress for yourself and your child. If the result of your interaction is always a big blowout, with tears and angry words, your child might transfer these negative feelings to you or to learning in general. In addition, when you explode you are depriving your child of success—the fifth basic point. Success is the most important ingredient in learning. Have you ever been highly motivated to learn something—maybe chess? The interest was there, but after you got into the game, you just weren't successful at it. There's a good chance you dropped it, despite your initial enthusiasm. On the other hand, have you ever been lukewarm about learning something new, like skiing? Someone encouraged you to give it a try and after starting out in a haphazard, bored manner, you began to experience some level of success. In no time at all you loved skiing and vowed to become an expert. Nobody likes to fail, and a source of failure is usually a source of stress. Program attainable success into your child's life.

As a member of the teaching team you must be familiar with your child's individuality. Sometimes parents need to remind themselves of their child's uniqueness. Resist the temptation to insist that your child perform exactly like the rest of the class or like brothers and sisters. Be familiar with your child's developmental level and don't program experiences or content materials inappropriate for that level. If you are unsure of what you are doing, ask the teacher or some other expert for guidance. If you think some activity should work with the child and find that it doesn't, table the matter for a short time. When you come back to it, you will probably find that the child has grown into it. If not, wait a little longer.

Following is a list of twenty old wives' tales about children and learning. Operating under these misconceptions can create stress for parent and child.

TWENTY OLD WIVES' TALES

1. **Children should be seen, not heard.** Verbal ability is closely related to success in the language arts, particularly reading. If that old adage is actually enforced, there's a good chance of difficulty in school.

2. **I must teach, teach, teach.** I think what you really want is for your child to learn. When you teach, teach, teach, you usually talk, talk, talk. Instead, concentrate on structuring the environment so that your child learns by discovery. Real learning is the result of finding out on your own, not of being told. Get your child to talk and ask thought-provoking questions to keep the ball rolling.

3. **Educational television can teach my child things I can't.** I am a believer in the merits of educational programming. However, some parents with preschool children have an exalted notion of what educational television has to offer. They sit their children in front of the set with not the slightest twinge of conscience, confident the programming has more to offer than they do. Although children can profit from carefully monitored TV viewing, particularly if the parent is at hand to reinforce learning, in reality they need to be active participants in their environment. They need parents to interact with and talk to.

4. **Once my child begins reading, I should stop reading to the child.** Parents should begin reading to children before they are a year old and continue throughout childhood. This activity transmits a love of learning and enthusiasm for reading. The key is to select material appropriate for the child's age and interest. Your librarian can help.

5. **I can't help my child with reading, math, or science because I don't have the training.** Your role is not to teach from scratch, but rather to reinforce and extend the mate-

rial that is presented by the teacher. If you study the work your child brings home, you will soon see the sequence of learning. Corrected papers and homework also tell you where the child needs help. Just listening to your child read and then asking some comprehension questions can be a tremendous benefit. If you hit a snag, don't hesitate to contact the professional—your child's teacher.

6. **Silence is golden.** Don't mistake your child's silence for understanding. Learning is noisy and animated. Watch for that fake nod of understanding or the silent plodding along.

7. **Difficult material is challenging.** Many parents select material that is beyond the success range of their children. Maybe it is the result of wishful thinking, but the results are disastrous. Rather than challenged, children are defeated and unable to cope. Reading material, in particular, should be below the instructional level at school and easy enough to read with fluency and understanding.

8. **If my child can do the work, the child understands it.** Children can correctly "call" each word when reading aloud and not read them. In other words, the child doesn't comprehend what is being read. It is also possible to memorize a process, such as carrying or borrowing in math, and not understand what you are doing. Many children can correctly complete a phonics worksheet and not know how to apply what was done on the sheet to decoding an unfamiliar word. It is not unusual for a child to get one hundred per cent on a spelling test and miss a word on the list when composing a story an hour later.

9. **If I want my child to get off to a good start in school, I should teach reading in the home or enroll my child in a preschool that does.** There are many heated arguments about teaching reading in preschool and kindergarten. As a policy, I am against it. I have seen many preschool children who were ready and actually taught themselves to read. In these cases I say fine! However, my experience has taught me that beyond these isolated cases most children are not ready. Instead, parents can provide a rich background of varied experiences and help the child develop a broad vocabulary and good verbal skills. What good is it to be able to read the word *silo,* if you don't know what one is?

10. **A child must know all the letters in the alphabet in order to learn to read.** Most children learn to read their first word before they have mastered the alphabet. My unofficial survey indicates that the word *McDonald's,* as in McDonald's

restaurant, ranks at the top as the first word read. Before formal reading instruction begins, children learn to read a number of words on "sight," or by recognizing the shape and configuration of the word.

11. **What happens at home is no business of the teacher's.** Children's learning is greatly affected by a number of variables—one of which is the emotional climate in the home. If your family is experiencing unusual difficulty or grief, inform the teacher.

12. **Children should be guided in selecting only the finest in children's literature.** A balance in reading material is desirable. However, particularly in the case of a reluctant reader, nearly any wholesome material is better than nothing.

13. **It's a parent's responsibility to help a child learn—not an older brother's or sister's.** Everyone in the family should work together to promote a stimulating environment. Sometimes, a younger child can even teach an older sibling. Besides, teaching something is a great way to really learn it thoroughly.

14. **It is better to provide new listening experiences, rather than to reread stories or recite poetry the child has heard before.** Children love repetition. They like to hear a story or poem until they know every word. There is nothing wrong with repetition. It helps the child develop a love for literature. Poems and rhymes help train the ear to pick out the rhyming elements, or endings of words that make them rhyme. This skill is extremely important for later reading ability.

15. **When reading aloud, it is important that the child read every word. Substitutions of one word for another should be pointed out.** The purpose of reading is to get meaning. If the child unconsciously substitutes one word for another similar in meaning or omits words, don't be alarmed—as long as the child is getting the meaning. Older readers, in particular, just get careless. Interrupting the fluency and train of thought can do more harm than good.

16. **My child is a straight-A student, so I don't have to worry.** Some parents get lulled into complacency by their child's past performance. Children can "hit the skids" in no time. In addition, the highest marks don't necessarily mean the child is achieving at full potential.

17. **Don't worry about why, just do it!** If children don't see the point to an activity, it is unlikely they will benefit much from its accomplishment. Resist the "because I said so!" attitude and explain the reason.

18. **You are created in the image and likeness of me.** Parents should stimulate the growth and development of new ideas and fresh approaches, rather than insist that the child adopt modes of thinking identical to the parents'.

19. **Children love praise.** Children do love deserved, sincere praise. Often-repeated, meaningless words, such as "great" have no effect. Children know when they have earned praise and when someone is patronizing them.

20. **Teachers and parents deserve respect.** While the statement is true, I see no reason for delineating who deserves respect. Everyone deserves it. Don't expect children to respect adults who don't earn respect for themselves and demonstrate it toward others. Respect can't be legislated.

Surefire Learning Boosters

Marie Martin arrives home from the parent-teacher conference worried, shocked, and angry. She has just found out that her son Ricky is reading at the second grade level, although the boy is in the fifth grade. The teacher seemed puzzled at Marie's total surprise on hearing the news. "Why, certainly you must have noticed he was having difficulty," Mrs. Jackson had said. Marie had tartly responded: "No, I wasn't aware there was a problem, and I don't understand why I wasn't informed. It isn't my place to interfere in the work of the school." Mrs. Jackson's only reply was: "Well, Ricky brings home four report cards a year and graded papers and homework each evening. Don't you help him at home?"

Ricky's problems cannot be blamed solely on the school or the home. Educating children requires a team effort. Parents pay taxes or tuition for the benefit of sending children to learn under the tutelage of trained professionals. However, it is an oversimplification, at best, to assume that a teacher can meet the total learning needs of each and every student in the class—especially when you consider that most children spend only nine or ten months a year in school and only about five hours a day in instruction. A child's failure is actually the shared failure of *both* home and school and produces stress for all concerned.

Obviously, no one expects you to take over the basic instruction that typically occurs in the classroom. What you can do, however, is reinforce and extend the learning that takes place in school. Graded papers and homework will guide you. In addition, you can provide rich, stimulating experiences that the school cannot possibly supply. You can take your child camping, apple picking, to see new places and new things. These experiences cannot be beaten for the quality and quantity of firsthand knowledge acquired.

You can also keep your child physically prepared to learn. A child who is suffering the stress of illness or who cannot see or hear properly is not ready to learn. Don't assume that because the child passed a vision or hearing test several months ago, there is no chance for a problem. Many perceptual difficulties go undetected in screenings and some do not manifest themselves until the child is fatigued. A number of children have regularly recurring earaches or colds which are accompanied by serious temporary hearing loss. Not all vision problems are physical. Such functional vision problems as coordinating the use of both eyes, difficulty with depth perception, or inability to move the eyes smoothly to follow an object or line of print are common. In fact, experts estimate that forty percent of all elementary school students have some type of visual problem. Watch for signs that your child cannot see or hear properly. For example, does your child insist on turning the television or radio very loud or turn his or her head when listening to something? Does your child reverse letters, confuse words, favor one eye, or frequently lose the place when reading? Maybe your child leans close to paper work, has difficulty remembering letters or words, or has poor handwriting. Any of these behaviors may be a sign of trouble.

Once you are certain your child is physically ready to learn, you can try some of the "Surefire Learning Boosters" that follow:

SUREFIRE LEARNING BOOSTERS

1. Set aside a quiet place for daily interaction with your child in learning activities.
2. Equip the learning area with desk or worktable, good lighting, pencils, paper, ruler, stapler, dictionary, scissors, glue, and other supplies.
3. Schedule a regular, specific learning time that doesn't interfere with after-school play or a favorite television time. Keep the span reasonably short.
4. Be consistent in your observance of learning time. Your child will benefit far more from fifteen minutes of your time each day of the week than from one two-hour session.
5. Discuss schoolwork and use it as a means for developing vocabulary and verbal ability, but avoid doing the work for the child.
6. Enrich school studies with magazines, reference books, maps, outings, and extra independent research.

7. Strive for understanding and guard against rushing.

8. If your child isn't bringing home any work, find out why. Is the child completing it at school, forgetting it, or failing to do it?

9. Insist that your child get to bed at a fixed time each evening.

10. Strive for good attendance at school. It is hard to catch up on new material once you fall behind.

11. Get your child a library card and use it.

12. Give your child books as gifts.

13. Subscribe to several high-quality children's magazines.

14. Utilize mealtime, time in the car, or time during meal preparation or doing dishes to discuss school, problems, current events, anything at all—just to communicate.

15. Show your interest in learning by letting your child see you reading, studying, and enjoying learning.

16. Play games and drill on the addition, subtraction, multiplication, and division facts. Many adults still experience momentary stress when asked, "What is seven times eight?" For a shortcut, work on facts in related groups—for example:

$$
\begin{array}{cccc}
2 & 7 & 9 & 9 \\
+7 & +2 & -7 & -2 \\
\hline
9 & 9 & 2 & 7
\end{array}
\quad \text{or} \quad
\begin{array}{cc}
6 & 7 \\
\times 7 & \times 6 \\
\hline
42 & 42
\end{array}
\quad
6\overline{)42} \quad 7\overline{)42}
$$

17. Teach your child to use referents in remembering basic addition and subtraction facts. For example, 9 plus 8 is almost the same problem as 10 plus 8, just one less since 9 is one less than 10.

18. Find books and learning activities that correspond with your child's interests. Leave appealing books lying about the house. Stick interesting news clippings to a bulletin board or the refrigerator. Encourage your child to play school with appropriate materials. Install a backyard mailbox so he or she can exchange notes with friends.

19. Make the most of everyday experiences—going to the grocery store, finding a number in the Yellow Pages, or watching a new home being built in the neighborhood. Teach new concepts, skills, and vocabulary words.

20. On long car trips, show your child how to map-read, plot the route, and compute the mileage.

21. Call attention to the many signs that now contain pictures only and play games to teach their meaning—for example:

those indicating no smoking, men, women, railroad crossing.

22. When traveling, let your child read timetables and guide
    the family to the proper ticket counter, gate, or taxi stand.

23. Involve your child in reading the newspaper. Clip coupons,
    read the funnies, or play games finding ads in the Classi-
    fied section.

24. Teach your child to count and handle money.

25. Pick up forms wherever you find them. As soon as your
    child can write, let the child practice filling in employment
    applications, bank withdrawal slips, income tax returns,
    driver's license applications, credit applications, or what-
    ever you can find.

26. When dining out, ask your child to read the menu and
    comment on the best value for the money.

27. Teach your child to read the various meters and gauges in
    the house and car (gas gauge, water meter, thermometer).

28. Comparison-shop. Compute price per ounce for various-
    size containers, prices from one store to the next, and price
    per pound for different cuts of meat.

29. Discuss light, water, and telephone bills. Figure out how to
    save money by conserving or making long-distance calls in
    the evenings or on weekends.

30. Practice emergency procedures, such as calling for an am-
    bulance, exiting the house in a fire, or seeking help if lost.

31. Encourage your prereading child to "read" familiar signs
    and logos to develop visual memory and a notion of what
    reading is all about.

32. Encourage a wide variety of activities in addition to aca-
    demic pursuits, but remember that developing independent
    reading skill is the most important interest of all. A disabled
    reader is truly disabled, in the strictest sense of the word.

Education Under Stress

For children with certain unique needs—the handicapped, the
learning-disabled, slow learners, the hyperactive, underachievers,
or the gifted—acquiring an education means facing peculiar
stressors. The following pages will discuss these children and the
means for helping them cope.

Stress and the "Special" Child

No one can help or harm the handicapped child more than the parents. The entire family is susceptible to the special stresses generated when one member is handicapped. Parents sometimes react in ways that increase stress for everyone concerned—viewing the child as an extension of themselves, for example. Parents feel guilt or shame and question what lies hidden deep inside that caused the problem. In the case of birth defects one spouse may blame the other. In other cases the response is fear—fear of people's reactions and fear of the future. Pity is another painful emotion. Some parents pity the child, as well as themselves. They ask: "Why me? I don't deserve this." Providing a lifetime of care makes some parents feel cheated. Anger can result in a prolonged stressful state. Hostility is directed toward self, the child, the doctor or professionals involved, teachers, or the world in general. Occasionally, parents will deny the existence of a problem. They tell themselves it is probably nothing, or begin making the rounds of professionals and clinics, trying to find someone who will tell them that it isn't so. This practice is expensive and exhausting, for parent and child alike. Many times the child experiences the stress of feeling that the parents don't want to accept the child as is. On the other hand, sometimes parents exaggerate the severity of the handicap, smothering the child with overprotection and making the child unnecessarily dependent.

The burdens of sadness, unceasing care, expensive treatments, and rejection by friends understandably create levels of stress that affect the entire family. The reaction is hard to predict and many parents undoubtedly suffer more than the child. Some parents turn to religion or adopt a martyred, "I've got my cross to bear" attitude. In some situations, the family breaks up as the tension leads to divorce or older siblings simply moving out. Happily, though, a great many families simply accept the handicapped child and are strengthened by working together to help the child maximize potential. They find that the child is more like other children than different. After all, what is a handicap, anyway? In our own way each of us has handicaps. Dealing with them is all part of the process of coping.

The term *special child* usually refers to children who are mentally retarded, autistic, deaf, blind or partially sighted, emotionally disturbed, orthopedically handicapped, cerebral-palsied, or the victim of a disease or birth defect. Despite their highly individualized needs these children have a lot in common. Most basic is their urgent need to accept and adjust to the disability. Special children need love, understanding, and guidance for growth.

If you suspect your child is special, don't bury your head in the sand. Get professional help! Call the local school district or a major teaching hospital in your area, and find out where to go for the best evaluation and treatment.

Once you have located an authority and are satisfied with the diagnosis, become well-informed about the condition. (If you are not satisfied with the diagnosis, do not hesitate to get additional opinions.) Ask the professional to clearly define the problem and implications for the future. You might want to join a local or national organization of educators or parents with a similar concern. In addition, ask the professional to suggest some reading material on the subject. Follow carefully the treatment or recommendations of the professionals, and avoid hopping from one expert to another, unless you are realistically convinced you can get better help. Take the sympathy and advice of friends and relatives with a grain of salt. Even family doctors have been known to lead parents astray with remarks such as "The child will probably outgrow it." Guard against spoiling the child or buffering the child from reality. Reduce stress for everyone concerned by realizing that the entire family is involved. Your spouse or other children often feel ignored or less loved than the special child. These feelings lead to a sense of resentment, which can ultimately produce deep-seated, stressful guilt. Sometimes family members are frustrated because they want to help, but feel powerless to do so. The whole family must understand the problem and openly express feelings. Everyone can learn to play a meaningful role in providing assistance, without surrendering their own specialness.

Raising a special child is challenging, but then isn't raising any child? Don't magnify your problems by assuming that everything would be fine if the child were normal. Children are individuals, and every child generates a set of special problems. Expect setbacks, backslides, and blowups. Allow your handicapped child to deal with stressful situations, but move in before tolerance is gone. Help your child put feelings into words, and suggest coping techniques for the future. Arrange a place of refuge where the child can rest or recover from stress. Gradually try to extend the time before you step in to help your child cope. Lastly, don't act embarrassed or ashamed when out in public. If someone asks you about your child, respond in a truthful, positive manner. If they don't understand, they have the problem—not you.

What Is a Learning Disability?

Jason arrives home from a frustrating day in second grade, where he has struggled unsuccessfully to understand ''borrowing.'' He bursts into tears as he crashes through the back door. His mother is shocked by his sudden explosion and rushes to put an arm around him. Jason shakes her off and says: ''There is something wrong with me. I can't do anything right. No matter how hard I try, I just can't. Why can't I be like the other kids?'' Mother wishes she could answer his question. Jason has had a complete physical. Everything, including vision and hearing, are fine. He has no physical handicaps, his IQ is measured at 110, and the home environment is excellent. What, then, is the boy's problem?

In recent years the vague term *learning disability* has been used in reference to many types of difficulties. Sensory inadequacies, poor motor development, perceptual problems, hyperactivity, and brain damage have all been termed learning disabilities. In addition, social or emotional maladjustment, language difficulties, special types of deafness, and particularly reading disorders, have been broadly included under this label.

Despite many published definitions, confusion still exists. In fact, the same child might be classified in many different ways, depending on the state of residence. The child might be called educationally handicapped, brain-injured, or neurologically handicapped. In other situations a child could be described as having a language disorder, specific learning disability, or sensory-perceptual-motor impairment.

There are wide differences in opinion regarding the incidence of learning disabilities, with estimates ranging from 2 percent to 30 percent of the school-aged population. But it is definitely known that a substantial number of children suffer from a decreased learning capability. The exact nature of the problem differs from individual to individual. In any case, children experience the stress of repeated failure and often feel rejected by parent or teacher. Recall your own childhood and the stigma attached to flunking.

Is My Child Learning-Disabled, or Just Slow?

In general, learning-disabled children show no evidence of uncorrectable vision or hearing problems, although in many cases they do have difficulty in accurately receiving and processing information. They have a normal level of intelligence and are free from handicapping emotional or social conditions. Learning-disabled children demonstrate erratic skill development. They attain in some areas, while experiencing difficulty in others. It is not easy to diagnose the specific learning problem. Somewhere in the series of events that includes receiving, processing, integrating, utilizing, and communicating information there is a breakdown. Diagnosis means finding that weak spot.

Margaret Jo Shepherd has pointed out that one possible source of confusion is another group of children who closely resemble the learning-disabled, demonstrating many similar characteristics.[8] There are no major physical, vision, or hearing impairments, and the emotional and social climate for learning is satisfactory. The big difference is that although the child is not classified as mentally retarded, intelligence level is at the bottom of the normal range. Slow learners, as they have been termed, experience difficulty learning and achieving. Actually, they are performing at a level consistent with ability. If your child is a slow learner, but is diagnosed as learning-disabled, stress can be the result. The diagnosis of learning disability assumes that with proper identification of the problem and corrective measures, skill development and achievement will improve. If, however, the child is actually a slow learner, goals and expectations set by optimistic parents may never be reached. The child's individuality is not recognized and accepted, and there is frustration from constant failure. Unfortunately, it is far easier to write about slow learners and disabled learners than it is to correctly identify them. Obviously, an inaccurate diagnosis in either direction is dangerous to the child. We often get what we expect from children. A learning-disabled child classified as a slow learner will probably stay a slow learner and not be assisted in maximizing potential. On the other hand, a slow learner described as learning-disabled might be expected to achieve at unrealistic levels, rather than being allowed to progress at a realistic pace.

Reducing Stress Through Identification

Although the slow learner is consistently slow, the learning-disabled child shows a highly uneven pattern of skill development. Slow learners are not as prone to impulsive behavior and hold on to a skill once it is learned, while a disabled learner is often highly active and apt to forget or regress. IQ tests alone cannot make the differentiation, since many children with learning disabilities do poorly on these tests.

Following is a list of symptoms that might mean your child has a learning disability. If you suspect problems, check with your pediatrician, who will probably arrange for a complete physical, vision and hearing tests, electroencephalogram, and blood and urine analyses. In addition, you should contact your local school district office. Even if your child is of preschool age, the school can probably arrange for a battery of tests which could include those for determining intelligence, gross and fine motor skills, and study of behavior and activity level. Once the problem is correctly identified, you will be on the way to reducing the stress experienced by both parent and child.

Symptoms of Learning Disability

_____ Difficulty following directions

_____ Difficulty understanding, even after having paid attention

_____ Inconsistent performance from one day to the next (gets a perfect paper one day and misses every item on a similar work sheet the following day)

_____ Confuses left and right

_____ Poor handwriting

_____ Difficulty spelling words (unfinished words, syllables omitted, words not spelled the way they sound)

_____ Loses place when reading because of difficulty in moving eyes smoothly from left to right

_____ Mixes up the order of words in a sentence when reading aloud or speaking

_____ Reverses letters or entire words (mirror writing)

_____ Short attention span

_____ Poor reading ability

_____ Poor language development

_____ Difficulty in sports activities, hopping, skipping, or jumping

_____ Apt to forget what has been learned

_____ Difficulty in copying from a book or blackboard

_____ Difficulty learning phonics

_____ Loses interest in school; withdraws

_____ Doesn't complete assignments or homework

If your child has a learning disability, you will probably receive suggestions from experts. There are also a number of excellent books available for parents. In general, stress can be minimized if you take learning in small steps, being careful to achieve one skill before moving on to the next. You should understand that your child may not always pay attention. If behavior is not disruptive, you shouldn't insist on one-hundred-percent conformity. Also, you can't presume that your child has heard and understood. Get an appropriate response or restatement of what was said. When working with your child, maintain an absolutely fixed time, place, and routine. The setting should be free from distractions and highly structured. You might make a private office by cutting a large cardboard box so it has only three sides and placing it on a table to surround the work area. Encourage your child to take time and to avoid jumping to conclusions, such as guessing at a word after seeing the first few letters. All children need success, praise, and encouragement, so reward diligence and accuracy. Above all, stay cool and make learning fun.

Is My Child Hyperactive?

Hyperactivity, hyperkinesis, and learning disability are all closely related. Hyperactive children, as the term implies, seem to be continuously active. Some experts believe that many children outgrow the problem between twelve and seventeen years of age. However, by that time the child is usually hopelessly behind in academic studies and suffering from a very poor self-image. Negative patterns of behavior are firmly entrenched. Hyperactivity, even if outgrown, can have lifelong adverse effects. Following is a list of traits common to hyperactive children:

Is My Child Hyperactive?

_____ Attends to everything—unable to ignore stimuli

_____ Continuously in motion, fidgety, unable to sit still

_____ Seems to touch everything

_____ Short attention span, moves quickly from one activity to another, leaves projects half-completed

_____ Distractible

_____ Forgetful

_____ Aggressive, hostile, irritable, or emotional

_____ Dismantles or destroys toys

_____ Low threshold for pain, temperature, or tickling—readily laughs or cries

_____ Demanding, insists on things "my way"
_____ Little self-control
_____ Disrupts class, talks during class, or teases other children
_____ Clumsy
_____ Impatient
_____ Often loses things
_____ Has nervous habit—such as sucking on blanket or clothes, biting or picking fingernails, or twirling hair
_____ Accident-prone
_____ Attempts reckless stunts
_____ Interrupts
_____ Talks loudly, excessively, or rapidly
_____ Panics
_____ As a baby, appeared to have colic
_____ As a baby, sucked thumb or pacifier
_____ As a baby, rocked crib
_____ As a baby, banged head when angry

Numerous studies of children with behavior problems have yielded some dramatic findings. Many children have chemical imbalances; food allergies; hypoglycemia; vitamin deficiencies; reactions to additives, colorations, or preservatives; or "addiction" to junk food or sugar.

Hyperactive children are treated in a variety of ways. In some cases doctors prescribe a stimulant, such as an amphetamine, which seems to slow the impulses to the brain. Other physicians don't believe in drugs, since drugs can produce many side effects. Dr. Ben Feingold is one of these doctors. In _Why Your Child Is Hyperactive,_ [9] Dr. Feingold details a specific diet for the hyperactive. Dr. Feingold's work began with allergic patients who also were hyperactive. He found that in clearing up the complaints associated with allergic reactions, hyperactive behavior also improved. Gradually, Dr. Feingold turned his attention to synthetic food additives. He developed the Feingold K-P (Kaiser-Permanente) diet, which excludes all foods and drugs that contain artificial coloring or flavoring. In addition, some preservatives are eliminated, as well as fruits and vegetables containing natural salicylates (such as apples, berries, grapes, or tomatoes).

Once your child is diagnosed as hyperactive, you should follow closely the suggestions for controlling behavior specified by your doctor and teacher. There are a number of books that deal exclusively with the subject and give useful suggestions for reducing stress for the entire family.

Portrait of an Underachiever

Twelve-year-old Melissa is often described as a lovely child. She has a winning personality, and it is hard for anyone to stay angry with her for long. All Melissa has to do is grin sheepishly and look out from under the tops of her big, brown eyes, and everyone is instantly charmed. Test scores indicate that Melissa has an extremely high level of intelligence. She has a keen wit, good sense of humor, and likes to read poetry. You'd never guess that her report card is a mess. Melissa is an underachiever.

There is great disparity when it comes to defining exactly what is meant by underachiever. However, for our purposes we will say that an underachiever is simply not achieving at levels commensurate with ability. The child should be doing more. Underachievers are experts at getting by. They often try to do the minimum in the least amount of time. It is heartbreaking for parents and teachers alike to watch as ability is wasted. Many underachievers refer to themselves as lazy, tired, depressed, disinterested, or bored. While parents are saying, "She just doesn't seem to give a darn," underachievers are muttering, "Oh, the heck with it!"

Many underachievers come from a home environment that appears highly conducive to learning. However, researchers have found that underachievers often have a low self-concept. They sometimes lack self-confidence or are dependent. Anxiety is another common source of stress. Many underachievers would like to succeed, but are afraid to try—for fear they will fail. Most underachievers are regularly under the gun at home. Parents prod, push, preach, and punish—all of which have limited effectiveness.

Determining the cause for underachievement is no simple task. The child may be preoccupied with social relationships, appearance, or problems that are virtually draining away available energy. Some children cannot bear to compete and lose, so they simply don't compete at all. Others haven't learned to cope with the frustration associated with mastering skills or learning new concepts and, therefore, withdraw when the going gets rough. If a child has never learned to delay satisfaction, it may be difficult to attend to learning instead of going out to play or watching television. Perhaps the quality of teaching is a turn-off. Little is done to arouse the student's interest. Maybe success doesn't seem likely, so the student reasons, why try at all?

Whatever the cause, underachievement is a phenomenon that generates extra stress for parent and child. I wish it were possible to neatly spell out a ten-point program for correcting the problem. Each and every situation is different and requires a unique solution. However, instead of berating your child, try reaching the child by building on current interests. For example, if the child likes automobiles, use this natural interest for motivation. Stimulate reading by getting books and magazines on the subject, encourage the child to learn how an automobile engine works, or enter into a contractual arrangement in which you promise to take your child to the auto show if certain responsibilities are fulfilled.

Underachievers need a fixed learning time and place. Bear in mind the child's learning style, and work with it. Break information into small chunks in which success is likely. Use a system of rewards as reinforcement, or try working out learning agreements, in which the child contracts to accomplish certain mutually established goals, one day or week at a time. Last, remember that you will accomplish far more by convincing your child of his or her self-worth and capability than by demeaning the child or instilling guilt and additional stress.

Intelligence, Creativity, and Stress

Some gifted children are easy to spot. They read at three or play concert piano at four. Mozart composed his first minuet at the age of five. On the other hand, consider Thomas Alva Edison, one of the world's greatest inventors. As a young boy he had an inquisitive mind and loved to experiment. In fact, one day he even tried sitting on eggs to hatch them. When Edison was seven years old, he entered public school. His search for knowledge led him to ask an endless stream of questions that annoyed the teacher, who finally told the school inspector that Tom was "addled." The boy overheard the conversation and told his mother. Mrs. Edison immediately took the child out of school, ending his formal education after only three months. Winston Churchill also had difficulties as a child. He was described as "lazy" and "rebellious," and his marks in school were a disaster. In addition, the eloquent statesman lisped and stuttered when he was a boy.

Both Edison and Churchill probably surprised their teachers with the accomplishments of their adult lives. They are just two famous examples of many who were difficult to identify as gifted when they were children. Yet, recognizing exceptional ability and talent is the first step in assisting children to maximize potential.

Gifted children may have a high level of intelligence or of creativity or both. Intellectually gifted children comprise 2 percent to 3 percent of the school population. Creativity is a way of thinking; it is not synonymous with a high IQ. Creative children engage in divergent thinking. They perk with fresh ideas and approaches for solving problems. When presented with a situation, the creative child is flexible and will look at it from many different perspectives. Rather than try to find the one right answer, the gifted child comes up with a number of original alternatives. The following checklist will help you determine if your child is gifted.

Could My Child Be Gifted?

Check any statement that applies to your child:

_____ Has scored over 125 on a test of intelligence

_____ Has special talent in a particular area, such as art, music, math, or athletics

_____ Learns new concepts or skills easily

_____ Often appears to teach himself/herself something new; finds answers to questions with little or no assistance

_____ Is very self-sufficient for age level

_____ Has an advanced vocabulary for age level

_____ Has an excellent memory

_____ Often surprises adults with what he or she knows

_____ Has a longer attention span than most children of the same age

_____ Often prefers to work alone

_____ Hates to be interrupted when concentrating on an activity

_____ Is inquisitive and asks many questions

_____ Easily puts together puzzles difficult for age level

_____ Rapidly adjusts to change

_____ Expresses ideas well in speaking, writing, or both

_____ Complains of being bored by routines or at school

_____ Seems to do well in almost everything tackled

_____ Has excellent reasoning ability (mentally works through situations, anticipating events three or four steps ahead; likes to plot moves in games such as chess)

_____ Learned to read early or very rapidly

_____ Has excelled academically in the past or is doing so currently

Interpretation

School districts differ in their definition of intellectually gifted. Usually the minimum qualifying IQ score ranges between 125 and 140. If you checked the first item, your child may be intellectually gifted.

The second statement is also a key characteristic. If your child shows unusual talent in a special area, you should consider further development or lessons.

If you checked more than seven of the remaining eighteen items, there is a likelihood your child is gifted. Obviously, the more you checked, the greater the possibility. Your school system has testing you can request. However, if you checked fewer than seven statements, don't automatically dismiss the possibility of giftedness. Remember Churchill and Edison—some children just seem to hide their potential. Also, everyone has creative potential which can be cultivated. Even if not identified as gifted in the strictest sense, your child can develop creative interests and thought processes.

But I Just Want My Child to Be Happy and Normal!

Identification of intellectually gifted children generates stress for many parents and leads them to insist, "All I want is for my child to grow up happy and well-adjusted." Many times they have a stereotypical image of the bright or talented child as being a bookworm, with no friends and limited interests. Although they are susceptible to some special stresses, gifted children overall are just as active in extracurricular activities as their classmates. They have more hobbies and a wider range of interests. In addition, research indicates that they have fewer illnesses and are taller, better-coordinated, and have greater physical endurance. Gifted children are popular with their classmates and have an excellent sense of humor. On the average they cause fewer problems at school or home and are more independent. They are less likely to cheat, steal, or take advantage of people. Gifted children are sensitive to others and better able to cope with stress.

They seem almost too good to be true! But wait, all these positive statements refer only to the hypothetical, average gifted children. On an individual level, giftedness can cause your child a great deal of stress. Don't assume that gifted children can fend for themselves. They need guidance and assistance, the same as other children. If your child is enrolled in a program for the gifted, development of capability is probably the major objective, with secondary attention given to emotional or coping problems. More than half of the gifted children in this country don't attend any special program, and some regular classroom teachers are ill-equipped to tailor a curriculum to meet the needs of the gifted. Being bright doesn't guarantee achievement. As Thomas Edison said, ''Genius is one percent inspiration and ninety-nine percent perspiration.'' For one reason or another, many gifted children are underachievers and a number ultimately drop out of high school. You can learn to recognize the special problems and stresses that accompany giftedness. Watch for these signs:

The Flicker-ing Flame
Creativity appears to peak at about four years old. Some experts believe that fading is not caused by maturation, but rather results from adult and societal influences. Creative behavior produces stress, and the child copes by stifling creativity. To keep the flame alive, guard against:

Making your child afraid to experiment or try a new approach for fear of failure.

Imposing rigid sex-roles that inhibit your child from exploring areas generally regarded as masculine or feminine.

Insisting on conformity (for example—telling your child, ''That's not how you are supposed to draw a house'').

Discouraging questions, curiosity, and experimentation.

Inferring that learning is programmed and play is the time for free thinking.

The Sinking Self-image
Children do not like to feel different. In an effort to be accepted by peers or parents, gifted children sometimes conceal their ability, become withdrawn, purposely fail, or act up in school. The following can contribute to the deterioration of self-image:

Classmates who engage in name calling and refuse to play with "teacher's pet" or "the brain"

Classmates who are more socially adept (some gifted children spend considerable time pursuing solitary activities and have less social experience)

Siblings or classmates who are jealous and react to the gifted child negatively or with hostility

Parents who continuously brag and boast about the child's accomplishments. Gradually the child begins to believe the parents care more about the special ability than the child as a person

Parents who insist that the child devote more time to an active social life rather than pursue the area of special talent

Parents or teachers who don't acknowledge the child's special ability and who, therefore, don't help the child actualize

Parents or teachers who expect too much and place unreasonable demands on the child, which can only lead to failure

The Lazys

Gifted children become lazy for a variety of reasons:

Slow pace of classroom instruction and frequent repetition of material

Presentation of material or skills the child has already mastered

Peer rejection which is handled by feigning laziness

The Domineering Demands

It is not uncommon for gifted children to be very demanding, particularly in the following situations:

Seeking attention from teachers, parents, and other adults

Becoming overbearing in activities with the peer group

The Pen-chant for Perfection	Some gifted children rely heavily on perfection and praise to maintain self-esteem. They become frustrated and upset when lofty goals are not realized.
The Snob Syndrome	Successful coping involves dealing effectively with the entire range of humanity. Gifted children can become intolerant and impatient with others they view as less bright, or can assume an air of superiority.

When you notice that your gifted child is having coping difficulty, take advantage of the child's ability to understand by discussing the matter in depth. In understanding the nature of the problem your child will grow in self-awareness. Engage in some structured problem solving and map out specific coping strategies with the child.

As the term implies, gifted children have been born with a gift. Whether or not they make full use of their gift is largely determined by environmental factors. You can help your child maximize potential by providing the right environment. Be careful not to stifle your child by insisting on total regimentation or practicality. Provide toys and experiences that stimulate free play rather than dictate it. Realize that the school is another big factor in your child's life. Prescriptive teaching, large class size, or an authoritarian atmosphere may cause giftedness to lie dormant. The big push today for "basic skills development"—namely, emphasis on reading, writing, and arithmetic—is a necessity for many students. However, most gifted children do fine in the basic skills and need an enriched program. If you sense your child is bored or wasting time, you might check with the school to see about advanced placement or see if your community has a school with a more challenging program. Dealing with success is an important part of coping. Gifted children should not be overpraised or allowed to develop an insensitivity to others. In addition, the gifted should be prepared for inevitable failures. Some gifted children just can't cope with failure and become frustrated or fall apart. You should avoid living vicariously through the successes of your child.

Your gifted child needs a realistic self-concept, coupled with the freedom and security necessary to maximize potential without fear of failure or worry about what other people think.

Student Stresses: The Big Two

The number and variety of stresses associated with formal education is inestimable, since stress is the result of each individual's interpretation of situations as threatening. However, there are two stressors that share widespread stress-producing capability. I have taught students from preschool to graduate school, and I know that you need only say one sentence to create classroom pressure—"We're going to have a test." The most commonly shared stressor among students of any grade level is test taking, followed at some distance by the second big stressor—math anxiety. I will try to explain sources for the math anxiety which torments so many students and will make some suggestions for relieving the tension of tests.

Test Stress

Testing begins before the child even enters school. Most districts have some type of preschool screening which initiates the student to the testing process, that most dreaded aspect of getting an education. Many preschoolers get right in the swing of things—frightened out of their wits by separation from parents, strange faces, and the school surroundings. The stress reaction differs among youngsters. They may cry, throw tantrums, cling to a parent and refuse to participate, or valiantly bite the bottom lip and give it their best effort.

Throughout a student's educational career there will be test after test after test—pretests, post-tests, aptitude tests, attitude tests, creativity tests, criterion-referenced tests, achievement tests, and IQ tests. Some tests are short, while the standardized types can take a whole day, or even several days. If you added up all the time spent in test taking, I am sure it would be substantial, and for many pupils it is time spent in sheer torture.

Let's analyze the cause of test stress. Basically, students are threatened because they perceive test scores as a measure of their value as individuals. A low score is a blow to self-image and self-esteem. Furthermore, students learn from experience that tests do not always accurately measure what they know or how much they have studied. Therefore, it is not always possible to protect oneself from failure through preparation and study. The student feels helpless and at the mercy of the test. The conditions under which tests are administered generate tension in many students. Rigid time limits, hour after hour of sitting in one place, the demanding job of recording answers from the test booklet onto a separate answer sheet—all these factors combine to create a real monster. Students become such a bundle of nerves that they are their own worst enemy. I have seen students go blank and forget material I know they know, or get so excited they misread the question, so although their answer may be factual, it doesn't respond to what is asked. Other students don't read the entire question and give only a partial answer. In some cases students panic if they don't remember reading or hearing the answer to the question. Usually, if they were able to keep cool and think about it, they could come up with an answer that would earn partial credit, at least. However, they freeze, and this condition can easily transfer to questions they do know.

You can help your child by teaching the why and how of test taking. Many times the students with the best scores are not smarter, just better at taking tests. Unfortunately, important educational decisions are made based on test scores. In addition, teachers, parents, and the child generalize about student ability and make placement decisions. Following are some tips which can relieve pressure from the testing scene:

Test-Taking Tips

1. Explain the purpose of tests, and make it clear that you expect the best the child can give, but no more. In this way, the child can prepare and relax going into the test, knowing that maximum effort is being expended.

2. When you know a test is scheduled, be certain your child gets a good night's sleep, eats a healthy breakfast, dresses in comfortable clothes, and leaves the house in a relaxed, unrushed state.

3. When the child brings home returned test papers, immediately go over them and analyze errors. Clear up any misunderstanding about directions, terms, or answers so the child will be better prepared next time.

4. Give your child experience working under rigid time limits. Play some games in which you time the child or allow a designated number of minutes for completing a work sheet.

5. Tell your child not to get hung up on a tough question, but instead to skip it and do it later, if there is time.

6. Teach your child to pace work by looking over the material to see how much needs to be done.

7. Play games that require following directions in which you give oral or written directions for making Jello-O, preparing for a party, playing a game, or whatever.

8. Design some multiple-choice questions that your child can make a good guess at answering by eliminating a few obviously incorrect choices and selecting from those that remain.

9. Have your child practice reading a question in one place and recording the answer on a separate sheet of paper.

10. Don't magnify the importance of tests by getting overexcited by good, or poor, scores. Let the child know that the learning that occurs in school is your prime concern. Hopefully, tests reflect that learning.

11. Help your child understand that a little test stress can motivate a student to study and achieve. However, if stress is extreme, it can cripple the learner. Work on using some of the relaxation techniques in the final chapter.

12. Help your child understand that test stress caused by not studying is inevitable and unacceptable.

Math Anxiety

Large numbers of students, particularly girls, experience what has been termed math anxiety. They typically grimace at the very sound of the words *arithmetic* or *mathematics* and will tell you quite definitely, "Math is my worst subject." These students begin to avoid math at every turn. Although in reality they have the skills and problem-solving ability to deal with most mathematical situations, past stresses have left them feeling incompetent and vulnerable. These students grow into adults who refuse to tackle anything mathematical. They unnecessarily turn to others when it comes time to prepare tax returns, measure for carpeting, or balance the checkbook. Sadly, many even make college and career choices based primarily on the desire to avoid math. There are some common stressful situations that can ultimately lead to math anxiety.

First, some children are threatened by the idea that in arithmetic there is only one right answer. They are overwhelmed by the odds against their locating that answer. In addition, even if the child has mastered the problem-solving process, a wrong answer means no credit. You only get credit for correct answers, even if you know how to do the problem but make a computation error. Many teachers use games, drills, and flash-card work in which success is based on getting the answer first or ask students to demonstrate their ability to the class by solving the problem at the blackboard. Working under pressure causes some children to experience stress. Earlier math failure is another cause for math anxiety. The student begins to feel incompetent and no longer regards success in math as a realistic option. Once you tell yourself you can't do something, you create a self-fulfilling prophecy and usually do end up failing. The following suggestions will help your child avoid failure:

1. Begin in the preschool years to develop arithmetic readiness through games, puzzles, building activities, or model construction which develops visual, spatial, and number awareness skills.

2. When you work on any new math concept at any grade level, first show it concretely—with real objects. Next, go back over the idea with pictures. Finally, demonstrate the concept with the more abstract numbers. For example, in working on the concept of fractions, first use paper plates to cut halves, fourths, or thirds. Next, divide circles drawn on a piece of paper. Last, write the abstract representation of the fractional parts—"½," "⅓," or "¼."

3. Never move ahead with new concepts until your child has a firm understanding of those you are presently working with.

4. Don't teach a process, such as how to carry, borrow, multiply, or divide, without an understanding of why the steps work. A thorough knowledge of place value helps.

5. Check returned work sheets or homework every day to be certain your child is not falling behind.

6. Eliminate demeaning situations in which the child is forced to work through a problem that is not understood until the correct answer is stumbled upon. Rather than putting your child on the spot, go back over the concept and demonstrate the steps.

7. Allow your child to see personal progress, rather than competing with friends or siblings. For example, when working on flash cards, let the child see how many can be learned per day rather than putting the emphasis on who knows the most or can get the answer first.

8. Structure situations in which your child experiences success in solving everyday, practical problems—such as doubling a recipe.

9. Avoid sex-typed generalizations, such as that boys do better in math, but girls do better in reading.

10. Teach your child to use some of the relaxation techniques presented in the final chapter.

11. Be on the alert for the corollary of math anxiety—science anxiety.
12. If you have math anxiety or are unfamiliar with the modern math, ask the classroom teacher for help.

Nice Place to Visit—But Would You Want to Send Your Child There?

It is not my intent to start taking potshots at the educational system. I have been a teacher myself, and believe that the vast majority of educators are dedicated, sensitive individuals. Currently the schools are under all-out attack. This situation is frightening and depressing, since education treats the causes of society's real problems—illiteracy and lack of skills—rather than the symptoms, such as crime and unemployment. Despite the difficulties faced by our schools, literacy in this country has never been higher. In fact, the United States has the highest literacy rate in the entire world. It is true that in some situations test scores are declining. However, this phenomenon is not isolated in the United States, but found worldwide. Factors beyond the school must be considered, particularly insufficient home reinforcement of learning and heavy television viewing. One study indicated that sixty-four percent of the seventeen-year-olds in this country spend less than five hours per week on homework. My guess is that these students watch a great deal more than five hours of television per week. America's schools are firmly committed to maximizing the potential of individual learners, but they cannot accomplish this task alone. The failure to do so must be shared by school and home.

While president, Lyndon B. Johnson once stated: "At the desk where I sit, I have learned one great truth. The answer for all our national problems, the answer for all the problems of the world, comes to a single word. That word is 'education.' " No matter what your political affiliation, I hope you believe those words. I believe that teaching is the most important profession. However, it is also one of the most stressful.

Recently, the subject of teacher "burnout" has received considerable attention. Teachers face a long list of stressors. Many schools are overcrowded, in the midst of a financial crunch, or facing racial tension. It is not uncommon for teachers or students to be physically attacked in their own buildings. Some school systems insist that teachers teach more in less time. Reading is introduced in the kindergarten. Since the teacher is held accountable, children are pressured to complete one book after another or to pass mastery tests. The classroom is tense, and the joy of learning disappears. Admittedly, this condition is often beyond the control of the teacher. A number of children sit daily with teachers who are suffering the effects of prolonged stress and are ill-equipped to cope with the needs of approximately thirty students—the slow learners, average students, gifted, and those with special problems. They have lost the ability to challenge children to work to their maximum, without pushing too far, too fast, or too hard. In a few cases teacher stress can even result in emotional abuse.

Signs of a Stressful Classroom

A visit to your child's classroom can give you some indication of the absence or presence of stress. Be on the lookout for the following signs of stress:

Unhappy children
Bored children
Children hesitant to talk
Frequent fighting or other aggressive behavior
A teacher who rules with an iron hand
Permission required—for *everything*
Harsh punishment
Fierce competition
Clutter, trash, or debris on the floor
Old or out-dated bulletin boards
Vandalism
A tired, burned-out teacher
Materials and equipment kept under lock and key
Dull assignments
Few papers returned to students graded
Emphasis on improving test scores, rather than on learning
Reading instruction for all kindergarteners or preschoolers
Large group instruction, with no provision made for ability grouping or individualized instruction
No instruction at all

How to Generate a Little Stress at School

Way back when you were an elementary school pupil, most parents shared a common attitude—the teacher is always right. You probably wouldn't have considered complaining to your parents that the teacher was unfair, unkind, or unprofessional. Today, few educators would subscribe to the "my teacher, right or wrong" philosophy. However, as parents we usually like to think that the stresses our children report are exaggerations or mistakes in the child's judgment. We have adopted a philosophy that gives the teacher the benefit of the doubt. Yet, teachers are human and make mistakes, the same as doctors, lawyers, you, or I.

Following are some steps for those times when your child complains about school or appears stressed:

1. **Don't jump the gun.** Although it is important to intervene before the situation is totally out of hand, give your child some time to cope with the problem before you step in.

2. **Check it out.** The stereotype of the doting parent who assumes the child is always right is familiar. Take time to carefully question your child about complaints. Even if you think the teacher is wrong, don't come in like gangbusters. You would be amazed at the large percentage of inaccuracies in the reports children relay home. Often it isn't a matter of lying; the child simply doesn't perceive the situation correctly or takes things out of context.

3. **Tell your child your plans.** Before making an appointment to confront or confer with school personnel, detail your plans to your child. Children often vehemently oppose parent involvement. Sometimes they feel competent to cope by themselves or realize they overstated the problem.

4. **Give your child your attention.** Many complaints are simply a child's attempt to capture a parent's attention. Once they have it, some children enjoy the feeling so much they embellish a bit. Frequent petty complaints about school or teacher can be a sign of other emotional problems or feelings of neglect.

5. **Teacher or principal?** It is sometimes difficult to decide who to see. If you are so upset with the teacher that you fear you might lose control, arrange to meet with the principal. The same holds true if you prefer that the teacher not know about the complaint. However, in the majority of cases, you should extend the teacher the courtesy of airing your concerns directly. You might feel the necessity of a later follow-up visit

with the principal, superintendent, or—ultimately—the school board.

Taking the Stress out of the Parent-Teacher Conference

The school does not have a monopoly on learning. In order to become meaningfully involved you should confer regularly with the teacher. You may find that report cards are confusing or that parent-teacher conferences by inference tell you: Look at how smart the teacher is. Look at how little you know about education! You don't need a teaching degree to join the teaching team. You can provide valuable reinforcement and enrichment by using your expert knowledge of your child, coupled with some good, old-fashioned common sense. Whenever you find that you are confused by a technical term or explanation, don't hesitate to question the professional and request a layman's definition. Included at the end of this chapter is a glossary of terms which may help you interpret testing results.

Before any parent-teacher conference, take time to carefully consider any areas of concern you may want to discuss. Use an index card to list the points you don't want to forget. If you have questions about any of your child's work, bring the work along. After you have presented your concerns and listened to those of the teacher, work together to develop a plan of action. Next, stick to your part of the agreement. If you agreed to help each evening with reading, do so religiously. Make plans to meet with the teacher again some time in the near future to evaluate the progress being made.

Occasionally, a parent may leave a parent-teacher conference feeling frustrated by the "expert handling" of the professionals involved. Stuart Losen and Bert Diament have identified some tricks of the trade used by a few educators during discussions with parents: [10]

Monopolizing the conversation and not allowing the parent to talk

Responding authoritatively and overwhelming the parent with technical terms and confusing explanations

Failing to admit a mistake

Failing to admit a lack of training which makes it difficult to handle the situation

Jumping to a conclusion, such as that problems are inevitable after parents get divorced

Blaming circumstances beyond the teacher's control for difficulties, such as cutbacks, increased class size, or the demands of the principal

Responding with artificial sympathy or understanding

Avoiding the problem by suggesting that the child is just "going through a phase," or will "probably outgrow it"

Becoming angry with parent, when in reality the teacher is angry with the child

Denying that there is a problem

Making "snap recommendations," which may or may not be beneficial

Telling parent to be patient and "trust me"

Parents also use a number of defense mechanisms in coping with conferences.[11] Guard against reacting with:

HELPLESSNESS: Well, I'm all alone, you know.

DENIAL: I really don't see any evidence of the problem at home.

GUILT: It's all my fault. I should be working with him more at home.

AVOIDANCE: Well, you're the teacher. I really don't know what you expect me to do.

MISTRUST: I never trusted those tests, anyway.

BLAME: I told my husband we shouldn't let our daughter play with those kids in the neighborhood.

GLOSSARY OF TESTING TERMS

The following definitions are adapted from the *Test Service Notebook 13* [12] and presented for those with little or no training in tests and measurement. These terms often create confusion for parents, and the most commonly accepted definition is presented, although among specialists there might be some variation.

Academic aptitude or academic potential—the inborn and acquired abilities associated with likelihood of success in academic studies

Achievement test—test that measures how well certain skills have been mastered or content information acquired

Age norms—tables of scores which provide information regarding the typical or average performance of children at particular age levels

Anecdotal record—a written report of an incident which is considered significant in understanding the individual

Aptitude—combination of inborn and acquired abilities which indicate a child's ability to learn or to develop proficiency in a particular area

Arithmetic mean—average obtained by adding up a set of scores and dividing by the number of scores originally added together

Average—a general term used to refer to the central tendency of a group of scores. The three most common ''averages'' are mean, median, and mode.

Battery—a group of tests usually used to measure academic achievement, with subtests for each of the separate curriculum areas

Ceiling—the upper limit of ability measured by a test. If a child earns the highest possible score, the child is at the ceiling, and a higher-level test should have been given

Correlation—the relationship between two scores or measures which indicates how they go together. For example, the relationship between IQ and academic achievement

Criterion-referenced test—test that is based specifically on the information covered in units of instruction and indicates whether or not the child learned the material

Culture-fair test—test that provides all children an equal opportunity for success, regardless of culture

Diagnostic test—test used to pinpoint a child's areas of specific strengths and weaknesses

Expected grade equivalency—expected score on an achievement test, based on the student's grade level and academic aptitude

Grade equivalent—the grade level for which a particular score would be considered average, usually stated in terms of grade and month (for example, 2-3 would be second grade, third month)

Group test—test administered to a group of children at the same time

Individual test—a test which is administered on an individual basis, to one person at a time

Mean—see *Arithmetic mean*

Median—the middle score in a group of scores which have been placed in rank order, from the highest to the lowest. The median divides the set of scores in half.

Mental age—age for which a score on a test of mental ability would be average. For example, if a score of 87 is average for a child who is six years, five months old, any child scoring 87 is said to have a mental age of 6-5.

Mode—the score occurring most often in a group of scores

Norms—after a test has been given to a large group of students, the average score of children at particular grade levels is determined and called the norm for each level

Objective test—test for which the correct responses are determined in advance so that scoring is unaffected by the personal opinion or judgment of the scorer

Percentile—a point in a group of scores at or below which fall the percentage of scores indicated by the percentile (for example, if a student scores at the 61st percentile, 61 percent of the scores in the group were below this score and 39 percent of the scores were above)

Performance test—a test involving some specific task and usually not a paper-and-pencil test (for example, a test of manual dexterity)

Personality test—a test designed to gain information about the motivational, attitudinal, or emotional aspects of an individual's personality

Quartile—one of three points that divide scores in a group into four equal groups (Q_1 at the 25th percentile sets off the lowest fourth; Q_2 at the 50th percentile is in the middle of the group; and Q_3 at the 75th percentile sets off the top fourth)

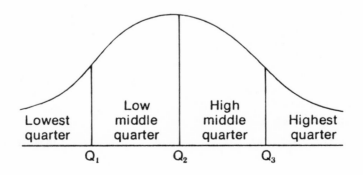

Range—the difference between the highest and lowest score in a group

Raw score—the uninterpreted, first score obtained after scoring a test

Readiness test—test that measures if a student has mastered the skills or concepts necessary to successfully begin a new learning area (for example, reading readiness tests measure if a child is ready to begin formal reading instruction)

Reliability—the extent to which a test produces stable, dependable, consistent results, with reasonable freedom from measurement error

Standardized test—a test that has been given to several thousand students who have been carefully selected so that they represent the national population—rather than all living in one area or coming from the same socioeconomic group. All the students' scores are analyzed to find norms for various age or grade levels. Then specific directions are written so that all teachers administer the test in the same manner. Upon scoring, educators can compare their students' scores to the national norms.

Stanines—nine points that divide a group of scores into nine groups. The fifth stanine includes the mean and is average. The first stanine is the lowest group, while the ninth stanine is the highest.

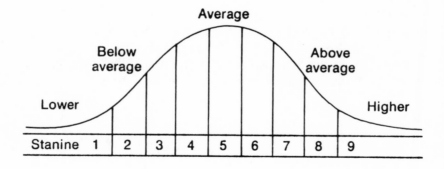

Subjective test—a test that involves personal opinion and judgment in scoring, such as an essay test. Different scorers may assign a different score.

Validity—the extent to which a test accomplishes the measurement or prediction for which it was designed

Chapter Eight

Recognize Modern-Day Stressors

Johnny Smith is in the sixth grade. He lives in a nice home, equipped with a microwave oven, dishwasher, and two color TVs. His parents often tell him: "You don't know how lucky you are. When we were growing up, we didn't have it so soft; times were tough!" You might say that Johnny has it soft. He owns a ten-speed bike, has been to Disney World twice, and never worries much about money. I guess it's true—growing up in current times does provide advantages for many children.

However, there is another side to modern existence which may not be as obvious. For example, several years ago Johnny's mother went back to work. Inflation had made it impossible for the family to enjoy their usual standard of living on one salary. Life changed with both parents working, and sometimes Johnny reminisces about the old days—when there seemed to be more time for family discussion and fun. Johnny is a good student. At school he has learned all about the energy crisis and air and water pollution. He worries about these problems and wonders if there will be any gasoline left to drive that sports car he has always dreamed of owning. When it comes to military service, Johnny doesn't know what to think. He fears he might be drafted and is terrorized by the stories that have come out of the Vietnamese War. "Well," he rationalizes, "I don't know why I let it bug me. Some guy will push a button and bang-o . . . there won't be anything left to worry about." Johnny stays well informed. He followed the story of Three Mile Island and has read the reports of assassination attempts on leaders throughout the world. He had trouble sleeping for a while after his house was burglarized and can't see why someone can't stop all the crime. Sometimes Johnny is anxious about the future. He wonders what the world will be like when he is ready to have children. They already have test-tube babies, artificial insemination, and women who have babies for other people. He has heard that scientists are now exploring the possibilities of children with four parents, artificial animal wombs for human babies, gene therapy, and humans with patches of chlorophyll used for making their own food. "Maybe they will just eliminate fathers altogether," reasons Johnny.

Yes, Johnny Smith has it soft. Technology has reduced the threat of infectious disease and improved the standard of living. I wonder why a boy who has it so soft has ulcers?

There Is Nothing Permanent but Change

Change is a part of life and always has been. Five hundred years before the birth of Christ, Heraclitus said that there was nothing permanent except change. Likewise, stress is not a new phenomenon. Earliest humanity experienced stressing conditions. However, it is only in recent times that stress has become a major threat to health and well-being on such a massive scale. This situation is probably linked to the fact that this era is marked by the most rapid change in history. Individuals seem to possess an almost natural resistance to change. Alvin Toffler has written that man is "a biosystem with a limited capacity for change. When this capacity is overwhelmed, the consequence is future shock."[1]

The many Johnny Smiths who are growing up today face some unique stressors, relatively insignificant in previous generations, which are causing them worry and anxiety. The common thread running through all these stressors is the threat to security and stability. Children have little to fall back on since our society has become progressively more disillusioned, resulting in the near collapse of many support systems previously used in times of stress. People have lost confidence in the government, and rather than relying on it to protect the nation from destruction, many fear that government itself might be a contributing factor to that destruction. Religion no longer provides the widespread comfort it once did. The attitude toward big business is often one of mistrust, and many Americans no longer derive great personal satisfaction from a job well done. Instead, they view employment as "just a way to make a buck."

Children are beginning to question the adult world. They wonder at the loss of values and lack of reason. They look to adults to help them find a sense of security and confidence in dealing with the world of today and tomorrow but instead find adults themselves are troubled. The family, previously the very heart of stability in American life, is undergoing drastic change. In fact, less than fifteen percent of the families in our country conform to the traditional model of working husband, and wife at home caring for the children. Thanks to the grown-ups our environment is in trouble, and machines, robots, and computers are taking the place of humans. Children get a firsthand acquaintance with technology in their own schools, where computer programs are hailed as more effective than teachers, and students are identified by code number, rather than name.

It is the strangeness, the uncertainty that accompanies change which is stress-producing. Ideally, change should solve problems or make life better, but in modern times the motivation often seems to be change for its own sake. Adults and children alike face mind-boggling options, wondering which way to turn. Traditional values and beliefs are pitted against conflicting current trends. For example, religion says one thing about sex, while pornography, peers, television, and movies say something else. Parents and teachers warn about the dangers of drugs, while friends, famous athletes, movie stars, and proponents of drug reform laws contradict their point of view. If you do opt to use drugs, which are the least dangerous? Should you try marijuana, cocaine, or amphetamines? Decisions of these types are being made by children at progressively earlier ages, as the option to experiment with sex or drugs is faced even by children in the elementary grades.

Often children do not fully understand the options our changing society offers. They make outward changes without making the corresponding internal changes necessary for comfortable adjustment. For example, an eight-year-old, given the choice, might opt to enroll with friends in a desegregated, innovative, magnet school requiring a fifty-minute bus ride, one way. If the change from the neighborhood school is not accompanied by a willingness to get up earlier, a new sense of maturity in leaving the immediate community each day, and an elimination of racial prejudices learned since preschool, the child will experience stress. Yet, in all probability the child was not aware of the full impact of the options when the choice was made. This awareness could have helped in making a more enlightened decision and paved the way for a speedier adjustment.

The accelerated pace of change in modern living sweeps us up, whether we like it or not, much as an overflowing river picks up small trees and objects in its rapid course. The child can feel like an insignificant branch caught in the current and moved swiftly along—twirling, bobbing, and colliding with others similarly adrift. Occasionally the child feels he or she will surely sink. The process of staying afloat begins with an understanding and acceptance of the inevitability of change, as well as the natural fear of it. In many cases children don't like the changes they see. Parents don't stay the same, for example. They grow with their children and their attitudes and interactions with the youngsters change. Many children long for the days when Mom was more interested in them and less interested in outside activities.

Young people with a strong self-image and feeling of control over their lives can usually cope and maintain order in life, even during times of rapid change. These children have a sense of security that comes largely from having been successful in coping in the past. In addition, they know someone is always behind them, standing by with love and support. The fear of failure is offset by the knowledge that there is someone to turn to in times of stress. The feelings of helplessness and panic during crisis are avoided because strategies for crisis coping have been learned and practiced.

The following confidence boosters may help your child deal with change. The age of the child will determine the manner in which you implement the suggestions, but each can be adapted for children from early childhood through the preteen years. Crisis coping will be discussed in future pages.

CONFIDENCE BOOSTERS

Help your child become sensitive to change by noticing the changing seasons, growth process, or improvements in the home or community.

Discuss how change can create a new interest, opportunity, or improvement.

Analyze the ways in which humans and animals prepare for life changes, such as a change in season or birth of babies.

Suggest different methods for coping with the same change. Highlight the fact that there isn't just one "right" technique.

Evaluate the desirability of various approaches for coping with change. Consider the freedom each individual has in selecting how to deal with change.

Discuss whether or not change is always for the better. Recount changes in the past that did not result in improvement. Ask the child if people sometimes make a change because they think any change is good.

Help your child understand the strength to be gained from good basic learning skills. If you know where to go for information and can teach yourself, you can cope with the knowledge explosion. (Incidentally, there is a new book published in the United States every 13 minutes.)

Don't immediately step in to facilitate or smooth the transition resulting from change affecting your child. Give the child an opportunity to experience success in coping.

Encourage your child to talk about the changes affecting her or his life.

The American Family—An Endangered Species?

"You're lucky you don't have a big family!" twelve-year-old Kim philosophically told her friend Gail. "The more people, the more problems—just look at my family. My grandparents are getting divorced and my grandpa is moving out because my grandma is having an affair and he found out and beat her up. Can you imagine, an affair at fifty? My oldest brother is joining some religious cult so he can live with his boyfriend. They're gay. My sister is expecting a baby in November. She won't get married or have an abortion and plans to stay right at home with us. She's only sixteen, so when she goes out on dates you know they'll make me baby-sit. My mom went back to work this year, and now she's never around. My dad is trying to look like Robert Redford, I guess. All he cares about is jogging, tennis, and exercise. I tell you, Gail, life is really the pits at our house."

Kim's description of her family may seem like an episode from a soap opera, but families at every social and economic level are facing major readjustments. Nowhere have the rapid changes sweeping our society been more drastically felt than in family life, and you may even know of a family like Kim's. The specific nature of their problems may differ, but families all over find that no sooner is one crisis over than another begins.

Sociologists, psychologists, researchers, and even politicians are concerned about the future of the American family. Is it growing weaker and possibly facing extinction, like the auk, whooping crane, or saber-toothed tiger, or is it in the process of mutation, changing its basic form in response to the changing conditions in society? Is the decline in morals, changing male and female roles, relaxed divorced laws, or even the economy to blame? No one knows for sure, but the statistics are alarming and indicate beyond a doubt that families are under stress.

Between 1960 and 1980 the U.S. divorce rate increased one hundred percent. In some metropolitan areas seven or eight out of every ten marriages end in divorce. Studies predict that half of the children born in 1978 will spend at least a portion of their childhood in single-parent homes. Changing values, lack of parental supervision, and permissiveness have resulted in greater sexual activity in teens. The number of babies born to unwed mothers of all races and nationalities is skyrocketing, and the number of unmarried couples living together doubled between 1970 and 1975.

Inflation and rising costs have hit the family. The enormous financial burden of housing, food, clothing, and education has forced many mothers into the work force. This decision affects the entire family. Mother usually has less time for house and family and expects husband and children to assume new roles. The return to work can also produce unexpected feelings of independence and enhanced self-worth. Mothers develop interests and friendships separate from family and neighborhood and begin rediscovering themselves. This process can be long and painful for mother and family alike. I recall the case of Margie F. She spent the first ten years of her marriage happily involved with the house, school, and community. She spent her days keeping her home spotlessly clean, baking, sewing, canning fruits and vegetables she grew in the yard, doing things with her children. Suddenly there was a shake-up in her huband's company, and overnight he lost his good job. After he had been unemployed for a few months and still had no prospects, she decided to take a job with the advertising agency where she had worked as a copywriter for a short time after college. Her years of experience as a homemaker and consumer had taught her something, because her ads were extremely well received and successful. She made an excellent impression on clients, and soon found herself getting one raise and promotion after another. When she came home, she resented wasting her valuable time on menial household tasks. Instead, she preferred to prepare her wardrobe for the following day, go to exercise class, or repair her manicure. When her husband got a new job, she refused to even consider quitting, saying: "I always thought I was happy and fulfilled all those years. Now I don't see how I could have been. I have a whole new life, and I love it." Margie began working longer and longer hours. Her husband hated to come home, and also began spending more and more time away from the family. The poorly supervised children were always getting in trouble, and neither Margie nor her husband could stand to cope with their endless problems. Margie often scolded them saying: "Can't you see how hard Dad and I work to make a good life for you? All we ask from you is that you behave, and you can't even do that." Finally, Margie met a man. He was rich, handsome, and totally devoted to her needs and problems. Not surprisingly, she found she preferred intimate candle-lit dinners in expensive restaurants to the hassle of contending with her messy house, delinquent children, and nagging husband. So, less than one year after going back to work, Margie left her family, reasoning that she had already given them the best years of her life. Everyone was shocked. Friends and relatives had always considered her the perfect mother.

Some experts believe that American parents, in general, are not as child-centered as they were in earlier times. In a study conducted by the firm of Yankelovich, Skelly, and White and reported in *Psychology Today,* parents with children under thirteen years of age were questioned. Two out of three said that parents should have their own lives and interests, even if it takes time from the children. Fifty-four percent indicated that when parents age or are experiencing difficulty, they have no right to count on their children. Sixty-seven percent said that children have no obligation to their parents, no matter what the parents have done for them. Nearly sixty-six percent said parents should not stay together for the sake of the children.[2]

Many parents are directing more attention toward their physical fitness and appearance. If you consider the time spent commuting, on the job, and performing necessary household responsibilities, you realize that time is a precious commodity. Yet, many parents, like Todd Baker, spend hours following personally fulfilling pursuits, leaving little time for their children. Todd stops at the health club three days a week after work. Instead of arriving home at six o'clock, he gets there at eight, just in time to say good-night to the children. At least one evening per week he stops for a drink with friends. On Saturday he plays golf. The Baker children hardly ever see their father. Although obviously affluent, they suffer from father neglect.

The phantom-parent syndrome has forced a generation of children to turn to their peers and to television for information and companionship. Teen-age problems are growing, and under extreme conditions children may even run away or turn to religious cults for the direction and coping assistance missing in the home. Even in more traditional families young people are questioning their parents' authority and asserting themselves. A number of books that address the issue of children's rights have recently been published, and courts have considered matters such as the right of a twelve-year-old to seek treatment for venereal disease or the right of a consenting thirteen-year-old to engage in sex. The issue of a child divorcing the parents is also under consideration.

How will families ultimately cope with rapidly changing modern-day existence? Many experts believe that the family is already changing, but not without additional stress. For example, Sally Combs has decided to simply go it alone. Bernice and Lonnie are lesbians who have established a household that includes both their children. Renie and Doug live together with Doug's eleven-year-old daughter. The entire Simpson family has joined a commune. Christopher Barnes is a six-year-old who divides his time between his parents, according to a joint-custody agreement. Bob and Bill are two gays looking for a surrogate mother so they can start a family. Linda Dixon moved back in with her parents following her divorce, while her friend Shana and Shana's children now share a rented home with Shana's sister-in-law and her three boys. Mary O'Donnell feels like a bride again. She plans to remarry in the spring, and her future husband wants to adopt her children.

All these alternatives to the rapidly vanishing traditional family model are a response to stress, which simultaneously create new forms of stress, at least during adjustment. However, as thousands of new-breed families are reporting, the stressors are not insurmountable, and the alternatives can work.

Does Divorce Equal Devastation?

Divorce doesn't have to devastate your child. However, this notion has become a self-fulfilling prophecy shared by parents, teachers, and society. Rather than accepting the challenge of this highly stressful event, adults often throw up their arms when a child is behaving badly and say: "What do you expect? The parents are divorced." The very term "broken home" connotes a hopeless situation. Undoubtedly, divorce is tremendously stress-producing for parents and children. It is probably one of the most traumatic experiences in life. Nonetheless, it doesn't doom a child to a lifetime of unhappiness and poor adjustment. Parents who can shake the usual guilt feelings and face the challenge of making it through the difficult "mourning period" can help their children establish emotional stability and acquire new coping skills in the process.

Studies show that less than ten percent of children affected by divorce think it was for the best. Despite the tension and problems, they wish their parents had stayed together. In spite of the high incidence of divorce, many children still feel there is a stigma attached and are ashamed. Society has helped to maintain this stigma, even though divorce has become common. Television often presents children with a model of the ideal family, which most children envy, but which rarely exists in the real world. In some classrooms thoughtless teachers still have the children make Mother's Day cards, arrange father-daughter banquets, or urge them to show their work to "Mom and Dad." The implication is clear, and such situations can be painful to a child without the requisite parent.

Most children feel alone in facing their parents' divorce. It doesn't matter how many friends have gone through the process or how widespread the phenomenon. The child feels forsaken and worries about being left with no one to provide care. Life has suddenly become unpredictable. The child questions just who can be counted on and wonders if she or he will lose the parent's love. The child longs for the happy days gone by and may become depressed or burst into tears without the slightest provocation. Schoolwork is affected as the child grows restless, is unable to concentrate, or fails to find any relevance in academic studies. Who cares about reading when one's parents have just gotten divorced? Some children become physically ill, and it is common for them to become aggressive and irritable. Or they may try to act indifferent, deny the whole mess, or become angry at their parents. Sensitive friends, relatives, and teachers can help ease the transition. However, studies show that when it comes right down to it, it is the parents who have the power to provide the greatest relief.

Yet, parents are also experiencing profound levels of stress. In some cases the new arrangements mean there is less time to spend with the child. Some children sense their parents' distressed condition and end up worrying more about them than their parents do about the children. If you are having personal coping problems, you might want to contact your local chapter of Parents Without Partners for assistance. Below are some considerations for coping with the stress of divorce. Many are difficult to implement. However, maintaining control over the tumultuous short term aftershocks of divorce can minimize long-term stress for you and your child.

MINIMIZING THE STRESS OF DIVORCE

Recognize that mother, father, and family life are the most important components of your child's life. The stress of divorce is understandable and unavoidable.

Don't try to hide the fact that there has been a separation. Your child will probably experience more stress from the anxiety of not knowing what is happening than in learning the truth.

Even if you are successful in hiding the fact, when the child finds out he or she may feel cheated or tricked and lose trust in you.

Preserve your child's love and respect for the other parent. When a marriage fails, parents often feel guilty and magnify their mate's faults in order to place the blame elsewhere.

Don't go into detail about the reasons for the divorce. Merely say you were no longer happy together.

Don't try to convince your child (or anyone else) that the whole thing is not your fault. Don't get upset when your child begins to recount all the other parent's good points.

Try not to expose your child to bickering, arguments, or long periods of silence. Don't allow your child to get involved in arguments or take sides.

Never allow your child to think for a moment that she or he was the cause for the divorce. Make it clear that no child ever causes a divorce. It is between adults. I cannot emphasize this point enough. Children are egocentric and tend to place themselves in the middle of everything. Don't let your child think that "Daddy left because I was bad."

Be sure both parents give the child an outpouring of love, affection, and reassurance.

Don't make the child feel that the divorce has placed impossible responsibilities on her or him by making comments such as, "You're the head of the house now" or "You're all I have left."

Spend more time listening to your child. Encourage the child to express feelings. Emphasize that it is natural to feel anger, fear, and sadness. Let the child know that sometimes there may be a feeling of wanting to be with the other parent. Tell your child that whenever feelings start to build up, it is time to talk about them. Allow him or her to freely telephone your spouse.

Don't let your child harbor false hope that you will all get together again. Although children often fantasize that it might happen, you should make it clear that in reality it won't.

Your child may develop temporary behavior problems in an effort to rebel, gain attention, or test your love.

Your child may regress and act more like a baby. Remember, those times were more comfortable.

Your child may become anxious or upset over anything that threatens security. Maintain stability in routine and relationships.

Don't confuse a young child's request for a "new daddy" or "new mommy" with loss of affection. The child simply wants to have a "normal" family like the other kids.

Some children do try to reject the absent parent and any qualities associated with that parent—such as a love for sports. The child, in turn, hates sports.

Don't compare your child's faults to the faults of your mate by making remarks such as "You're just like your mother!" The child may fear rejection.

Point out that there are many different types of families, but that they still are families. Point out specific examples of families that include two parents, only a mother, only a father, grandparents, or other relatives. Depending on your philosophy, you may want to include living-together arrangements.

If you move, be sure to let your child keep comfortable, familiar possessions.

Don't ever use your child to hurt your spouse.

Don't ask your child to express a preference for custody. The child is placed in a no-win situation in which any choice creates guilt for not having chosen the other parent.

Don't try to compensate by becoming overindulgent or allowing your child to "get away with murder."

Let the school know what is happening.

Make plans for both parents to stay involved in school affairs.

If you find the school is dealing with the family in a stereotypical fashion or otherwise discriminating against single-parent families, call the matter to their attention. Few teachers intentionally hurt children.

Don't expect your child to have massive adjustment difficulties. Don't blame every problem the child has in the future on the divorce.

Make it clear that you never divorce a child. Mommy will always be Mommy, and Daddy will always be Daddy. Divorce doesn't change the love between parent and child.

Divorce can actually improve the quality of life for a child. It is hard to grow up in a household that is constantly stressed. The child gets mistaken notions about adult adjustment and life in general. Good parenting exists when a child lives in peace, happiness, and security, knowing that both parents love and care. Unfortunately, in some cases it takes a divorce to provide this setting.

A Tale of Two Houses

Ten-year-old Meredith has two bedrooms, two complete wardrobes, two sets of friends, and two parents who both love and care for her. Although her mother and father are divorced, they have worked out a co-parenting agreement, in which the custody of their daughter is shared. Merry spends weekends, summers, and a portion of the winter holiday vacation in her father's home, ninety miles from the house she shares with her mother the rest of the time. She is enthusiastic about the arrangement, explaining:

"When my parents separated, I wanted to die. I thought about living with my mother, and I missed my father so much I decided I wanted to go with him. Then I would think about being away from my mother and was sure I wanted to stay with her. I just kept jumping back and forth from one parent to the other. I was really mad at Mom and Dad for goofing up all of our lives. Maybe they wanted to divorce each other, but I didn't want to divorce either one of them. Finally I made up my mind. Even though they hadn't asked me, I told them I had decided I wasn't going with either one of them. I was going to live at Grandma's. A few days later they asked me how I would like to live with both of them, by dividing my time between their two houses. I loved the idea! We had a few problems getting organized in the beginning, but now everything works just fine. The way I look at it, I have double fun. I get two sets of toys, two vacations, and two birthday parties. The best part is, I didn't lose either parent. I still wish Mom and Dad didn't have to get divorced, but since they did, the way we run things works fine!"

The concept of co-parenting, which is also referred to as joint parenting, joint custody, co-custody, or shared custody, is not new. Although mothers still receive sole custody of nine out of every ten children, joint custody is being considered as an option by more and more divorcing parents. In one interesting case, the divorcing parents both moved out of the family house and established their own separate households. The children remained at home, with the parents dividing their time between their new residences and the old one. In an article appearing in *Time* magazine, Susan Whicher, who heads the Boulder, Colorado, American Bar Association's special committee on joint custody, is quoted as saying, "Legally it's terrifying for a lot of lawyers and judges, but by the end of the 1980s it [joint custody] will be the rule rather than the exception."[3]

The surge of interest in joint custody is largely the result of the changing roles of men and women in today's society. The traditional stereotype of a woman's place being in the home is rapidly changing in light of the vast numbers of women entering the work force. Economic conditions often require that a divorced mother go to work outside the home. In addition, society is becoming more tolerant of the male who expresses an interest in assuming domestic and child-rearing responsibilities, previously reserved for women. Men are finding that raising children is extremely rewarding and satisfying and are going into court to fight for their rights as fathers.

Many husbands and wives realize that father neglect is a very real and serious problem. They believe that everyone benefits when both parents share the responsibilities for meeting the physical, emotional, and financial needs of their children. They have worked out co-parenting agreements that reportedly work. *Time* magazine cites a New York study of forty divorced men conducted by Judith Brown Greif, a psychiatric social worker, which showed that the joint-custody fathers were "happier, closer to their children and had fewer problems with ex-wives than did noncustodial fathers."[4]

While minimizing some of the stressors often associated with divorce, the growing phenomenon of joint custody can generate certain types of stress. The charts below compare the stresses that can be created with those that can be reduced. The first chart deals with children, the second with parents.

JOINT CUSTODY AND CHILDREN'S STRESS

Can Minimize Stress Associated with:

Can Generate Stress Associated with:

Can Minimize Stress Associated with:	Can Generate Stress Associated with:
Conflict regarding child's choice of custodial parent, whether that choice is expressed by the child or not	Regularly readjusting to the particular rules and lifestyle of the parent currently in custody
Loss of one parent	Confusion regarding conflicting values and rules
Feeling of being abandoned by one parent	Confusion regarding who is in authority
Negative impression of marriage in general, formed as	Disruption of friendships

JOINT CUSTODY AND CHILDREN'S STRESS (continued)

Can Minimize Stress Associated with:

a result of the child's bitter experience

Delinquent behavior stemming in part from the absence of a parent

Can Generate Stress Associated with:

Determining a sense of primary loyalty.

Having time carefully programmed for them, particularly in the case of preadolescents and adolescents

Spending large portions of time traveling from one home to another

Transporting favorite toys, items of clothing, or other childhood paraphernalia from one location to another

JOINT CUSTODY AND PARENTS' STRESS

Can Minimize Stress Associated with:

The profound sense of deprivation associated with loss of custody

Friction between ex-spouses created in part by the hostility of one parent at having lost custody

Anxiety about facing important child-rearing decisions alone

Financial aspects of raising a child alone

Locating top quality child care

A lack of free time for career, social life, or leisure activities

Can Generate Stress Associated with:

Organizing life-styles, schedules, and priorities to accommodate the coparenting arrangement

Worrying about the quality of care being provided the child, particularly on the part of the mother when the father has custody

Lack of preparation for the diverse range of parenting responsibilities, particularly on the part of the father

Fear that the child will ultimately choose one parent over the other

Disapproval of friends, relatives, or teachers

Constantly juggling the arrangement to take into ac-

Can Minimize Stress Associated with:	Can Generate Stress Associated with:
	count special happenings in the lives of the parents or child
	Placing the divorced parents in frequent contact
	Attempting to cope with problems when the divorce has left the parents barely on speaking terms
	Differing values, rules, or lifestyles
	The expense of each parent maintaining a bedroom, wardrobe, toy shelf, and so on for the child

Obviously, joint custody is not for everyone. Before making such a decision, parents should consult a co-parenting support group in their area or read some of the books concerned solely with this issue (see Suggested Reading Section). These resources can help the separating or divorcing parents focus on important aspects, such as whether or not the arrangement would prove stable for the child; the ability of each parent to assume custody; the compatibility of values and disciplinary techniques; and the likelihood that the arrangement could be efficiently organized.

However, the most important variable is the willingness and ability of the parent to adjust and work through the inevitable difficulties. As one co-parent put it: "My husband and I get along much better now than we did when we were married. Necessity dictates that we see each other often, and the situation motivates us both to work at maintaining the relationship. Many of our friends who see our joint custody working marvel at why we ever got divorced in the first place."

The "Brady Bunch" Myth

In response to the accelerating divorce rate, stepfamilies are emerging as a growing alternative to the traditional family. Remarriage results in stepparent-stepchild relationships that generate a set of very unique and complicated stressors. However, research findings indicate that children raised in stepfamilies do not differ significantly from their counterparts, reared under the traditional family structure. Once the initial adjustment is over, they share the same problems, behaviors, successes, and failures. Some experts believe that the older the child, the greater the adjustment difficulty, but it is dangerous to generalize. In dealing with your specific situation, you might find that your three-year-old cannot cope, while your twelve-year-old eases into the new relationship.

The stresses experienced by a child affected by remarriage are complex, in that they cannot be totally separated from the anxiety produced by the original divorce. The child has helplessly watched as his other world was shattered and may be fearful of it happening again or leery of making a commitment to a stepparent that might end in heartbreak. Sometimes the youngster blames the stepparent for contributing to the divorce—even irrationally, as when the stepparent and parent weren't even acquainted at the time. This tendency might be precipitated because the child has been clinging to the idea that the parents would ultimately reunite. Remarriage completely obliterates this last shred of hope. If the child has made a satisfactory adjustment to the divorce, chances are the single-parent arrangement is quite comfortable and intimate. There may be jealousy or fear that this special bond will become weakened.

It is important to deal with the stressors mentioned above before the remarriage, because once the new family structure is in place, everyone involved is bound to experience some difficulties. You can help ease the transition by waiting a reasonable length of time before considering remarriage and informing your child of the decision well in advance. Remarriage should not be considered during the child's painful "mourning" period. It is also wise to plan for a gradual get-acquainted period, in which the possibility of marriage is discussed. When the announcement is made, it is important to warn the child to expect everyone to have some adjustment problems, rather than painting a rosy picture of living happily ever after. Allow the child to vent hostile reactions and express fears and concerns. Your child should realize that the new relationship will take time, and that he or she will be involved in making it work. Most children can accept the challenge, since a warm, secure family situation is equally important to them.

Once you're settled as a new family, don't be inclined to attribute every problem to the stepfamily arrangement. All parent-child relationships go through some sticky times.

You can expect the new relationships between child and stepparent, child and stepbrothers or stepsisters, and stepparent and ex-spouse to result in some friction and accommodating adjustments.

You may even find that you and your new spouse differ on some of your ideas regarding the functioning of your new family. Differences in values, backgrounds, life-styles, and disciplinary techniques will require a certain amount of give-and-take. The children may experience confusion over such minor matters as the term used for going to the bathroom or the manner in which a holiday is celebrated. The following suggestions may help you cope with some of the more common stress-producing situations:

Emphasize the idea of being a family, rather than delineating all the various step-relationships. However, don't insist that a child use "Mother" or "Dad" against his or her will.

Don't have unrealistic expectations of immediately becoming a model, "Brady Bunch" family.

Realize that as a stepparent you may have to change some of your parenting practices or alter your life-style.

Be honest with yourself about your emotions. You may even be feeling guilty because you sense you don't particularly like your stepchild, although you love the mother or father.

Acknowledge the fact that if you have natural children in one household and stepchildren in another, balancing your attention, love, and money can be a difficult feat.

As a stepparent expect resentment from the ex-spouse, stepchildren, and even your spouse.

Don't come in like gangbusters, immediately asserting your authority. Live with the existing rules and regulations until the child has settled into the new relationship.

Recognize when your stepchild is testing your love. Uncharacteristic misbehavior may be calculated to find out just how deep your feelings run.

Don't compete with the natural parent, and don't allow the child to make comparisons. Tell the child nothing can ever change the special bond between natural parent and child. However, you hope to develop another type of special relationship.

If the child informs you that you are not doing something like the "real" mother or father, thank the child for the information but explain that every individual is different.

Don't take sides in disputes between your stepchild and the ex-spouse or between your spouse and her or his ex-spouse.

Realize that initially the child may be looking for a carbon copy of the absent parent and expect you to fit the mold.

If the absent parent was neglectful, the child may resent you for being too good, in order to defend the parent's image. The image of the natural parent is often linked to the child's self image.

Don't leave discipline matters solely to the natural parents. Slowly become involved and assert yourself, explaining to the child that you are responsible for his or her well-being too.

Expect the angry child to challenge your authority by retorting, "You're not my real mother [or father]!" You might respond by saying, "You are absolutely right, but that doesn't change the fact that I love you very much and that I am concerned about you."

Don't be surprised if the child is embarrassed because his or her mother now has a different last name.

Understandably, children who are not faced with the added stress of moving, adjusting to a new school, and finding new friends often adapt more easily.

A cooperative ex-spouse can be of immense assistance in the coping process by discussing the matter with the child, easing some of the resentment, and dismissing questions of loyalty. A positive relationship can also reduce the tension associated with child-centered social occasions, such as school programs, tournament games, or religious ceremonies, when stepparent and natural parents want to be present.

Stepchildren and stepparents rarely experience love at first sight, but by working together to cope with the stresses of the new family life, they can grow to love one another.

. . . And Baby Makes Two

A number of other factors are contributing to the dramatic increase in single-parent families besides the high divorce rate. Many unmarried individuals are adopting, and sometimes they are even preferred to married couples, particularly when older children are involved. Some unwed women deliberately become pregnant and never inform the father, while others opt to keep babies rather than get an abortion. Whatever the reason, single-parent families are no longer regarded as unusual, and the stigma once associated with this life-style is gradually disappearing. In recent years society has become more interested in the plight of the single parent and committed to assistance. The possibilities of providing single parents with more flexible working hours; part-time employment with full-time fringe benefits, such as insurance; sick leave in the event of a child's illness; paternity leave; and child care on company premises are all being considered.

Single parents and their children experience stress on a number of fronts. The adult is often overwhelmed by the additional responsibility of providing economic and emotional sustenance. The largest percentage of single parents are women, and many suffer serious financial cutbacks in this new family style. They must locate housing, child care, and employment—all strategically related to one another. While society is definitely becoming more supportive and accepting, single parents still face major social readjustments. They may no longer fit in with the old set of married friends or even have time to socialize after meeting all the family responsibilities. Money is usually in short supply, and socializing can be expensive. In addition, some parents are afraid to get involved with members of the opposite sex.

Parents can become resentful of their children for imposing this tremendous burden. They don't think it's fair that one person should be required to make all decisions, assume full responsibility, provide all the attention, and be the sole source of love. They are forced to cope with problems for which they have no training. Single parents are often frustrated by their continuously harried condition, feeling they are spreading themselves too thin to be effective in any area. They worry that they may make a serious child-rearing mistake, are failing to furnish both a male and female role model, or are incapable of providing the emotional support, sex education, or open communication needed. When you consider that all these new stressors are being faced at a time when many parents are already experiencing the shock of being alone, it adds up to double-trouble.

The parent's condition largely determines the child's. When a single parent doubts personal coping ability, the anxiety and lack of confidence is transmitted to the child, who in turn feels insecure and similarly unable to cope. Following a divorce parents may overcompensate for guilt feelings by spoiling the child. They may tire of being the sole dispenser of authority and discipline and let behavior problems slide. If the parent does reenter the social scene, the child's world is often threatened for a second time. Just as the youngster is beginning to feel assured again in the snug, intimate new relationship shared by parent and child, it all starts over and the child thinks, "Here we go again!" Remember, the child may also face the new stressors of the single-parent family with a slight hangover, resulting from the parents' recent divorce.

At first, coping may seem impossible for both parent and child. However, in a short time most families find they are doing just fine and experience pride at having made it. A parent's first step is to understand the child's feelings and to provide reassurance. The child touched by divorce has just watched as the loving relationship between mother and father crumbled and fears the same fate in his or her relationship with the single parent. Delinquent or unusual misbehavior is a cry for help. Don't futilely assume that it is the direct result of living in a single-parent family, but instead blame a lack of supervision, attention, or affection.

Children can be naturally jealous and resentful of a parent's new social life. First, it takes precious time away from the child. You might be able to minimize some of your child's stress by arranging dates at times when the child is with your ex-spouse. Second, some children don't feel their mother or father has the right to love again. If it didn't work before, too bad. You had your turn. Although you may be divorced, your child is not and remains faithful to the other parent. Children have a variety of techniques for sabotaging your new associations. For example, Ann Avery complained that her nine-year-old daughter was suddenly rude, hostile, and insulting to her dates, traits she had never before exhibited. Six-year-old Bruce Dillon refused to talk to his father's girl friend, while Candy Poole, nine, refused to cooperate and never approved of any place her mother wanted to take her if the boyfriend was going too. Ricky Schroeder had the best technique of all. When his mother had a date, he became violently ill and proved it by vomiting. Sometimes parents allow the child to win, rationalizing that if the child takes it so badly, dating really isn't that important. If you do make this decision, don't let your child score a mental victory. Having learned that the technique works, next time the child will use it with even greater vigor. You will have created a real tyrant.

You can prepare a child to cope by including the possibility of either parent dating, falling in love, and remarrying in your earliest discussions of an impending divorce. Parents renewing their social life should adopt a go-slow approach. Allow a reasonable length of time for your child to recover from the grief of a divorce or death. Children accept dating better if the parent is not immediately embroiled in an all-consuming romance. Some children are upset by physical signs of affection. Expect your child to ask if you plan to get married. You can explain that dating does not necessarily equal marriage, but is a way to get out and have some fun with other adults. Last, be patient.

How you handle sex is up to you. There is no pat answer. Living-together arrangements are in the same category. However, realize that children learn by your example, and your child will probably form attitudes based on the model you set. If you move from one marriage or living-together arrangement to another, your child may learn to take commitment lightly, distrust the opposite sex, or doubt the possibility of a meaningful, sustained relationship.

Many experts believe that single parenting is usually a transition stage. Within five years many single parents make other arrangements. In previous years single parents often established family life closely tied to a relative, often sharing a household. Today many parents marry or remarry.

The important thing to remember is that even with limited options and income single parents can and do meet the needs of their children. Once they are able to coordinate child care, employment, housing, and their own leisure activities, they find single parenting begins to work. But making it work can mean choosing between disposable income and disposable time, since time is a precious, yet scarce, resource. Children also cope if family life includes opportunities for frequent parent-child interaction, particularly during the difficult stages of early adjustment. Some children spend many long hours without the benefit of adult supervision or companionship. Their model of grown-up behavior lacks examples of adults in a give-and-take relationship. These disadvantages can be avoided if the parent manages to locate excellent child care, structures a variety of social experiences, and spends quality time with the child. In the case of a child affected by divorce, it is also important that the divorced parents maintain a relatively conflict-free relationship and that there are regular visits with the noncustodial parent, which are encouraged by the custodial parent.

Although single parenting undoubtedly requires extra effort and gives the parent few breaks, experts report that single parents can raise their children successfully if they recognize the magnitude of their task and work at it seriously.

Do Working Mothers Really Have More Stress?

The mother who goes to work, returns to school, or begins doing volunteer work will understandably experience stress generated from her concern over the effects of the decision on husband and children. If the mother is functioning in a constant state of disorganization and distress, this condition will transfer to those most dear to her. However, chaos certainly is not inevitable. In fact, there are nearly two and a half million working mothers with babies under three, three million mothers with youngsters from three to five, and nine million with children from six to seventeen. These mothers share special stresses and many have learned to cope effectively with them. In fact, research indicates that a mother's level of satisfaction regarding her life is a more crucial factor in determining her adequacy as a mother than employment status. A dissatisfied mother will transmit her unhappiness to the entire household, and it is immaterial whether the source of her discontent is employment or home. In some cases women actually become better mothers when they find meaningful employment, while other mothers would be better off if they were able to quit their jobs and stay home. It is a purely individual matter. Sometimes the working mother finds that her family is a major source of her stress. Husband, children, or both simply refuse to accept the new situation and cope with it. Obviously, the woman who must contend with an uncooperative, sullen family while simultaneously adjusting her life to efficiently manage home and job has a real challenge. One study estimated that working mothers do four times more work than their husbands, when home and job are included. In most cases the situation does improve. Necessity and human compassion force the family to share in more of the household responsibilities. In many cases the extra income soon loses the "extra" label and becomes an important source of funds, which helps to adjust family attitudes.

There are many causes for family stress when Mother becomes involved outside the home. In some cases the decision is a poor one from the onset: there is no pressing financial urgency, and the mother really hates the idea of leaving her child. She is plagued by guilt and fear of losing control over the child. Perhaps it is difficult to locate child care that minimizes stress for parent and child. Or, maybe the problem isn't with working but with the nature of the job. If a mother works in a high-pressure occupation, she may be totally drained when she arrives home. The time spent with her child won't be quality time. The job may lack flexibility and make her life extremely difficult when the child is sick or has a special program at school. Some jobs have odd hours and demand overtime or evening work.

The whole family suffers when the mother is under stress. Many mothers get off to a bad start before the baby even arrives. They work up to the last minute and are too busy to prepare for the infant. After delivery these women are exhausted and spend their few days at home trying to catch up with the neglected household. It seems they never really have time to relax before it's time to go back to work. Once back on the job, personal expectations are set too high. The mother strives to be perfect in all ways. She keeps up a good front for a time, but living under perpetual stress takes its toll. Instead, she should set realistic goals and seek assistance from her husband, since studies show that employed mothers do, in fact, spend more combined time working on the job and at home than their spouses.

Occasionally, a critical grandparent, neighbor, or teacher may cast a disapproving eye on the working mother or attribute a child's misbehavior to lack of maternal supervision with a remark such as "Well, his mother works, you know." All children have problems. You can't blame yourself or your job for that fact. You can help reduce the stress your child experiences by being available to help and by adopting a drop-everything policy when a child is in obvious need.

The biggest source of stress for the child is probably staying alone or feeling lonely before parents arrive home from work. In facing this stressor you should realize that every child must develop independence and self-assurance. You are not guilty of neglect if the child is mature enough to be left alone and has been properly prepared. The first time this arrangement is made, you will probably be more nervous than the child. Mature children are usually eager for the experience. If you know it is an inevitability, begin by leaving the child for short stretches while you do an errand. Gradually extend the length of time. Clearly establish a set of rules, which might include:

No guests in the house.

Never open the door for any stranger, no matter who they tell you they are.

No cooking.

Never try to extinguish a fire; immediately run from the house and get help.

Never enter a burning house for any reason—not even to get a pet.

If you aren't sure something is permissible, don't do it unless you contact me and get permission.

Encourage your child to use the telephone to discuss any unusual situation or emergency. It isn't a bad idea to have the child check in by telephone when he or she arrives home. It relieves your mind and breaks the loneliness of the empty house. Let neighbors know when your child stays alone, and tell the child what neighbors to contact if there's a special problem. Rehearse a possible conversation to be used in the event a stranger phones. Post emergency numbers, and practice making effective emergency calls. If your child does complain of loneliness, perhaps you can arrange for participation in an after-school recreation program or some type of lessons. Check the school and park district offerings. You might even consider getting a pet to share the lonely hours.

Studies have shown that there were no significant differences found in social development, intellectual growth, and ability to form close interpersonal relationships between children cared for at home and those receiving high-quality day care. A working mother need not experience the unnecessary stress of fearing her family will suffer if she:

Is able to arrange for good child care.

Organizes her life and spends quality time with her children.

Doesn't confuse quality time with ignoring misbehavior.

Manages to avoid compensating for working by overindulging children with expensive toys or clothing.

Takes time every day to talk to her children.

Sets aside special time each week for family fun.

Recognizes and copes with her feelings of guilt.

Realizes that it is normal for her children to occasionally object to her working.

Specific suggestions for locating child care and organizing time are presented in Chapters Ten and Eleven.

Some working mothers find they can't cope with employment and child raising, particularly when they have more than one small child. They give up their jobs to stay home. As one mother put it: "After my twins were born, *I* felt like a baby. I couldn't seem to do anything right. I was overeating out of frustration and constantly gaining weight. I felt my body and personality turning ugly. Juggling employment and household responsibilities made me feel like a martyr, and I found myself reverting to childish behavior—throwing verbal tantrums. The twins were a handful, I didn't know what I was doing, and there never seemed to be time to learn. Finally the pressure was clearly too much. My husband couldn't stand me, and I was a pain in the neck at work. I didn't even like myself, so I just decided to quit.'' It all sounds simple, but working mothers who make the decision can experience substantial stress. Friends at work may disapprove of the action or lose interest in maintaining friendship. Many mothers miss the stimulation of daily interaction with the outside world. Their sense of self-worth declines. The family's standard of living might of necessity be cut. In spite of these stressors, many mothers find they prefer their new situation. As one close friend explained after the birth of her baby: "At first I was unsure about quitting the job, but after a month at home, I realized how much the stress at work had been getting to me. I actually hated the demands made at the office and was bored getting up each morning. Raising my son is the most important job I ever had, and I want to work at it full-time!''

When Too Much Is Too Little

Children come into the world wanting very little. Beyond their basic physical needs they crave security, the companionship of other human beings, recognition, and most importantly, love. During the first few years of life parents and the media teach them to want a great many other things, which might include designer jeans, an Atari game, or a six-hundred-dollar dirt bike. Many parents are questioning the speed with which today's youngsters are experiencing life, acquiring possessions, and growing up. They worry that the fast pace of childhood is leaving many children jaded, bored, and spent by adolescence.

Children today are different from children of the past. They are sophisticated and informed and probably know more of the world than their parents did at the same age. One mother made the following comparison:

"I had my first airplane ride at twenty-six, my son had his at six weeks. I got my first two-wheel bike from Sears in the spring, when I was in fifth grade. My son got a two-wheeler for his third birthday and a ten-speed in second grade. My parents took me out to eat three or four times a year; we go out three or four times a week. I never knew anyone who drank wine; my son knows Lancers is a good brand. I didn't know about sex until eighth grade; he knew in third. I have never seen a *Hustler* magazine; he tells me they're gross.''

Childhood changes have been for both the better and the worse.

Many of the opportunities do provide added stimulation and enjoyment. However, when too much is given to compensate for a parent's inability or unwillingness to provide enough personal attention, then too much is actually too little. Spending money on children can never be a substitute for spending time with them. Conversely, some parents have been brought up believing in self-denial and self-sacrifice so the family can have more. They dutifully deprive themselves to fulfill their children's every want and avoid infringing on the carefree days of childhood by demanding little and waiting on their offspring.

In either case the children ultimately come to believe that they are entitled to whatever their hearts desire. They equate gifts and lavish expenditures of money as a sign of love. They develop a need for acquisition, in order to feel worthwhile. Fulfillment does not come from self-actualization, but rather from satisfying selfish whims. However, the sense of fulfillment is momentary, since it is the act of acquisition that is rewarding—not the thing that is being acquired. For example, Brandon nags his father for an expensive pair of gym shoes, although his old pair are in good condition. Brandon's father works late every evening for an entire week, but on Saturday he takes the boy to purchase the shoes he has so desperately wanted. Dad is surprised when Brandon begins asking for a new component for his stereo system before they are even home from the shoe store. Neither Brandon nor his father realizes that the child is dependent on gifts as tangible proof of love. It is not the thing that is important, but the father's willingness to provide it. Therefore, as soon as one need is satisfied, another must take its place in order for the child to have continuing evidence of his worth. This vicious cycle obviously places stress on all concerned and results in frustration when satisfaction seems impossible.

There are warning signs. Parents notice that children pay little attention to their acquisitions once they are in the house. In fact, like Brandon, their interest might not even be sustained during the ride home. They may appear bored with a vacation or outing they planned. These children seem to be constantly searching for something else to want, and can find something to buy in any kind of store. They seem confused about short-term and long-term goals and are basically discontented.

For want of a better term, the overindulged are often referred to as spoiled. Spoiled children are aware of their condition, as evidenced by the anecdote reported by a mother in the middle-income bracket. She was teasing her seven-year-old about running away and being out on his own. She asked, "What in the world would you use for money?'' The child replied, ''I have money in my drawer and in the bank.'' ''Oh, yeah,'' said the mother. ''Well, just how long do you think that would last?'' To which the seven-year-old responded: ''A lot longer than you think. I wouldn't spend money on myself the way you spend it on me.''

Take the following self-test and see if you might be a spoiler.

DO YOU SPOIL YOUR CHILD?

Answer each question by circling "Yes" or "No."

1. Do you have an "if one is good, two are bet-ter" philosophy? (Example: Your child asks for one package of baseball cards, but you insist on buying two, or even three.)   Yes   No

2. Do you give in to your child's demands even though you know they are unreasonable, simply because you are too tired to fight? (Example: You purchase an item at the gro-cery check-out counter rather than deal with your child making a scene.)   Yes   No

3. Does your "squeaky wheel child" get more than others by making more of a fuss?   Yes   No

4. Do you sometimes give in against your bet-ter judgment to your child's arguments of "Everybody's doing it" or "Everybody has one"?   Yes   No

5. Do you intercede when your mate is disci-plining your child because you can't stand to see the child suffer?   Yes   No

6. Do you allow your child to boss you around or wait on the child, reasoning that you really don't mind doing things for the child?   Yes   No

7. Do you compete with other adults in the child's life to appear the most generous?   Yes   No

8. Do you accept almost any excuse when it comes to letting the child off without doing assigned chores?   Yes   No

9. Do you rush experiences or toys, providing them before the child is really mature enough to understand or appreciate them?   Yes   No

10. Do you go along with the kiddie version of keeping up with the Joneses by buying articles that are currently fashionable, even though you sense they are foolish?   Yes   No

11. Do you find that your child has no concept of money or feels the family supply is limitless?   Yes   No

12. Does your child keep you in emotional bondage by appealing to your sense of guilt at working, getting a divorce, whatever?   Yes   No

13. Do you create wants by calling your child's attention to the latest in toys or fashion?   Yes   No

14. Do you let your child know you think it is cute when the child makes demands that reflect a sophistication far beyond his or her years? (Example: telling you she can't possibly start first grade without a new pair of Jordache jeans.)   Yes   No

15. Do you find yourself frequently disposing of toys, clothing, or shoes that have barely been used?   Yes   No

16. Does it take months for your child to get around to playing with Christmas or birthday gifts?   Yes   No

17. Would you buy your child a television rather than struggle with negotiating a family viewing schedule?   Yes   No

18. If your child enjoys going to McDonald's to eat, do you reason that a more expensive hamburger pub would be better yet?   Yes   No

19. Do you freely and absentmindedly give your child money to make purchases and act unconcerned about getting change or counting it?   Yes   No

20. After experiencing a loss, is your child's first reaction "Oh, well, we'll just get another"?   Yes   No

Scoring

0–3 Yes answers   You overdo it occasionally but probably not enough to do any real harm.

| 4–6 Yes answers | You probably sense that your child has a good set of values. However, once in a while you may be shocked at some selfish behavior, which you may unintentionally be reinforcing. |
| 7 or more Yes answers | You should reconsider your own values, as well as the means you typically use to show your love. |

We all love our children and work hard to be able to give them the best. We may be anxious for them to have experiences, opportunities, and tangibles we did not have as children. If both parents work, it is easy to feel guilty and want to make it up to the child in any way possible. It is fun to show our love with gifts and warm to a smiling face. Sometimes we are just too tired to cope. With limited time to share between parent and child, it is easy to overlook behavior problems rather than spoil an evening with discipline. With all the temptations, it becomes imperative we keep an eye on the scale and watch for the tipping, when too much becomes too little.

Opting to Choose

Children today are freer to choose than their parents, according to a recent study by the research firm of Yankelovich, Skelly, and White. Their poll of 1,500 Americans revealed that 73 percent felt they had more freedom of choice than their parents had. A mere 8 percent thought there were fewer choices, while 17 percent said the levels were about the same, and 2 percent were uncertain.[5]

Options are naturally introduced early in life. Possibly beginning with self-demand feeding, children progressively are given a wider range of options of gradually increasing importance. The decisions span a host of circumstances, some generating little or no stress (for example, selecting new gym shoes) while others are extremely tense (such as choosing a custodial parent in a divorce).

Parents are affected by the increased options in child raising. Inevitably, they face disagreements concerning the best parenting approaches. Children are usually aware of these conflicts, and parents worry that the friction might harm them. Actually, the opposite can be true. Children can understand that the choices available to both young and old have never been broader. When individuals are faced with options, they sometimes disagree. Children should accept the right of their parents to differing opinions. Even an angry exchange between mother and father can furnish a valuable lesson, provided it isn't explosive or vicious. The child sees a firsthand model of adults respecting each other's opinions and resolving thorny issues by negotiation and discussion. It is reassuring to learn that a stormy exchange isn't synonymous with the breakup of a relationship, provided the child is secure in an atmosphere of love and support and not forced, or even permitted, to take sides.

Childhood choices are the proving ground for adult decision making. By the preteens many children have already faced issues dealing with sex, religion, relationships, drugs, alcohol, athletics, and education. The profusion of options in modern life produces stress. When a situation is perceived as threatening, often a decision is required for adaptation. For example, if a child is spending a large percentage of his free time playing basketball and consequently is doing poorly in math, the threat of failure forces him to consider many options: ignoring the whole mess, dropping out of basketball to have more study time, getting tutorial assistance, or just accepting failure. Some of these options produce new threats such as answering to parents and teachers after failing or suffering peer disapproval after dropping out of basketball. The more threatening the situation, the more stressful the decision-making process. Sometimes the prospect of having to make a decision is more stressful than. actually making it. If the choice must be made quickly, the time restraint can also create stress, particularly if the child feels there may be other, less threatening, options not yet known to him or her. Options relating to morals or values can also be stressful. For example, if Benny's friend suggests they skip church in order to get to the tennis courts before the Sunday crowd, morals and values are involved in the choice. In addition, Benny is concerned with the social approval of his actions and must consider how his friend will react, as well as how his parents will react to his decision—if he chooses to tell them. Ultimately, he must answer to his own conscience.

In summary, the stress of choice can be caused by:

The prospect of making a choice in the near future.

A threatening situation requiring a choice.

All negative options.

Knowledge that a threat will remain, even after the choice is made.

Pressure to make a quick choice.

A sense that other, less threatening, alternatives are available—yet unknown.

Issues involving morals or values.

The desire for social approval.

The desire for self-approval.

When a decision is made under stress, the child often lacks confidence and conviction that the choice was a good one and begins to prematurely anticipate negative consequences. A lack of commitment may cause the child to fall short of the follow-through necessary to make an option work.

Parents unwittingly contribute to a child's lack of effectiveness in dealing with choices and increase levels of stress by failing to give the child practice and support in decision making. Consider nine-year-old Julie Evans, who was carefully supervised since infancy. Her mother routinely selected her clothing, meals, and most of her leisure activities. When Julie did express a choice, such as her preference for a birthday gift, her parents immediately questioned the wisdom of her decision and urged her to rethink the matter. If she refused to change her mind, they made her feel guilty and anxious by subtly withdrawing signs of love and affection. Julie began to believe she wasn't smart enough to handle the normal options of childhood. She lived her life like a windup doll, waiting for her parents to crank the lever and aim her in one direction or another. Julie felt no sense of control over her life. At school she followed the crowd rather than choosing for herself. When a problem surfaced, she whined and complained about it until her parents resolved it or directed her course of action. On the few occasions when she was forced to make her own choice, she was overwhelmed, particularly if there were a large number of options or great many decisions in one day.

Parents can help children deal with choice efficiently, effectively, and with confidence. Initially, a child must realize that relying on others to decide for you is tantamount to turning control over to others. A series of careful steps can guide a child in making choices:

COPING WITH CHOICE

Phase 1: Focus on options.   Consider only one choice at a time. If a child is faced with several decisions, deal with them separately and individually. Once the choice area has been specifically identified, define each and every option available.

Phase 2:
Focus on
yourself.

Determining the best option is like finding a pair of shoes—it must fit the individual. In order to know if an option is suitable, the child must be able to analyze it in terms of his or her:

Needs.

Values.

Morals.

Abilities.

Interests.

Temperament.

Short-term and long-term goals (arranged in order of priority).

Phase 3:
Focus on
conse-
quences.

Each option must be methodically dissected to discover its value, relative to all the others. Parents can help the child objectively list the pluses and minuses, perhaps even performing the task on paper. In focusing on the consequences, it is important to weigh the gains and losses to self and others, as well as the approval of self and others.

Phase 4:
Focus on
new infor-
mation.

At this stage a concerted effort is made to locate new information, outside opinions, criticism of the tentative choice, and guidance in general. Parents can be a valuable resource, provided they serve in an advisory capacity and resist the impulse to take over the entire operation.

Phase 5:
Focus on
choosing.

Finally, it is time to make the actual choice of option.

Phase 6:
Focus on
implemen-
tation.

After an option has been selected, it is necessary to determine how it will be implemented. In some cases the choice may be to do nothing, while in other situations a detailed plan is required.

As an adult you have undoubtedly faced decisions at a time when you felt inadequate or too tired to cope. Perhaps you were already under great stress. Postponing a decision under such circumstances is advisable for both adults and children, provided it is possible. Also, don't go overboard by insisting your child make decisions that are beyond her or his maturity level, range of interests, or proper domain. Practice in decision making should be gained in a personally meaningful context, rather than in a setting in which the child senses her or his lack of preparation. No one wants to be responsible for a poor choice, particularly if it affects others—so be fair when you ask a child to choose.

Everyone makes a poor choice now and then. When it happens to your child, help the child uncover the cause. Below are some questions the child can ask to locate the weak link in the decision-making process:

1. Did I forget to consider some of the options available?
2. Did I take too long to make my choice because I wanted to be absolutely positive I was on the right track?
3. Did I take too long to make my choice because I didn't know what was the best option?
4. Did I make my choice too quickly so I could forget the stressful matter?
5. Did I make my choice too quickly because it seemed there was only one option when actually there were more?
6. Did I make my choice too quickly because I thought the matter wasn't important anyway?
7. Did I make my choice too quickly because others were pressuring me to hurry up?
8. Did I make my choice too quickly because I didn't think any of the options available had any negative consequences?
9. Did I make my choice too quickly because I didn't want to take time to look for new information?
10. Did I choose to let someone else make my choice because I have had bad experiences in decision making?
11. Did I choose to let someone else make my choice because I wanted to be able to shift the blame if the choice was a bad one?
12. Did I choose not to consciously make a choice in order to avoid the stressful issue?
13. Did I make a careless choice by settling for "good enough," rather than looking for the best option.

14. Did I overstate the advantages or understate the disadvantages of a favored option?

15. Did I tell myself that the choice wouldn't really matter until a long time in the future?

16. Did I blame someone else for causing me to choose the option?

17. Did I tell myself no one would know about my choice but me?

18. Did I use faulty logic; for example, reasoning that one situation is exactly like another when it isn't; following the lead of someone who doesn't fully understand the options and their consequences; telling myself "everybody does it"; or assuming a cause and effect relationship between my choice and my goal which doesn't, in fact, exist.

19. Did I categorize all my options as either good or bad, instead of looking for the good and bad in each option?

20. Did I choose an option and then fail to implement it?

Decisions are not irrevocable, and once a child realizes a mistake has been made, it is time to do something about it. In some cases it may be possible to undo what has already been done and begin the process of choosing anew. If not, the child may want to stop the current course of action in midstream and consider the options available for change. After careful consideration it may be that the original choice was a good one after all, but simply needs more time or more effort in implementation.

Everyone has options, and it is impossible not to make choices, although we can choose to let others take control. Help your child gain confidence by making it clear that everyone has the right to make mistakes and change their mind. You also have a right to react on impulse, decide that you really don't care, or that you just don't know. Your choices are personal, and reversing yourself is not a sign of weakness or equivalent to breaking a promise. It shows that you have acquired flexibility and evaluative skills necessary for meeting the challenge of life in our changing times.

My Dad's Stronger Than Your Dad

Competition is a way of life in this nation, and many chain-smoking, tranquilizer-popping parents provide their children with a model of competitive behavior. They return home each evening with accounts of how they "murdered Smitty on the monthly sales chart," "crucified Eddie in racquetball," or "made Miller drop his teeth when he saw the new family car." The children sense that the object of each day is to win at someone else's expense.

Children are indoctrinated into competitive thinking from infancy. Parents make comparisons, rankings, or ratings such as:

"Billy is taller than Bobby, and they're the same age!"

"Matt scored higher than Mindy on the reading test the teacher gave."

"Cathy did better in the ballet recital than Katie."

"Michelle hit more Little League homers this season than Mandy."

In moderation, competition can prove stimulating, but many children face situations in which competition is no longer exhilarating because self-image is on the line. An article in *The Wall Street Journal* quotes a recent high school graduate as saying that at her high school "there was so much competition for places on teams and things you pretty much had to pick one activity and give it everything you had." What a pity competition so limits the students' range of usual extracurricular high school interests! Also, how do students feel if, after giving it everything, they fail?

In one study where twenty stressful childhood events were listed, being picked last for the team or losing the game were cited. Organized children's athletics all have a potential for generating stress, but perhaps the most notorious is Little League. Little League is designed to improve gross and fine motor skills, teach sportsmanship, and give children the opportunity to win or lose gracefully. It is supposed to be fun, and in many cases it is. Unfortunately, some parents and coaches push too hard. Individual performance and winning become all important. When a child's self-image is in jeopardy, it is no longer harmless sport. Even the children themselves apply pressure. I asked a few Little Leaguers what made losing so hard, and they told me it was facing the ridicule of their friends the next day. An eleven-year-old admitted he threw sand in his face on the playing field to hide his tears after making a fielding error. One mother interviewed advised me that if parents intend to have a child participate in Little League, they had better arrange for the child to learn basic batting and fielding skills in Peewee League during the years prior to eligibility, or "Otherwise the child just can't compete."

Competition is not limited to athletics. Teachers run contests, offer awards, and rank students. While a few children do experience the ecstasy of succeeding, consider how the other twenty-five or more children in the class feel. Alternatively, sensitive teachers arrange activities in which everyone can be a winner by fulfilling a specified goal or improving their own past level of performance.

Competition at its worst is a dangerous trick to stimulate achievement, which is risky since a loss may whittle at self-image. Many adults mistake competition with competence. Winning doesn't guarantee proficiency, and some very competent children freeze during competition. Competition is also confused with drive. Competitive children do not necessarily have more drive than non-competitive children. In fact, they may actually have less. The competitive youngster may not be a self-starter and may require others for motivation—it isn't vital to read until there is a reading contest; it isn't important to be a good roller skater unless you can be better than someone else. Competition at its extreme is ugly. It is based on boosting your morale with another's loss.

Children can find it difficult to come to terms with the seemingly contradictory emphasis on competition and cooperation. They get conflicting messages when told to "get out there and beat the other kids—be better than they are," and then alternatively, to "get along with your friends and respect them."

High levels of competition can work against the child's developing independence. The child becomes dependent on the praise and recognition that come from winning or being the best and suffers a blow when a loser. The individual's self-worth is determined on a comparative basis, rather than in terms of the self-satisfaction that should be a part of maximizing innate potential. The child relies on others for fulfillment and is unable to feel self-fulfilled.

Children do, in fact, have a lot to lose in competitive situations. Not only does their own self-image decline but the nature of our competitive society sometimes actually causes others to think less of the loser. A loss can also mean you don't get the reward, which might range from a trip to Philadelphia for the playoffs to stopping for ice cream on the way home.

Children cope with the stress of competition in a number of ways. Following are some examples of behavior which can signal difficulty:

Full speed ahead   Jarrett is bound and determined to win first place in the trumpet competition. He knows he is up against some tough opposition, so for months he devotes every minute of his spare time to practice. He develops headaches and loses his few friends. Although Jarrett ultimately does take first, one might wonder if the end justified the means, a question no one can answer for sure.

Retreat, retreat   Francine is the only girl on the soccer team. It seems the coach, spectators, players, and parents all expect her to not only be as good as the boys, but better. Francine can't stand the pressure and quits, although she loves the game.

Who cares?   Andy talked for weeks about making the all-star team, but when the coach read the list, his name wasn't on it. The next day at school one of his friends proudly proclaimed he was an all-star, to which Andy offhandedly replied, "That's nice, but as far as I'm concerned, I'm sick of baseball and glad it's over."

Sick and tired   Troy wanted to win the costume contest at the park Halloween party. He worked on his Flash Gordon costume for weeks, but a few days before the event he learned that another child had a "really neat" R2-D2 costume. The evening of the party his family was astounded when Troy announced he thought he was getting sick and felt very tired after the long day at school. He stayed home rather than risk losing.

Excuses, excuses   Donna is only eleven, but she aspires to one day be a professional tennis player. She has a tennis coach and spends many long hours practicing. In a very close match she lost the local championship. Although she never mentioned any ailments before the competition, after her loss Donna complained that her elbow had been bothering her for about a week.

Sorry, not interested   A group of neighborhood children are forming a Saturday morning bowling league. Randy has never bowled before and when asked to join, replied, "I am really not interested in bowling, but if you want, I might keep score for you guys.''

It ain't fair   Anna worked for a month on her weather station for the third grade science fair. She was sure her project would take first. When she earned an honorable mention, she replied: ''It was a fix, and it's not fair. Jeff only won because he is Mr. Mueller's pet.''

Premedi-   Eric's fourth grade teacher had a spelling bee each
tated   Friday. By Wednesday the boy had already begun
failure   dreading the weekly event. All day Friday his stomach was uneasy, and during the contest he felt clammy and weak. He only found relief when he missed a word and finally sat down. Eric ultimately solved the spelling bee problem. Although he was a fairly good speller, he simply missed his first word. Once he settled on this strategy, he no longer worried about Fridays.

Planned   From the time Gloria was three years old, her par-
punishment   ents pushed her into ice skating. Her father had been a professional hockey player, and her mother had done figure skating in college. By the time she was in sixth grade, Gloria hated the pressure of competing at skating meets. She resented her parents for putting her through the ordeal and was perversely delighted at their disappointment when she lost. Gradually, she began sabotaging her own performance.

If you recognize any of the coping strategies above, perhaps you can help your child deal more effectively with competition. First, help the child realize the difference between sport and battle. Prepare the child for losses by encouraging a ''let's give it a shot'' attitude, in which the child experiments with a number of competition situations without feeling pressured to win or be the best. Let your child know what you think being tops is all about. It is enough to be pretty, without being the prettiest. It is terrific to be a great skate-boarder, without being the best.

Most parents would not intentionally abuse their children with physical injury or a vicious verbal attack. However, parents do contribute to painful feelings of worthlessness when they put more stock in a competitive situation than is due. If every loss chisels a tiny piece from your child's emerging self-image, you must determine if the thrill of victory outweighs the agony of defeat.

"Bang, Bang . . . You're Dead, Fifty Bullets in the Head"

You may be familiar with the charming childhood chant printed above. If not, you have probably heard your children recite another, equally brutal one. Violence is a part of childhood.

The dictionary defines violence as the use of physical force to inflict injury, or cause damage to, persons or property. Most of us will admit that at certain times we feel violent. We wish we could "belt that guy in the mouth," or smash the malfunctioning television set. However, reason usually prevails. We have learned to control our violent impulses.

Violence is a reaction to stress. Effective coping means controlling violence and relieving stress in other ways. However, our children grow up seeing violence portrayed on television and in movies as a common coping technique. Many of the toys they play with encourage violent behavior. They see that violence is not limited to the fantasy worlds of movies, television, or play each time they watch the news or read a newspaper. Accounts of brutality abound. Some children have already been victims. They have been attacked by gangs of other children or even by their own parents. Sibling violence occurs in sixty per cent of the families with more than one child.

Children learn violent behavior. Unwittingly, many parents provide the lessons. Below is a checklist. Complete it and see if you are unconsciously approving of violence as a response to childhood stress.

DO YOU VETO VIOLENCE?

Circle "Yes" or "No" for each question below:

1. Do you monitor television viewing and discourage viewing of violent programming?   Yes   No

2. Do you check the ratings for movies and find out why a movie is PG? Do you discourage viewing of violent films?   Yes   No

3. Do you usually avoid using physical punishment as a means for dealing with behavior problems?   Yes   No

4. Do you check the comics and books your child buys to be sure they are not the "horror" variety?   Yes   No

5. Do you usually avoid violent reactions to personal stress—such as throwing or kicking things?   Yes   No

6. Do you discourage your son from fighting, rather than approving and considering male violence part of being manly?   Yes   No

7. Did you make it clear to your child from the time the child was a toddler that violent reactions to stress are unacceptable?   Yes   No

8. Have you placed in storage or disposed of guns or other weapons that were once kept in the house?   Yes   No

9. Do you try to limit your purchase of toys that involve violent play?   Yes   No

10. Do you encourage the expression of violent feelings in words and help your child find nonviolent means for relieving stress?   Yes   No

Each "Yes" answer counts as a veto. If you had ten "Yes" answers, you are actively working to make your child's environment less violent. Nine or eight "Yes" answers is pretty good, but seven or less indicates there is a potential for making your child's world less violent by changing some of the behaviors for which you circled "No." (See section on "Aggression and Hostility," Chapter Six.)

Television

Our children can hardly imagine a time when families read, listened to the radio, or played games in the evening. In a relatively short time television has become a pervasive influence in our society, and in particular on our children. Let's see how much you actually know about television and its effects on children. Take the quiz below and find out.

1. The percentage of two-year-olds that sing commercial jingles is approximately

    a. 25 percent   b. 46 percent   c. 62 percent

2. The approximate number of commercial messages the average twelve-year-old has seen is
   a. 50,000   b. 100,000   c. 300,000

3. Television can generate stress in children resulting from confusion or fear.
   True   False

4. Television has been criticized for contributing little to a child's gross motor development.
   True   False

5. Teachers are complaining that television doesn't provide children with an opportunity to develop verbal ability.
   True   False

6. Preschool children have been injured attempting to imitate "superhero" feats seen on television.
   True   False

7. Teachers report that students' attention spans seem to be getting shorter.
   True   False

8. Television viewing is most heavy during the month of
   a. February   b. September   c. August

9. The average preschool child watches television how many hours per week?
   a. 14   b. 28   c. Over 40

10. Upon graduation from high school the average student will have spent 11,000 hours in classrooms. How many hours will that student have spent watching television?
    a. 5,500   b. 11,000   c. Over 15,000

11. The percentage of cartoons on Saturday morning network programming is approximately
    a. 25 percent   b. 40 percent   c. 90 percent

12. Which two of the following products are most often advertised on programs designed for children?
    a. Peanut butter   b. Toys   c. Fruit
    d. Sporting goods   e. Cereals

ANSWERS

1. c	5. True	9. c
2. c	6. True	10. c
3. True	7. True	11. b
4. True	8. a	12. b and e

SCORING: Give yourself ten points for each correct answer.

INTERPRETATION:

120	**Genius**
110	**Above average**
100	**Average**
90	**Slightly below average**
80 or below	**So maybe you don't watch TV.**

Most parents recognize the good and bad in television. There is no doubt that a number of programs are of excellent quality and can stimulate children's curiosity and expand their knowledge as well as entertain. The problem seems to be that parents do not limit viewing to this type of programming, and children spend hours watching shows that contribute nothing to their development.

Unfortunately, when children watch television, they usually do little else. They don't move about—except to change the channel or tuning—they don't talk, and they don't interact with other individuals. In other words, the time spent in front of the television is not contributing to gross or fine motor development, verbal ability, or social skills. Children learn best through firsthand experiences, but everything on TV is secondhand. A few experts have even criticized television for contributing to the problem of hyperactivity with the constant changing of cameras and scenes. They theorize that young children become so accustomed to having concentration interrupted every few seconds that they attempt to duplicate the sensation with their own hyperactivity.

In addition to the poor motor skills, inadequate verbal ability, and difficulty with social interaction, students are reported by classroom teachers as having unsatisfactory listening skills. Despite the fact that they spend hours listening to the television set, the level of programming that youngsters prefer (situation comedies, cartoons, quiz shows as well as frequent reruns) does not encourage children to listen carefully and precisely. Preschool teachers have also reported that many children don't seem to know how to structure their own play activities. Teachers in all grades are often surprised at how late children stay up watching television on school nights. Homework often takes a backseat to viewing and ends up sloppily done or not done at all.

How Do You Catch the Gimme-gimmes?

The "gimme-gimmes" is a common childhood ailment, which if left uncontrolled, can remain with an individual into adulthood.

It is characterized by a desire for an endless number of products and a demand for immediate gratification. Once the need for an item is perceived, there is an impulse to run out and satisfy that need. The need, however, is usually artificially created—rather than natural. Commercials and advertisements tell us that we need their product to cope with life. We may need a pill to feel better, a drink to relax, or a toy to have fun. As a result, we begin to believe that we must look beyond ourselves for products to help us cope, and the well-being of the self-image becomes linked to the satisfaction of mass-produced standardized needs. The gimme-gimmes are a source of tension between parent and child. In addition, a frustrated child who finds he or she can't make a toy do the things it did on the commercial may be angry at the parent for buying the item, rather than at the ad for misrepresentation.

Television has managed to reach the children's market in a way salespeople, magazines, or newspapers can't. The local sponsor's cost per thousand consumers for reaching the young audience is extremely low. These commercials are aimed at children who do not have the maturity to view them critically. Instead, the purpose seems to be to persuade the child to pressure the parent into making the purchase. Advertisements portray a materialistic society and create wants and artificial needs. Any parent who has been nagged to buy a box of cereal to get the prize inside can attest to their effectiveness. Commercials create stress associated with the threat that if the need is not satisfied, an individual's well-being is jeopardized. A parent who simply doesn't have the money to buy a child an item can feel inadequacy or guilt.

Viewing and Values

Some people believe that television violence can confuse a child's values. Brutality and death are viewed so often that they lose their emotional wallop. If, as one study suggested, the average four-teen-year-old has seen 11,000 murders, how upset can we expect the child to become at murder 11,001? Victims recover miraculously from serious injuries and near-fatal accidents. They may even die one evening and reappear the next. Considering the constant exposure to violence, it is no wonder many children take it for granted—as the way society copes.

Television sex has become more explicit in recent years. Children are indoctrinated into promiscuity and the notion that to be attractive and "sexy" should be their ultimate goal. The stereotypes portrayed on television are rarely encountered in the real world. However, many children spend a lifetime wishing they could look like one of Charlie's Angels and have a family like the Brady Bunch.

Put Your Family on a TV Diet

Addiction to television is not unlike addiction to food. Both are a means of immediate pleasure and escape. Your first step in dieting is to realize that, like food, too much television is unhealthy. Next, although television may have gradually been gaining ground and influence in your home, understand that you are still the parent and have the power to change the situation. Any diet is difficult at first. When you begin to limit viewing, to guide program selections, or to refuse to purchase any more products hyped on Saturday morning, you can expect resistance. Once you control the electronic baby-sitter, you will also find you are spending more time with your children and less money on junk.

THE FAMILY TV DIET PLAN

Day 1   Discuss the diet plan and resulting daily decrease in television intake. Agree to cut back on viewing.

Day 2   Review the weekly schedule, and mutually determine those programs most intellectually nourishing. Implement your efforts to decrease daily television intake by watching only high-quality shows.

Day 3   Continue efforts to reduce TV portions, and stick to a nourishing diet. Add a program of daily mental exercise. The following exercises are recommended:

Discuss programming. Follow up on new concepts or ideas.

Talk about how the program made viewers feel. Upset, happy, angry?

Analyze commercials and their appeal, and vow not to purchase junk.

Identify the differences among the real world, the world of television, and all-out fantasy.

Be on the alert for violence, and realistically question how it might affect a real person and the family.

> Discuss whether or not the characters on TV are like people in real life.

Day 4 and thereafter
Continue with the plan, as you did on Day 3. After turning off the set, follow up with activities centering around:

> Reading—parent to child, child to parent, or independently.

> A hobby.

> A walk or bike ride.

> Board games.

> Records of old radio dramas.

> Physical exercise.

> A community activity offering.

> Playing with friends. (Discourage or limit viewing when guests visit.)

You will notice that this diet does *not* call for a specific number of viewing hours per day—*and no more*. It does not dictate acceptable programs, but calls for mutual decision making. It has been my experience that rigid demands rarely work for long, and that "forbidden" programs become that much more appealing. The simple objective is to reduce viewing time each day from its previously large portions and to improve the quality of programs you do select. Be sure you know what your children are watching and join them, if possible—so you can follow up with discussions. Credit yourself with success if you are able to break your child's habit of turning on television with near reflex-action. Don't expect to revolutionize your family overnight.

The Great Melting Pot or the Great Stew?

Philosopher René Descartes wrote, "The chief cause of human errors is to be found in the prejudices picked up in childhood." Few children under the age of three even notice racial or ethnic differences. However, from the age of four on, children learn prejudicial attitudes and behaviors as part of their value system.

I believe that the common reference to our country as the "great melting pot" overlooks the fact that we are actually still a very multicultural, pluralistic society. It might be more accurate to refer to the United States as the "great stew," in which people blend together while maintaining some distinct characteristics. Your child will undoubtedly attend school, work, or otherwise interact with individuals representing a wide cross section of humanity. If the child has inherited a value system that includes prejudice, these relationships will be stressful, since the child will approach the various racial and ethnic groups with hostility. This hostility makes the child feel uncomfortable, insecure, mistrusting, or apprehensive.

I would not be so foolish as to suggest that all parents reading this book can immediately rid themselves of attitudes and bias held since childhood. I am suggesting that you consider the stress you will inevitably place on your child by indoctrination to your way of thinking. You force the child to cope with unnecessary conflict, which is not even of his or her own making. What can be done? Realistically, you can accept the fact that you are prejudiced and clearly define your areas of bias. By facing your prejudices squarely, you can make an active effort to avoid passing them on to your children. While an occasional negative attitude may surface, your efforts will certainly contribute to a higher level of tolerance and acceptance than you learned as a child. You can also help your child understand different cultures by visiting ethnic festivals, food-tasting fairs, and the old neighborhoods in your area.

War and Nuclear Threat

Children know about war. They read about it in history and see it on television and in movies. They play games with tanks, soldiers, guns, and various types of ray guns. In one study over half the children questioned stated they felt war was sometimes needed. Children accept the prospect of a war in the future, and their involvement in it, as a very real possibility. In the early sixties children became more aware of the threat of nuclear war. Adults can sense the heavy weight these children carry when the children ask, "If America gets in a big war, will it be the end of the world?" Some children carry a mental image of a forboding foreign leader with the power to push "the button." In fact, in one depressing study, children were asked about the world in the future. Although no mention of war was made by the questioner, seventy percent of the children brought up the threat of nuclear destruction, with many indicating they thought we had a fifty-fifty chance of survival. Some children have expressed uneasiness at the possibility of surviving a nuclear holocaust, only to find this planet uninhabitable. They fear having to move somewhere in space to live the rest of their lives.

Children face the stress of war with few mechanisms for coping. Like adults, they feel helpless. After all, how can they stop a war? Most can't comprehend the causes and matter-of-factly ask, "If so many people get killed, why don't the bosses just get together and stop the war?"—a question most parents can't answer.

The idea of the total devastation of nuclear war is difficult for children to handle. The age of your child will determine, for example, the amount of detail you should use in discussions of fall-out. In general, you can help your child cope if you:

1. Provide a secure home environment and as much reassurance as you can that the likelihood of nuclear war is remote.
2. Encourage your child to ask questions and openly express fears. (The cause of most of their fears is that old standby, separation anxiety. They are afraid they will lose Mom and Dad and be left with no one to provide care.)
3. Don't overexplain or go into grisly details about the effects of fallout or nuclear destruction. Monitor movie and television viewing.
4. Correct misunderstandings. For example, a child might fear a nuclear war as the result of a rather minor international incident.
5. Foster feelings of brotherhood, rather than condemning entire groups or countries. An atmosphere of hatred is stress-producing in itself.
6. Realize that you are an important model for your child. Don't go on about how the world is coming to an end, or how we'll all end up destroying each other. If you say things like that, expect your child to believe them and react accordingly.

A Stake in the Future

Children today are more concerned with the environment than their parents were as children—and with good reason. They sense that if we aren't careful, the world of tomorrow won't be worth inheriting. Water pollution is killing fish and wildlife, destroying beautiful beaches, and rendering portions of our water supply unfit to drink. Every day we fill the air with hundreds of different types of pollutants. Carbon dioxide, hydrocarbons, sulfur dioxide, nitrogen dioxide, and dust fill the air. Air pollution causes headaches, breathing problems, nausea, or vision problems. We are also running out of space. We are a nation of consumers and regularly replace clothes, cars, cans, and any number of other items. Disposing of these discarded items is becoming a real problem. In addition, we must worry about sewage disposal and radioactive waste, and everyone knows energy is in short supply. In some schools, children even participate in nuclear accident drills.

The schools have done an excellent job of making children aware of the problems. Students are genuinely concerned about the environment, but feel helpless to protect it. Children do have the power to make a difference, but concern for the environment is often merely a classroom exercise. Follow-up in the home, becoming constructively involved, makes the lesson meaningful. Show your children that you care by discussions and in practice.

When it comes to air pollution, don't burn trash or leaves. Avoid buying products in aerosol cans whenever possible. Don't smoke and report pollution to the proper authorities.

Encourage your children to notice signs of water pollution and to report them. Observe laws regarding water pollution; for example, don't dump your garbage or cans into the water when boating. Get involved with your child in working with volunteer groups to support clean-water legislation and clean-up campaigns. Even the youngest child can understand that you can save water by using less at bath time or by not flushing the toilet unnecessarily.

Help the whole family become conservation-conscious. Find new, creative uses for junk. Try to buy soft drinks in the reusable bottles, rather than in cans or throw-away bottles. Don't waste paper (it has two sides!). Save plastic bags and foil for reuse, and try not to use as much toilet paper or so many paper towels. If your community has a recycling center, collect newspapers or aluminum cans. Shop for toys and books at garage sales, rummage sales, or thrift shops.

Protecting the environment is a challenge. Remember that the example you set for your children says something. If you waste resources, disconnect the pollution-control devices on your car, or foul the water with the waste from your boat, you are sending your child a message. In effect, you're saying, "I don't care what's left for you."

The following "Energy Audit," which appears in *Al Ubell's Energy-Saving Guide,*[6] can help make your child more aware of the cost of being energy-careless. If your child is in the second grade or beyond, let him or her be your family's energy auditor by completing the inventory below. You might have to help with some of the items, but the very process of completing the form will make the child more energy-wise. Remember, doing something about a stressful situation helps to relieve the stress. Guide your child toward constructive behavior.

YOUR ENERGY AUDIT

HEATING

Usual thermostat setting:

Winter Day	Possible Points	Your Score
74°F	0	____
73	3	____
72	6	____
71	9	____
70	12	____
69	15	____
68	18	____
67	21	____
66	24	____
Winter Night		
65°F	15	____
64	18	____
63	21	____
62	24	____
61	27	____
60	30	____

You use an electric blanket to allow you to lower thermostat at night	6	____
You wear two sweaters indoors so you can lower thermostat during the day	9	____
You've installed an automatic flue damper	30	____
Your heating system has been serviced within the last six months	15	____
You change or clean your heating system filters every month	3	____
Your heating ducts have no leaks, or leaks have been taped	4	____
All heating ducts or steam pipes are insulated	4	____
Your oil burner burns without smoke or signs of carbon on its surfaces	9	____
You have a working draft adjuster in your oil burner	9	____

	Possible Points	Your Score
Your gas burner burns with a clear, blue flame	9	____
Your gas burner has an electronic ignition system, not a pilot light	10	____
Your oil burner is a new one with a retention head	30	____
You use a humidifier during the winter	9	____
Your radiators or air supply registers are not blocked by drapes or furniture and are clean	27	____
You close off rooms not in use and turn off the heat in them	25	____
You keep your fireplace damper shut, or you have glass fireplace doors	25	____
On winter days you open your drapes on the south side of the house and close them at night to take advantage of radiant heat from the sun	10	____

INSULATION

	Possible Points	Your Score
Attic insulation		
None	−15	____
2″ or R-4	0	____
4″ or R-11	15	____
6″ or R-19	30	____
8″ or R-24	45	____
10″ or R-30	60	____
12″ or R-38	75	____
All your insulation has vapor barriers	15	____
Your attic door is insulated	6	____
Insulation in your exterior walls:		
None	−6	____
3″ or R-11	25	____
Insulation in crawlspaces		
None	0	____
6″ or R-19	30	____
Your attic and crawlspace are ventilated	15	____
No basement crawlspace	30	____

	Possible Points	Your Score
All outlets and switch plates are insulated	6	____
Your foundation wall is insulated	30	____
Vapor barrier on foundation wall	9	____
You have storm windows	25	____
You have storm doors or a vestibule	15	____

WINDOWS AND DOORS

	Possible Points	Your Score
Your windows are not drafty	30	____
Your doors are not drafty	15	____
Cracks at doors, windows and where wood and masonry meet are caulked	30	____
All window glass has full putty	15	____
Broken windows (deduct for each)	−9	____
Double-glazed windows	25	____

WATER HEATING AND USAGE

	Possible Points	Your Score
Water heater insulated	**15**	____
You've set your water heater temperature at:		
110°F	12	____
120	9	____
130	6	____
140	3	____
150	0	____
160	−3	____
170	−6	____
180	−9	____
You drain sediment from water heater every month	5	____
You've installed solar water heater	44	____

AIR CONDITIONING AND VENTILATION

	Possible Points	Your Score
Your air-conditioning thermostat is set at:		
74°F	0	____
75	3	____
76	6	____

	Possible Points	Your Score
77	9	____
78	15	____
79	15	____
80	18	____
No air conditioning	20	____
You use natural ventilation and wear light-weight clothes in summer	5	____
You close drapes on hot, sunny days	5	____
You close windows and doors on hottest days	5	____
Your air conditioners all have 8 or higher EER (Energy Efficiency Ratios)	9	____
Central System	9	____
Window units—per unit	1.5	____
Your air-conditioning units are shaded or on north side of house		
Central unit	5	____
Window units—per unit	1	____
You have an attic ventilation fan	15	____

LIGHTING

	Possible Points	Your Score
You've installed fluorescent lights in kitchen	15	____
All closet lights on auto-switch or timer switches	8	____
You replace multiple low-watt bulbs with single high-watt bulbs for same light value but lower total wattage	9	____
You habitually turn off lights when leaving a room	15	____
You have energy-saving (solid state) dimmer switches (per switch)	5	____

TELEVISION

	Possible Points	Your Score
Instant-on TV sets (deduct per set)	−5	____
You turn off TV and hi-fi when not in use	15	____
You fall asleep with TV on	−30	____

	Possible Points	Your Score

THE KITCHEN

Your refrigerator is in a cool spot	5	____
The EER of your refrigerator is above 7	9	____
You close the refrigerator door quickly, rather than dawdle	5	____
You have a manual-defrost refrigerator	10	____
You defrost it regularly	5	____
You clean the back of the refrigerator	5	____
The refrigerator door gasket fits tightly	9	____
You air-dry dishes rather than use your dishwasher drying cycle	6	____
You have a flow restrictor in your kitchen faucet	6	____
Your gas range has an electronic ignition system, rather than a pilot light	29	____
All the gas burners have a clean, blue flame	15	____

THE LAUNDRY

You wash with cold water	9	____
You use a clothesline, rather than your dryer	9	____
You turn off the iron when you're not using it	9	____
You forget to turn off the iron	−18	____

THE BATHROOM

You shower rather than bathe	15	____
You have a flow restrictor in your shower	6	____
You fix leaky faucets promptly	15	____

OUTSIDE THE HOUSE

Trees and shrubs are placed to allow sun in winter, block wind in cold weather, but shade house in summer	40	____

	Possible Points	Your Score

BONUSES

Installing a clock thermostat with day and night settings	15	____
Installing a clock thermostat with double set-back capacity	20	____
Installing a heat producing greenhouse on the south side of the house	44	____
Installing an energy monitor	45	____
Installing a wood-burning stove (if wood is inexpensive in your area)	55	____
Installing a windmill, solar heating and/or cooling, or any other renewable energy source	150	____

Possible total: approx. 1350*

Your total

HOW WELL DID YOU SCORE

If your score was	Here's how much you can save on your energy costs
0–99	50 to 75 percent
100–199	45 to 70 percent
200–299	40 to 65 percent
300–399	35 to 60 percent
400–499	30 to 55 percent
500–599	25 to 50 percent
600–699	20 to 45 percent
700–799	15 to 40 percent
800–899	10 to 35 percent
900–999	5 to 30 percent
1000 or more	You win a gold star! You've gone about as far as you can go.

*Possible total will vary from house to house, since points are given for gas furnaces which oil-heated houses won't qualify for and vice versa

A Nation on the Move

Americans just don't stay put. The refinement of modern transportation has contributed to the decline in our sense of community. Parents work miles from home and may shop in a new plaza far removed from the neighborhood. Many adults have more friends scattered throughout the metropolitan area than they have on the block. Relatives may also be spread far and wide. In addition, families relocate frequently. At least one in five moves each year.

Our national mobility has brought about a decline in the sense of security and belonging we once associated with our neighborhood. The community is no longer a prime source of support in times of stress, and conversely, we don't feel particularly responsible to our community. In fact, the composition of the neighborhood may change so often that you hardly get acquainted before you find you have new neighbors.

Adult transiency affects children. Some youngsters worry because their parents work all day so far from home. They miss their relatives in distant cities, or have never really gotten to know them. They aren't able to turn to neighbors in times of stress, because they don't know them. You can help your child by becoming more involved yourself. Find that hard-core group of citizens who are generally interested in the community, and offer your services. Enroll your child in clubs or organizations. If you see a child playing outside, find out where he or she lives and help your child make friends.

Moving is a big stressor for children, and even if you don't move, the departure of a dear friend can prove heartbreaking for your child.

If you do plan a move, sit down and spend some time explaining the matter to your child. Some children just pick up on bits and pieces of overheard information and are never extended the courtesy of an official explanation. Obviously, the timing of your announcement is important. Don't select a time when the child is already under stress. Bedtime may seem like a cozy time. However, many children feel more vulnerable and insecure at night. Next, try to understand how the child feels. Ask questions, and rephrase the child's statements so she or he knows that you do understand. Acknowledge the many insignificant, but very special parts of the environment the child hates to leave (like the big tree in the yard or hill at the end of the road). Tell your child it is perfectly natural to be afraid, and that yes, friends will certainly be missed. Let your child help you accumulate boxes and participate in the packing. *Don't* insist that the child pack up a favorite toy or security object or discard a lot of personal belongings. Toys and other souvenirs from earlier stages of development provide a sense of comfort. There are a number of children's books that can help prepare your child for the move. You can also talk about the new friends and nice places to discover at the next house. Discuss when you will move and how the move will be accomplished. Some children like to make a scrapbook of photographs to take with them. In summary, the two key ideas in handling a move are discussion and participation.

New School

Transferring to a new school is often a source of stress for children, particularly if the move is made once the school year is already in session. Not only is the child saddened at the loss of many old friends, but the process of adjusting to a new home in a strange community must be faced.

While you can assist in making the adjustment, you cannot make it for the child. For example, if you walk or drive the child to school each day, you are not helping matters and you may invite peer ridicule. Take extra time with your child to provide a warm, secure, loving home atmosphere and actively listen to the reports of the child's day. Discuss feelings and emotions. If possible, try to make connections with at least one new friend before the first day of school. In some cases the counselor, principal, or teacher may provide the child with a "buddy" for a few days to help the child get acquainted.

If your child resists jumping into the mainstream, don't overreact. Some children are satisfied with making one or two close friendships at a time. If the child doesn't seem to be making any friends, perhaps you can invite some of the local children for lunch or to go on an outing. Enrollment in youth activities in which everyone is new to the program puts your child on an equal footing and provides opportunities for social interaction. However, suggest—don't push, or you will only increase stress levels.

A few children may develop a school phobia, particularly if they are shy to begin with. If your child is unhappy, seems to dread school, or feigns illness, look out for trouble. Sympathetic parents sometimes encourage the phobia by allowing the child to stay in the safety of the home. Obviously, this temporary relief from stress only impedes adjustment.

If your child fears school, consider the causes. Have you transmitted your stress to the child with words, facial expressions, or body language? Perhaps you are suffering from separation anxiety, as well. Have you given your child an opportunity to practice independence, or have you smothered the child with overprotectiveness? Are there some real reasons to fear school? Maybe the teacher is unduly harsh or the other children engage in teasing or bullying. These abuses cannot be tolerated, and you should complain. If the problem does not improve, or gets even worse, consider transferring your child. Some children hate to leave home because they feel they are needed there. For example, six-year-old Benjy kept refusing to attend school for about a month before his mother was scheduled to have a baby. He was afraid she would go into labor with no one there to help her. In other cases a history of school failure has conditioned the child to hate school.

Whatever the cause, all children must go to school. You can ease the stress by facilitating your child's adjustment. Get to the root of the problem by discussing the matter with your child and the teacher. Make it clear that getting an education is very important and that the child has no choice in the matter. Visit the new school before the first day, and make it an exciting event by involving the child in shopping for new clothes or school supplies. Make sure the time before school is unrushed, and try to be available after school until the problem subsides.

It's a Small World, After All

Firsthand experiences rank above all else in promoting learning. Travel is one of the best sources of knowledge, and more and more families are doing it these days. But it can be stressful for parent and child alike. Following are a few suggestions for making your trips together less taxing:

1. Involve your child in planning the trip.
2. Learn about the sites, history, or language of the area before you go.
3. Board the plane, bus, train, car, or boat with a collection of activities to keep the child entertained.
4. Dress the child in comfortable clothes.
5. Pack a supply of medicines your child *just might* need.
6. Plan activities appropriate for children, and don't program too much into one day. Let your child participate in the planning.

7. Take time to stop at parks or playgrounds, and allow your child to play with other children.

8. Get your child a small notebook to use as a journal.

9. Let your child begin a collection of mugs, figurines, or other typical souvenir items, so there will be a specific purpose to browsing in shops.

10. Let your child help pack and select the clothes to wear each day.

11. Plan nightly room parties so your child can unwind.

12. Find a hotel or motel with a swimming pool.

13. Encourage your child to collect postcards of the places you've been.

14. After you are home, have your child make a trip scrapbook with postcards, snapshots, ticket stubs, and so on.

15. Use the trip as an opportunity to teach new words, concepts, map-reading skills, or to practice a hobby, such as bird identification or photography.

16. Use time in transit to teach the child a new skill (like knitting) or for discussions.

17. If you are using a common carrier, advise them you will be traveling with a child. If your child is small, request permission to board in advance of the other passengers.

18. Find out in advance if the hotel/motel has cribs.

If you are not taking your child with you on a trip, discuss your plans, as well as the child care arrangements in depth. Phone as often as possible and promise your child a special gift upon your return.

Crisis Coping

Every human being experience crises. The first exposure may be during childhood. During a crisis, stress levels reach a high. Panic is the first reaction in many people. During panic the physical symptoms of stress are dramatically apparent. The body is in a highly aroused state, although the person may actually be paralyzed with fear.

When any family member is facing a crisis, the reaction usually spreads rapidly to all other members. For example, if one of the parents faces unemployment, layoff, or reduced work week, the children will hear the parents worriedly discussing their financial condition and usually react adversely. If your family has financial problems, discuss the matter as a group. Children accept financial restraints more readily when they realize the reasons for them. In addition, if they do hear you talking, they will probably jump to conclusions and think the situation is worse than it actually is. Family problems can help your child develop important coping skills. Show your child you respect his or her ability to understand the problem. Get it out in the open and reduce stress for everyone concerned. Remember that your reaction to the crisis will be a model for the child.

In addition to personal crisis, children are bombarded by the media accounts of societal crisis. For example, crime is on the increase, and virtually everyone knows someone who has had a burglary or robbery, or otherwise been the victim of crime. Children are basically trusting, and the firsthand realization that people do commit crimes in real life, and not just on television or in the movies, is stress-producing. It may be difficult for you to reassure your child when you are experiencing identical fears, but again your model of calm coping can help steady the child. If you have a burglary or are otherwise victimized, talk out the feelings of anger, fear, and humiliation.

A crisis is truly the test of fire when it comes to coping. Children who are able to look back and see they were effective in handling their stress come away from the crisis stronger than ever. The following pointers may help your child:

1. When facing a crisis, your first reaction is usually your worst. Panic will only prolong the stress reaction and does nothing to resolve the situation.

2. You must ultimately cope with any crisis. You can't avoid it.

3. Coping usually takes the form of some type of adaptation, or change.

4. In deciding on a course of action follow the steps suggested in the earlier section entitled "Opting to Choose (see p. 233)." Carefully consider each option for coping with the crisis.

5. Deal with resolving one crisis at a time, rather than becoming confused by simultaneously anguishing over several at once.

6. Try to move through the crisis as quickly as possible, arriving at a carefully conceived coping plan and implementing it. Don't listen to rumors.

7. Realize that people differ in their reaction to a crisis. If you are already under high levels of stress, your reaction will be more severe than if you were unstressed prior to the crisis. Facing a number of crises simultaneously is extremely difficult.

8. Realize that your attitude will largely determinine your reaction. Try to accept the challenge, rather than becoming overwhelmed by it.

9. Use the stress-management techniques in the final chapter to control your reaction.

10. Get support and help!

Growing Up in a Pressure Cooker

People have always faced stressors generated by the times in which they lived. Consider the words of Abraham Lincoln: ''We live in the midst of alarms; anxiety beclouds the future; we expect some new disaster with each newspaper we read.'' However, at no time in history has stress proven the threat to health and well-being it does today.

Family and societal changes have altered the very nature of childhood. Improvement in media technology bring vivid accounts of world disasters into the living room, often overdramatized or sensationalized. Children as young as five years old are aware of and frightened by the news. Their egocentric nature results in an internalization of the threatening events, resulting in an almost non-stop, subconscious sense of danger. For example, during the hostage crisis in Iran, my own daughter asked me if our trip to New York brought us anywhere near the Ayatollah. Older children frequently ask questions about the likelihood of a Communist take-over.

Despite their increased vulnerability to stress, we seem to be expecting more from children at earlier ages. We assume wisdom and maturity that isn't there. Yet, we often aren't available to provide it, and children today encounter paradoxical adult models, particularly in the areas of drug use, sex, violence, and honesty. In fact, some parents seem intent in modeling their behavior after the children's—setting aside responsibility in favor of immediate gratification of personal wants. Our children are trying to cope with the stresses of childhood in a society marked by indifference, detachment, and lack of concern for others. They rely on television as one of their prime sources of information, entertainment, and companionship.

Modern youths are seeking coping assistance from psychiatrists, psychologists, counselors, and therapists. They are turning to alcohol and drugs for relief from stress. Since 1958 we have seen the suicide rate triple among children.

What does it all mean? Maybe the current slang of children can offer a clue. We all know that young people of any generation have their own vocabulary. In modern childrenese, *bad* can mean good, *ex* obviously stands for excellent, and *boss* is tops. But perhaps the latest term to be introduced is the most significant. *Decent* has come to mean great, and maybe it's because children think that a decent chance at a decent life is great.

Chapter Nine

Heart to Heart

George Bernard Shaw wrote, "Beware of false knowledge; it is more dangerous than ignorance." From the moment of birth children begin their search for knowledge. First, they try to figure out their own bodies and how they work. They also strive to understand the people and things in their immediate environment. Infants quickly learn the power of crying and use ingenious techniques for overcoming their physical helplessness. As children grow and mature, the quest for knowledge continues. Every stage of development creates new horizons, where children discover added dimensions of their ignorance. The process of learning continues throughout childhood, indeed, throughout life. The knowledge gained provides children with the information for dealing with life and planning for the future. Childhood is a time to find out, and children will get answers to their questions—with or without parental assistance. They pick up bits and pieces of information wherever or from whomever they can. And today, their source is often television, which has become a great influence in our children's lives.

Are You a Cowbird or an Ostrich?

The cowbird is a lazy bird. It lays its eggs in the nest of another bird and then flies away—leaving the nest's owner to raise her babies. Some parents are like the cowbird. When it comes to explaining delicate subjects to their children, they prefer to leave the job to teachers, books, media, friends, or clergy. Or like the ostrich, they bury their heads in the sand and wait for someone else to explain such crucial concerns as sex, drugs, pornography, or senility. From the first time your child turns to you for answers, it is imperative you provide them. If you do not, they will rely on television and other questionable sources and their natural curiosity may turn to fear and stress. But don't be like some well-meaning parents and go overboard. Listen carefully to the exact nature of the question, consider the level of the child, and provide the information requested. I am reminded of an old joke, in which a boy goes to his mother and asks, "Where did I come from?" The mother becomes visibly upset and sends the child to his father, who proceeds to explain about the birds and bees. As the boy leaves the den and walks past his mother, she asks, "Well, did Dad answer your questions?" Her son responds: "Not really, Mom. Bobby came from Philadelphia, and I was just wondering where I came from." Your answers should match the interest and comprehension level of the child. If a very young child asks, "Where do babies come from?" the best answer may be simply, "They grow inside their mother." Later, as the child matures and seeks more precise information, more details can be given.

If you furnish false information, you will soon lose your child's trust and confidence. The child won't come to you with important questions, but will instead rely on questionable sources for answers. It is also possible to promote undue curiosity, magnified importance, or an aura of intrigue by refusing to deal with some questions. Responding with "Wait until you're older" or "That's for grown-ups to know—mind your own business!" only intensifies the child's search for information. Last, if you project negative attitudes by appearing disgusted or offended by inquiries, your child's adult adjustment can be marked with "hang-ups." So when children ask a question, be sure to analyze just exactly what is being asked and how you feel about answering. You may find that there is more to the child's question—or your answer—than meets the eye. (As when the child asks if you'd like to get married again, but actually means "please don't.")

A few of the more common areas in which children ultimately have questions are discussed in the pages that follow. Some of these are subjects children have always been curious about—death, for instance, or sex. Others are newer concerns, subjects that were rarely discussed in the old days—divorce, drugs, homosexuality, and the like. The suggestions provided are brief and meant to stimulate your thinking rather than prescribe a precise course of action. If you have serious concerns in any area, I recommend that you find a book dealing in depth with the subject and consult your pediatrician. You may even want to contact a child psychologist or psychiatrist for assistance. Remember, answers to questions must be highly individualized and based on your expert judgment of your child's current needs. Most importantly, use these exchanges as a time for warm communication, heart to heart.

Abortion

Children hear the word *abortion* with approximately the same regularity as they hear the term *nuclear reactor* and have about the same level of negligible understanding of both. I have heard first-graders make offhand insults by referring to one another as "abortions," or repeat jokes dealing with crude abortion procedures. As children approach adolescence, they often develop an interest in the clinical aspects, or techniques, of abortion. They get together for schoolyard symposiums and share information—some of which is bizarre. Ultimately, your child will probably ask you about it. Depending on your child's level, you should deal honestly and directly with the request. Your religious or moral background will no doubt influence your discussion. Very young children will probably be satisfied with learning that abortion ends a pregnancy. As children mature, they will become more interested in the reasons for wanting abortions and the manner in which they are performed.

Although abortion has been legalized, illegal and do-it-yourself abortions are still common. Children as young as twelve years old have terminated pregnancies. Desperate children have been known to take desperate measures in time of stress. Young girls often feel totally alone—afraid to go to parents, mistrusting of friends, and abandoned by boyfriend. To ensure that this will never happen in your family, you should begin early to establish lines of communication and demonstrate to your child that the job of a parent is to share the good and the bad times. And the time to provide accurate information is when inaccurate information is being received. Don't wait for the situation to arise. Tell your child that illegal and home-remedy abortions can result in serious infection, sterilization, or even death.

The stress potential of explaining abortion is magnified when a member of the family plans one. Children often experience disappointment, loss, and fear. Some adults choose to shelter the child from the entire matter. However, that is easier said than done. Don't underestimate your child's sensitivity. Most children have a kind of sonar that detects family tension. Couple these "bad vibes" with an overheard remark, and the child will probably come to some real or imagined conclusions.

Abortion is a serious matter, but children cannot be expected to recognize that fact until they have some information. The amount, of course, must be gauged by the level of the child.

Adoption

It is not possible here to include a comprehensive discussion of the special stresses of being adopted. There are a number of books devoted entirely to the subject. In addition, families contemplating adoption are usually provided with expert counseling services.

However, children do sometimes think they have been adopted because "real parents" would never treat their own child so poorly. And sometimes young children fear being put up for adoption. In both cases there can be temporary stress.

The subject of adoption should be dealt with honestly. It is understandable that children may wonder about their status when you consider the joking remarks made by parents, such as "Let's take him back to the orphanage" or "They really gave us a lemon when we got you."

Don't tease about adoption. It is not to be taken lightly and certainly should never be used as a threat. Your child should understand that adopted children are very special. They have been chosen by their parents. In addition, you should never encourage the use of phrases such as "real parents" or "as much as their own child." If the subject comes up, impress upon your child that adopted children are their parents" "own children," and that the parents are "real parents." The words "mother" and "father" are more closely associated with love, rather than biology.

Alcohol

Bertrand Russell wrote that "drunkenness is temporary suicide: The happiness that it brings is merely negative, a momentary cessation of unhappiness." Alcohol does provide temporary relief from stress, but as Russell points out, the effect is not sustained. Stress reappears when the liquor wears off. Nevertheless, alcohol abuse is near epidemic in our country because *it does work*—briefly—to reduce stress.

Since statistics show that one out of every twelve people in this country is an alcoholic, your child can hardly escape coming in contact with alcohol abuse. If there is an alcoholic in your family, the problem is not isolated in that individual. Alcoholism is a family problem and should be treated as such. A number of alcoholism treatment programs provide family service. Even if your family has no alcohol-related problem, you probably have a relative or close family friend who does. Your child may well experience confusion, fear, embarrassment, and stress when confronted with obvious drunkenness. Children of four or five sense that "Uncle Bill is acting crazy." As children mature, it becomes more and more obvious to them that alcohol is the cause. Youngsters are uncomfortable in the presence of drunkenness. They often don't know if they should cry or laugh, since drunks are almost always portrayed in a humorous fashion on television.

Children should be given an honest explanation of drunken behavior and be guided in viewing it as a problem without losing respect for the individual. They should not be allowed to mimic or poke fun at the person.

Recent years have witnessed an alarming increase in alcoholism in women and children. In fact, half of the alcoholics in this country are women and over one-half million are children and teenagers. In past generations parents didn't worry much about their children drinking until the teen years. However, statistics show that drinking in elementary-school-aged children is on the increase—with severe alcohol problems reported in children as young as nine years old. Today's children seem to prefer drinking to other forms of substance abuse, such as marijuana smoking or glue sniffing. (Incidentally, the average age for glue sniffing is between eight and twelve.)

Too often, children don't even have to go underground to get the stuff; they simply raid the family liquor cabinet. Eleven-year-old Wayne Richardson has been drinking since he was nine. He never has any trouble getting liquor; he just takes what he needs from the family-room bar. He fills a Thermos with vodka every morning and begins drinking before his first class. Wayne drinks throughout the day and in his room in the evening. On a few occasions his parents noticed he was drunk but let him off with a warning. One day Wayne overheard his father joking with his poker buddies: "You want another drink? You might as well have one before my kid drinks it up. You know I caught that rascal drunk, at his age?" Finally, the school took action. Wayne was frequently absent with a hangover, and his teacher noticed the symptoms of alcoholism. When the principal met with Wayne's parents, their first reaction was, "Thank God it's not drugs."

The Richardsons' attitude is prevalent among parents, who believe that since alcohol is not illegal, it is somehow safer and less serious than drugs. In reality, the opposite is true. Alcohol causes worse physical damage and withdrawal symptoms than drugs do and can be fatal if mixed with certain drugs. And the statistics on alcohol-related automobile fatalities are staggering.

Cultural factors are closely linked to alcohol use, and children tend to follow in the footsteps of their parents. Youths who drink in defiance of their parents are even more likely to develop problems than if the parents accept their drinking because, some experts theorize, stress is generated when the parents are defied. The youth finds that by drinking, the feelings of guilt and anxiety are relieved. Childhood drinking is not limited to lower socioeconomic groups. In fact, one study found that the higher the economic level, the greater the chance of alcoholism in children.

Don't wait until the wolf is at the door. Teach your child the dangers of drinking, and consider the model you set. Most children learn about drinking at home. They start drinking because they want to feel glamorous or "big," and adults and the media have shown them that alcohol is one way to accomplish these goals. They should be warned that friends may pressure them to drink in order to prove themselves or to be one of the group. Opinions vary as to whether or not parents should let their children sample alcoholic beverages at home. Some families allow children as young as five a tiny serving of wine at extra-special occasions. Their logic is that as children are naturally curious, experimenting at home takes some of the mystique out of drinking, and most children find that they don't like the taste, for the time-being, at least. Also, "kiddie cocktails" and nonalcoholic wine served to children is a questionable practice when you consider that one study found that adults will act in stereotypical ways when they merely think they're drinking alcohol—even if they're not.

The following suggestions may help you deal more effectively with the problems associated with children and alcohol. Although peers play an influential role in childhood drinking, it is the parents' example that is most important.

Don't tell the family you "need a drink" to cope.

Don't allow your children to have or to attend parties when no adult is in the home.

Don't nag a guest to have a drink after he or she has refused.

Don't be afraid to turn down a drink now and then.

Don't make jokes about being drunk, and especially about driving drunk.

Don't isolate young children from family discussions concerning alcohol.

Don't have drinking parties, rather than dinner parties.

Observe your child every day. It isn't a bad idea to keep an eye on your liquor supply, as well. If you suspect the child has a problem, seek professional help immediately. Alcoholics Anonymous provides free services.

The following list of symptoms, which was prepared as a part of a special project entitled Students and Alcohol, can alert you to the symptoms of alcohol or drug use in children:

BEHAVIORAL SYMPTOMS OF ADOLESCENT ALCOHOL/DRUG ABUSE AND ADDICTION[1]

TABLE 1—PHYSICAL

Physical Changes

1. Weight change
2. Change in complexion
3. Change in sleeping habits
4. Difficulty sleeping at night
5. Increase in visits to the nurse with complaints about stomachaches, headaches, "not feeling good" at the beginning of the week
6. Early signs of major illness
7. Alcohol/drug intoxication
8. Acute alcohol withdrawal
9. Tremors
10. Bloodshot, puffy eyes
11. Lethargy

Changes in Personal Care-Taking

1. Skipping lunch or other meals
2. Change in eating habits and diet
3. Deterioration in personal hygiene, dress and grooming, particularly at the beginning of the week
4. Wearing outdoor coats, vests, and hats in the class

TABLE II—PSYCHOLOGICAL

Impairment in Cognitive Processes

1. Distorted perceptions of social interactions and social stimuli
2. Decreased concentration
3. Decreased short-term and long-term memory
4. Blackouts

Change in Emotional Responses

1. Increased irritability if student "binges" on the weekend
2. Erratic shifts in mood
3. Overreactions to situations
4. Low frustration tolerance

Impairment in Cognitive Processes

5. Decrease in motivation; student has an "I don't care" attitude
6. Organizational ability deteriorates
7. Deterioration in judgment and problem-solving abilities
8. Increase in accidents
9. Flexibility decreases; rigidity increases
10. Distorted, illogical thinking

Personality Change

Marked observable change in personality from passive to belligerent and hostile

Change in Emotional Responses

5. Depression—observable either in withdrawal or in a high level of acting-out behavior
6. Nameless anxieties and fears
7. Nervousness and anxiety
8. Increased dependency on adults and peers to make decisions or think for them
9. Increased feelings of inferiority and inadequacy
10. Increased anger, defensiveness
11. Increased passivity
12. Denial of responsibility for actions increases

TABLE III—SOCIAL

Human Relationship Problems

1. Increased isolation; distances self from teachers, peers, family members
2. Changes in peer group
3. Increase in fighting behavior
4. Always "hangs with" same person or group, never alone
5. Increase in rowdiness, belligerence, hostility
6. Increased suspiciousness of others
7. Strained family relationships
8. Unstable peer relationships, moving from group to group
9. Evidence of impulsive,

School Performance Problems

1. Increase in alibi system, excuses and passes, forged notes, phone calls, etc.
2. Tardiness, study hall and class cutting, leaving school early, an increase in in-school absenteeism
3. Increases in out-of-school absences, particularly on Mondays and Fridays
4. Deterioration in handwriting
5. Late assignments
6. Inconsistent, sporadic task performance
7. Increase in errors, decrease in quality of work

TABLE III—SOCIAL

Human Relationship Problems

uncontrolled behavior which violates the rights of others

Community Problems

1. Apprehension by police for law violations
2. Episodes of uncontrollable behavior, resulting in property damage, theft, and physical injury

School Performance Problems

8. Class grade drops, grade point average drops
9. Academic growth slows down or stops
10. Inappropriate responses to supervision and discipline
11. Avoids detention or other disciplinary consequences
12. Avoids teachers and authority figures
13. Avoids classroom discussion
14. Sleeping in class
15. Disruptive behavior in class
16. Leaving a school-sponsored activity and then returning to it later
17. Avoids school-related activities

Child Abuse

It would be reasonable to assume that any parents concerned enough about the welfare of their child to buy this book would certainly not be a child abuser, but child abuse has many forms and sources. It is not limited to physical harm inflicted by parents. Abuse may be emotional and perpetrated by any adult or sometimes other children. Even if your family is not directly involved, abuse of a playmate can prove a painful source of stress for you and your child.

Widespread interest in child abuse is relatively recent, although evidence of abuse dates back hundreds of years. You may recall some of your own childhood friends who were often disciplined harshly or whipped with a belt, which left bruises, cuts, and welts. Neighbors may have lifted an eyebrow, but unless damage was severe, most people felt that parents had the right to determine a means of punishment.

The most common form of child abuse is sexual abuse, which is dealt with separately, later in this chapter. Second in frequency is physical abuse, which can include bruises, cuts, burns, head injuries, abdominal injuries, or broken bones. Neglect is the third type of child abuse and can be failure to meet nutritional needs, maintain a sanitary household, provide a safe environment, or care for a child's hygiene. The final type is emotional which many people fail to identify as child abuse. It always accompanies physical abuse but may occur in situations in which the child is not physically harmed or otherwise neglected. Emotional abuse leaves marks that can scar the personality long after the signs of physical abuse have disappeared.

Child abuse is certainly not isolated in poor families in underprivileged communities. I once served as a consultant for a very prestigious private school and was appalled at the reports of emotional abuse and neglect reported by faculty. Children can suffer deprivation in the richest of households.

A number of factors contribute to child abuse, but stress is an active ingredient. Most child abusers have themselves been abused as children. In fact, many abused children grow up thinking there is nothing wrong with their parents' form of discipline. In some cases the abusive parent is experiencing failure and feels helpless. Abusing a child gives a temporary sense of power. Other parents misinterpret their child's behavior. When a six-month-old baby is scalded as punishment for "deliberately wetting his pants," it is obvious that the parent doesn't have an accurate knowledge of normal child development or a realistic set of expectations. Often, child abusers are suffering frustrations ranging from economic difficulty to chronic illness to alcoholism, or are emotionally disturbed. A large number of abused children are actually very difficult children with various types of behavior problems. And some parents just find their child unattractive, disappointing, or unlovable.

Parents are not the only ones guilty of child abuse. Be alert for the signs of abuse by baby-sitters, relatives, siblings, older children, playmates, and even teachers. Tell your children to report any situation in which someone has hurt them—no matter who it is. I have seen a number of adults in child-oriented occupations who consistently abuse children emotionally or who are experts at hiding the signs of pinches or pressure applied to sensitive spots. Many children experiment with games that inflict pain, and if it will get attention, some children will even abuse themselves by falling down or banging their heads against the wall. Impress upon your child the delicacy and sanctity of the human body. Hurt and injury should never be accepted willingly, self-inflicted, or unreported.

If you suspect that a child is being abused, you should not try to take action yourself. Report the matter to your local police. You will not be held responsible if the report turns out to be inaccurate. However, don't overreact. My own personal philosophy of discipline does not include physical punishment. I have found that when I strike my child (and I have done so a few times), I am actually responding to my own stress rather than to my daughter's behavior. You can imagine my surprise when one of her teachers told me that Carly had been present during a discussion of child abuse and had announced: "I know what child abuse is. My mother abuses me." A teacher replied: "Oh, Carly, you don't know what child abuse is. Your mother wouldn't abuse you!" "Yes I do," said Carly. "It's like when she came up to me when I was watching television and kicked me." I was mortified, but I did recall playfully kicking the bottom of her shoe one day as she watched television. A kindergarten student at the time, she must have heard about someone abusing a child by kicking and pigeonholed her experience under the category of "child abuse"—not really knowing what the term meant. Although a child's report of abuse may be exaggerated, it certainly merits attention without overreaction. In addition, you can look for the following signs:

PHYSICAL ABUSE

Frequent bruises or cuts

Bruises that obviously date back to several different occasions (you can tell by noting the varying colors of the bruises)

Scratches, especially on the face

Slow or stiff movement, caused by soreness resulting from a beating

Evidence of burns resulting from cigarettes or scalding water

Imprints of objects used to beat the child (such as a belt or extension cord)

EMOTIONAL ABUSE

Constant attention seeking

Sadness or withdrawal

Loss of appetite

Overeating or use of drugs or alcohol

Failure of parents to attend school or sports events or to take an interest in academic achievement

NEGLECT

Dirty, torn, or poor-fitting clothing

Clothing that is not appropriate for the season or weather

PHYSICAL ABUSE	**NEGLECT**
Apprehension or fear; refusal of child to discuss the matter	Cuts or bruises that have not been cleaned or treated
Reluctance of parents to take the child for medical attention	Filthy home
	Unsafe home
Aggressive play behavior, in which the child may beat a smaller child or doll	Hunger—meals unprepared; no lunch sent to school
Withdrawal	Materials, supplies, equipment, or money not provided for school or social activities
Fear of adults	

Abused children not only experience stress at home, but often they are teased or insulted by friends. Children can be cruel. The neglected child is ridiculed, taunted, and becomes the class joke. Youngsters insist they will die if they have to be seated next to the unfortunate child. It gives children a feeling of protection when they are united against an isolated child. The logic is that when they're picking on him or her, they're not picking on me. However, if you have raised a child with values, your child probably knows that this conduct is wrong and extremely unkind. Spare your child the stress of guilt by nipping such behavior in the bud. Even young children are capable of understanding the golden rule: Do unto others as you would have them do unto you. They can also realize that neglect is not the fault of the child. Abused children find comfort and peace among friends who understand and care.

Death

Children have a natural, healthy curiosity about death. Yet, many parents are taken completely off guard when a child says, "Mommy, I am afraid you are going to die and leave me," or "Daddy, am I going to die?" The mere thought of a child dying, or a parent dying and leaving the child, is so stress-producing for them that many parents react with anxiety or try to avoid further discussion. The child may become more upset or frightened by the parent's reaction than by a discussion of death. If parents aren't candid on the subject, the child is forced to rely on other sources for information—namely friends and media. Many children develop a distorted view of death from television. They see an actor die on one show, only to find the performer alive and well on the next program. Television has caused some children to associate death with violence. When they are told of a death, they automatically ask, "Who killed him?"

When families face the death of someone near and dear, it is difficult to avoid the issue. At this point parents are facing double stress. Not only must they cope with their own grief, but also must explain to their children what happened. The following suggestions might help:

Don't wait for your child's life to be touched by death to deal with it. Use the natural life cycle of plants and animals to discuss the transition from birth to death.

Use the death of a small mammal or fish to teach about burial.

Accept your child's curiosity about death as natural and healthy. Don't be shocked if the child asks probing questions, such as how someone looks after death, or wants to see or touch a dead pet.

Openly discuss death. In the event of death don't hesitate to communicate your grief or sense of loss.

Encourage your child to talk about personal feelings. Explain that it is natural for children to experience a fear of death. Tell the child that you know how it feels to worry about death.

Don't offer explanations of death that confuse the child. For example, telling the child that "God took Grandma" can make the child angry with the Lord. Saying "Grandma went for a long sleep" may make the child fear bedtime. Some psychiatrists feel that telling a child, "Grandma went on a long trip," may make the child wonder why Grandma deserted them without even saying good-bye. Ultimately, the child reasons that it must be because he or she was bad.

Don't shelter your child from death. Allow the child to experience the loss and grief, and tell your child you are feeling it too. A reasonable period of mourning is important for everyone. Don't rush out and replace your child's dead pet with an adorable puppy or immediately distract the child from the sorrow of losing a loved one by arranging a vacation. I know one young lady who lost her mother at five years old. Solicitous relatives provided one diversion after another. Finally, as a teen, the guilt-ridden girl said: "I must be an awful person. You know I never even cried when my own mother died!"

Don't be upset if your young child doesn't show grief at the loss of someone close. Children under the age of six really don't comprehend the finality of death. Many young children keep the relationship alive by fantasizing, and may not understand the loss for months. In the death of a mother or father, reality only hits some children when the surviving parent begins dating again.

During times of mourning, children rarely find the comfort in religion experienced by adults. In fact, some children become confused when told: "Uncle Paul was a very good man. God took him up to heaven." They wonder how wise it is to be "good."

Realize that your child may fantasize about death by role-playing a death, discussing how he or she would cope with the death of a parent, or speculating about life in the hereafter.

Avoid being hard-boiled or overly clinical about death. Children need reassurance that the likelihood of a parent's death is remote. Oftentimes questions about death are really their way of asking, "Who will take care of me?"

Allow children of five years or older to attend funeral services if they want to, provided the service will not be extremely emotional and the child will be cared for by an adult not experiencing intense grief.

In the case of a terminal illness prepare the child by talking about the seriousness of the illness and the possibility of death.

Since young children are egocentric, make it clear that the child had nothing to do with causing a death.

Much as we'd like to, we cannot insulate our children from death. Avoiding the issue or sheltering children does not prevent them from thinking and worrying about it. In order to teach our children love and respect for life, they must begin early to develop the concept of death, fortified against stress with emotional security provided by the family.

Drugs

All drugs are harmful when taken to excess. Even if your child is small, drug abuse is something to worry about. For example, the entire Chicago area was in a state of alert when comic transfer tatoos containing L.S.D., which was absorbed through the skin,

were distributed on elementary school playgrounds. Drugs are ped-
dled daily in elementary schools throughout the nation—in wealthy,
middle-income, and poor neighborhoods. Children get started on
them out of curiosity, rebelliousness, or pressure to be one of the
group. They think drugs are a sign of maturity or of being "with
it." Drugs are also sometimes used to relieve stress.

Your child will probably mention drugs to you sometime in the
kindergarten or first grade. That first conversation should begin
your drug education program. Provide factual information. Explain
how children, teen-agers, and adults get started using drugs. Inform your child without exaggerating of the health hazards and
legal danger. Children are very sophisticated these days, and your
child, when older, may well know more about drugs than you do.
Your credibility will be lost if your child finds that you were only
using scare tactics. And if your child watches you ignore the warnings against smoking or daily pop an assortment of tranquilizers or
diet pills, your sincerity may be questioned. Children sense the
hypocrisy of those who condemn drugs while abusing cigarettes,
liquor, or prescribed medications themselves.

You cannot shelter your child from drugs. They are easily available in our society. Young children have even abused airplane glue,
paint thinner, gasoline, or the common kitchen spices, nutmeg and
mace. Be careful you don't create the impression that drugs have
wondrous powers to solve any problem. Some children grow up
looking for a pill for every physical or emotional ill. Youngsters
should be taught to respect drugs by storing them safely and only
following doctors' prescriptions.

As your child matures, watch for signs of drug abuse (see section on "Alcohol" earlier in this chapter). Know your child's
friends and be alert for any evidence of drugs or strange disap-
pearances from the medicine cabinet. I have heard of eleven-year-
olds and twelve-year-olds experimenting with large doses of any
pills they could find. Last, realize that your strongest defense against
drug abuse is based on the foundation of love you build from the
child's birth. If you have done your best to raise a well-adjusted
child and to maintain open lines of communication—relax. Nagging, preaching, or cross-examining your child won't prevent drug
use and can backfire and cause alienation, which can only contribute to the problem.

Grandparents

Grandparents are a wonderful resource, better than a shelf of
child care books, and they are an important part of the support

system both you and your child can use in times of stress. Unlike most other sources of support, grandparents usually couple their assistance with unqualified acceptance. They have already experienced the stresses of parenthood and approach children in a more relaxed manner than parents. There is no substitute for experience, and grandparents are experts in recognizing symptoms and treating the physical and emotional ills of childhood. In addition, many grandparents have more time than parents. They can afford the hours it takes to teach a child chess or to spend leisurely afternoons in the park. Best of all, most grandparents never seem too rushed to stop and listen. They have learned the importance of taking time to communicate. They have wonderful stories to share, which can make children more aware of their heritage. In some cases grandparents can provide important medical and developmental history regarding the parents that might be important in understanding a child's medical or developmental problems.

In any relationship there is bound to be friction. Relationships with grandparents can create a host of stresses. The charge most often leveled against them is that they spoil, or overindulge, the grandchildren. My position may be unpopular, but I believe that a tiny bit of "spoiling" can be extremely uplifting for the child's developing self-image. Excesses are never good, and what I am referring to is the tendency of most doting grandparents to go just a little bit overboard, indicating to the grandchildren, "I think you are very special." Most children are adaptable. They understand the differences of one household and another. If grandparents allow your children to behave differently than you do, tell the children in your house you are the boss. If you sincerely believe that grandparents are detrimentally affecting your children, express your feelings. Under the worst conditions, you may have to limit visits, but I certainly hope that doesn't happen.

Another source of stress can be the fact that grandparents raised their children in another era. Considering society's drastic changes, you may have major philosophical differences in matters such as racial equality, sex, or teaching traditional sex-roles. You should make your position clear to both your children and their grandparents. If your children pick up grandparents' attitudes that you deem undesirable, tell the children you disagree and why.

Some children have difficulty coping with elderly or ill grandparents, refusing to admit that their grandparent is aging or sick or that the situation is hopeless. In other cases children are confused about roles. They always looked to adults for care, security, and support. Suddenly the grandparent may become childlike and rely on the child. Such a change in roles may cause children to become angered or saddened at their personal loss. Fear is also generated when children face the inevitability of a grandparent's death or are called upon to provide care or service they aren't sure they can handle. These added responsibilities can result in resentment, which in turn causes guilt. I am reminded of one twelve-year-old who required therapy when his grandmother died the day after he angrily thought, "I wish she would die. She's no good to anyone, anyway." He actually loved his grandmother dearly and had the thought just briefly when she embarrassed him in front of his friends. Children are often ashamed of the childlike behavior, hygiene, or disoriented behavior of the elderly. They experience frustration when the grandparent can't hear, can't see, moves slowly, is suspicious, or complains constantly. Stress results when grandparents begin functioning as a second set of parents, often treating the child's parents as children, too. Children reason: "It's bad enough to have to answer to one set of parents. I don't owe you any explanations!" Often the grandparents are responding to their own stress. They find it impossible to watch helplessly, when every instinct tells them that the parents are making a mistake. Some parents are basically insecure and automatically reject any suggestion made by the grandparents, in an effort to prove who's boss. They adopt trendy child-rearing practices that grandparents have difficulty accepting.

There are various stressors that can cause your child to resist interaction with grandparents, moaning, complaining, and arguing when asked to visit or talk with them. Family tension results. You can help ease these stresses. First, if you are considering asking your elderly parents to move in, assess your ability to cope with the inevitable stressors. Do you get along with them? If your relationship has always been bad, there is no reason to think it will improve. Do you really want them to come, or are you acting out of a sense of guilt or responsibility? Do they want to leave their home, giving up their independence, house, friends, and life-style? How does the rest of the family—your spouse in particular—feel about the decision? Do you have the time to devote to their needs?

If you sense that grandparents are a source of stress for your child, consider the model you set. If you regard them as troublesome, your child may adopt your attitude. Do you accord them dignity or treat them like children, caretakers, household help, or baby-sitters? Have you taken the time to help your child understand how it feels to stand in their shoes, to explain the special problems of the elderly. If Grandpa continually complains of being cold and turns the thermostat to 87 degrees, tell your child that poor circulation often makes elderly people feel cold when everyone else is warm. Since the most common problem of seniors is poor hearing, instructing your child to speak in a normal voice, slowly, and directly facing the elderly person can easily eliminate some frustrations. Develop your child's admiration and respect for the grandparents by talking about their life and achievements. Don't allow your child to patronize the elderly, assume all are senile (senility affects less than ten percent of the population over sixty-five), or treat them as if they were helpless. Instead, provide guidance in finding ways your child can help the seniors cope. A child can help ease the pain experienced by a grandparent who has lost loved ones, meaningful employment, social life, and financial security by simply sharing his life. Grandparents thrive on the vitality of young people, involved in their joys as well as their sorrows. The fear of death or total dependence fades when the young care enough to include Grandpa in a joke or party or give Grandma a good-night kiss, and in helping grandparents cope your child will be coping him or her self.

Homosexuality

Despite the advent of gay rights groups, many Americans have a repulsion to homosexuality. The fear of raising a homosexual child (homophobia) is a real source of stress for many parents. In fact, many males worry about latent homosexuality at some point in their lives. Young boys in kindergarten and first grade giggle if asked to hold hands and refuse to kiss their own fathers.

If your child is over five, the child probably smirks at the word *gay,* and is familiar with terms such as *fairy, faggot,* or *sissy.* However, the child may not know the exact meaning of the words. I gasped when a most prim and proper six-year-old girl referred to one of the children on her bus stop as a "gay ball." When questioned, it became apparent she was using the term to mean "a big baby."

Despite the many theories advanced by psychologists and psychiatrists, the fact is no one knows what causes homosexuality. The explanations that suggest heredity, Oedipus complex, maternal attachment, hormone imbalance, homosexual-producing family environment, lack of father figure, or dominant mother all have flaws. Early in life anxious parents teach boys to be "masculine," while girls are urged to be "feminine." However, these stress-producing, traditional sex-role stereotypes do nothing to prevent homosexuality. No one knows for sure what can prevent it.

Many young children engage in experimental sex play, sometimes with playmates of their own sex. Of course, you will want to discourage this practice, but realize that it is quite common and doesn't mean the child has homosexual tendencies. Don't blow the situation out of proportion, creating unnecessary stress for everyone involved.

Most informed parents today discourage their children from name calling. Depending on the child's level, homosexuality and terms referring to it such as *gay, lesbian,* and *bisexual* should be explained and unkind references eliminated. Meanwhile, don't be a source of stress for yourself or your child. Homosexuality can't be worried away. Instead, concentrate on raising a happy, healthy, well-adjusted child in a secure, loving home.

Masturbation

Initially, parents worry more about masturbation than their children do. Pleasurable handling of the genitals begins in infancy. However, between the ages of three and six masturbation becomes very common. It tapers off between seven and twelve, but increases again during adolescence.

Despite the fact that many parents recognize masturbation as perfectly normal and healthy, it is often excluded from the family sex-education program. Parents will discuss reproduction, birth control, and venereal disease, but omit any mention of masturbation. While children are interested in all aspects of sex, masturbation is the subject that is most timely and relevant. It is the one component of their sexuality that is here and now.

There are many different parental attitudes toward masturbation. A few parents encourage it, others ignore it, a great many try to distract the child, and a few outright forbid it. Your level of acceptance will no doubt be linked to your upbringing and sexuality. However, you should be aware that masturbation and orgasm (which many researchers believe is experienced by some children in the first year of life) are perfectly normal means for releasing tension. In addition, all children are going to masturbate—with or without parent approval. If parents succeed in instilling feelings of guilt or making the act stressful, children will continue the activity, but do so in fear. The disapproval or disgust parents associate with masturbation can cause confusion. Children think that sex is dirty and pleasurable feelings are wrong. Even today, some children still believe that masturbation can prove harmful, cause pimples, stunt growth, or adversely affect adult intercourse.

No one can tell you exactly how to handle this matter, but I urge you to provide your children with information regarding this very real childhood concern. Tell your child that the urge to masturbate and fantasize are perfectly normal. From there the rest is up to you. Many parents just look the other way, while others tell children that even though masturbation is normal, there are better things to do with one's time. A few parents say, "Go ahead, enjoy yourself." Nearly everyone agrees on one point: Children should realize that masturbation is a private act.

Meanwhile, unless masturbating becomes a continuous activity through which the child is trying to find relief or distraction from other stresses, don't let it become a source of parent stress. Some experts think that it is a form of sexual education, in which a child learns about the body.

Nervous Breakdown

In these highly stressful times we hear more and more about nervous breakdowns. I remember telephoning a friend who had just had a fourth baby, and when I asked how she was doing, she responded: "I'm not sure. How can you tell if you're having a nervous breakdown?" Children have an even more difficult time telling when someone is having a breakdown. Although they hear the term frequently, most don't know what happens during a nervous breakdown and can be frightened as a result.

If a close friend or relative has a breakdown, don't attempt to hide the fact from your children. It is amazing how much they can understand and empathize. Tell your children that a nervous breakdown is the body's way of saying, "It's time to slow down and rest." Someone who suffers a breakdown just can't take any more pressure or cope with any more problems and needs a doctor's care. As with any illness, when the individual is ready, life will go back to normal.

Parent Sex

Parents often worry that a child might "catch" them making love. Most experts agree that intercourse should take place in private. However, should one of your children surprise you, it's not the end of the world. The best approach is to calmly ask the child to leave the room. As soon as you have yourself back together, talk to the child about what happened. Try not to react with guilt, shame, or anger. Instead, explain that being close together in bed is one way of expressing love. Many children are frightened and think parents are hurting each other. Use only as much detail as the situation requires. You may then want to set some rules to prevent recurrence of this incident.

Pornography

Much modern pornography portrays violent or coercive behavior. Men, women, and children are portrayed in degrading situations or as "victims." Nonetheless, racks of pornographic magazines are found throughout most communities—from drugstores to twenty-four-hour groceries.

The sickening pornography pervading our society troubles me. If I could, I'd shelter my child from every last bit of it. However, I realize that's impossible. Restrictions and taboos cannot curb a child's natural curiosity. If you don't show your child what pornography is all about, the child will take the first opportunity to find out. I prefer being in control of this educational experience, with the opportunity to point out that the portrayal of sex is distorted and commercialized. I have found that children who grow up in an atmosphere in which parents in effect say, "If you want to know anything about sex, just ask me," quickly become bored with pornography and go on to the more wholesome aspects of childhood.

Sex Education

Sex education is one of the most difficult jobs of parenting. It is not surprising that some parents avoid it, rationalizing that the schools have experts with special training who can do the job better. That notion is dangerous. The sex education that takes place in most schools is designed to present facts about reproduction, birth control, and venereal disease. The question of morals and values must be considered within the home setting. And it is the parents who wrestle with the difficult task of simultaneously telling children, "Sex is normal, healthy, and wonderful," and "But don't do it."

Timing is another problem. I was amused by one manual that said, "Teach your daughter about menstruation about two months before her first period." The importance of providing just the right amount of information on sex at just the right time has already been stressed. I recommend that you take advantage of experiences in daily living, such as diapering a baby, the birth of puppies, or an episode on television to stimulate discussion. If you are expecting a baby, nature has provided you with a wonderful opportunity for sex education. Depending on the level of your child, you can use this event for some very meaningful instruction. Watch for signs of stress, though, especially when it comes time to discuss the hospitalization and birth process. Older children are sometimes embarrassed by this obvious evidence of their parent's sex life. Incidentally, telling your child that babies grow in their mother's stomach is a mistake. Even the youngest child is capable of understanding that babies grow in the womb, which is right below the stomach. The thought of a tiny baby mixed up with digesting food is stress-producing.

Expect your child to be sexually curious. Most young children play doctor at some point in their childhood. Rather than lecturing or punishing your child or ignoring the whole matter, tell him or her that interest in sex is natural, and that you will be happy to answer any questions. Children often feel guilty or frightened if discovered experimenting in this way, and a discussion of moral values is highly appropriate. Most children outgrow the activity in a relatively short period of time. However, if your child has a playmate who persists in initiating this game, you may want to supervise their playtime for a while.

It is never too early to begin sex education. Sadly, studies predict that four in ten girls will become pregnant at least once during their teen-age years. The information and moral values you transmit can help your son or daughter deal responsibly with sexuality.

Last, remember that a strong self-concept is the foundation for self-respect. Much promiscuity is the result of self-contempt, rather than the new morality.

Sexual Abuse

Sexual abuse is the most common type of child abuse, affecting as many as one child in every ten. It has been reported with children as young as two years old. Friends, baby-sitters, neighbors, fathers, stepfathers, brothers, sisters, cousins, uncles, grandfathers, or total strangers might be the abuser. Seventy-seven percent of all rape victims under twelve knew their attacker. Mothers rarely engage in sexual abuse, although they may deny it happened and fail to adequately protect a child.

Sexual abuse can take the form of incest, rape, violent or non-violent molestation, and often occurs after an adult has been drinking. Many times the child is threatened and warned not to tell.

Suffering in silence, the child may never reveal what happened or may wait until after a divorce, family fight, or leaving home. Some abused children become confused adults and end up in therapy.

Sexual abuse creates fear and guilt in children. Many experience insomnia, depression, school failure, or other obvious signs of stress. Some children assume the blame and feel they are "no good."

Occasionally an older child may lie about sexual abuse. However, I urge you to take any report seriously. Younger children, in particular, don't make up this kind of story.

A single bad experience need not devastate a child—provided the child goes immediately to a parent who effectively handles the situation. I recommend that any parent faced with this traumatic stressor remain calm and promptly seek assistance. Arrange an appointment with a child psychiatrist or other specialist, and discuss the matter in the child's absence. The professional may then recommend a visit with the child.

Parent hysteria, ranting, or raving can harm the child. Don't make remarks like "Never let anyone touch you again!" An abused child must understand that what happened was wrong and the fault of the adult. If the child says he or she knew it was wrong, you should make it clear that although it was wrong for both parties, it was much more wrong for the adult who knows better, initiated the action, and should be responsible. Reassure the child despite what the molester said, telling about the incident was the right thing to do. Try to act as though you are sorry or angry that someone would do such a thing, but don't behave as if it were the absolute end of the world, which will only make the child more stressed. Tell the child you plan to report the incident so that it won't happen again, but don't be surprised if this information generates stress in a child who has been threatened with harm should the matter become public knowledge. Provide comfort, support, and understanding.

Lastly, with all the press given this subject lately, some parents have gone overboard. Fathers, in particular, are hesitant to engage in any close contact with their children, particularly their daughters. Children want and need healthy, loving relationships. Don't let any unhealthy paranoia deprive them of this closeness.

Smoking

Preschool children roll up bits of paper and pretend to smoke. When given the chance, many elementary school children will actually try smoking. Cigarettes are associated with the adult world. They are portrayed as glamorous on television and in ads.

A combination of factors makes smoking an exhilarating experience for some children. They are able to show off or be one of the group. Matches, forbidden during childhood, are another exciting contraband item. Holding a cigarette gives some children a sense of power. I once found a pack in a second grade student's desk. When I questioned the child, she said: "Honestly, I don't even want to smoke. It just makes me feel big to have a pack of cigarettes."

Presenting your child with the health hazards of smoking is a good start. However, don't expect your child to be terrified about the possibility of lung cancer in the remote, adult future—especially if the child is surrounded by adult smokers. In some cases the antismoking campaigns launched by the American Cancer Society and local school systems have successfully influenced children. Your child might be adamant about the dangers of smoking and urge you to stop. Parent stress can be generated by the child's continual nagging, particularly when the parent is already stressed by the inability to quit smoking. In this situation parents must decide if they are going to regard their child's concern as healthy and constructive, or consider it harassment and discourage further lecturing.

Venereal Diseases

Elementary school children have heard about venereal diseases and loosely associate them with sex. When you hear your child offhandedly throw around terms such as "VD" or "the clap," use this opportunity for discussion. The media has been successful in pointing out that venereal diseases are at epidemic proportions. In swapping information children sometimes exchange fantastic notions that can cause them to fear they might catch venereal disease or already have it. It may sound comical to adults, but many children suffer for months after a classmate says: "That sore is VD. I know it, my friend had a sore just like that and she had it. Did you sit on any public toilets?" Free and open lines of parent-child communication are effective in preventing this type of stress.

If You Want the Job Done Right, Do It Yourself

Growing up is tough. It becomes even tougher when children don't have accurate information or are troubled by serious concerns and don't know where to turn. In desperation many children will seek information wherever it is available—on television, in magazines, from friends, or in fragments of overheard conversations. Often, the information they receive is erroneous, confusing, or incomplete. The child's reasoning becomes too greatly affected by his or her imagination and the child increasingly operates from a base of faulty knowledge. Such knowledge can lead to stress.

When it comes to the heart-to-heart matters discussed in this chapter, if you want to guarantee that your child is receiving quality information, do the job yourself.

PART III

Control and Manage Stress

Chapter Ten

Get Your Act Together

A significant amount of childhood stress can be prevented by parents who are in control of the family life-style. Children learn by imitation. As a parent you are your child's most important teacher. You provide a model of behavior. This model covers a range of areas, including coping. Your reactions to stress, tolerance level and means for minimizing, controlling, and preventing stress are noted by the child. In addition, children are extremely susceptible to tone and atmosphere created by adults. If you are continually in a distressed state, this condition is unsettling and unnerving for the entire household. Consider seven-year-old Carol. She is the daughter of two busy, carefully scheduled parents, who used to plan their time down to the minute. If church services began at 9:00 A.M., they attempted to arrive precisely at 9:00—not a moment earlier. Usually they were right on time, but predictably the unexpected sometimes occurred and they arrived late. The parents gradually noticed a pattern of behavior and questioning emerging in their daughter. Carol asked for reassurance with queries such as "I'll get to school before all the other kids, won't I?" or "I'll have plenty of time to eat before the bus, right?" In addition, Carol often complained of stomachaches when her parents were responsible for delivering her for an appointment. Luckily, one afternoon as her mother was setting new speed records driving to ballet lessons, insight struck. Carol nervously said, "Of course, I'll be there before class starts," and her mother realized that arriving late or at the last minute was a very real source of stress for her daughter. She vowed to alter her rushed life-style whenever her daughter's schedule was concerned.

No one needs a book to tell them that a household in a state of continual confusion, clutter, and chaos creates stress. In the pages that follow are a number of practical suggestions to help you reduce stress by controlling your time and your life.

Organization: The Key to Reducing Household Stress

"I'm only one person," shrieks Kathy Conlin. "Why don't you just take a knife and cut me into little bits. Every minute of the day, someone wants something from me." Kathy's children look shocked. All Tommy did was ask his mother to sew on his latest Boy Scout patch. Tommy's father nervously sends the children to their room, nodding his head in those short shaking movements that are supposed to signal: "It's all right. Everything will be okay." He turns back to his wife and in an understanding, fatherly tone says: "Now Kathy, Tommy didn't mean to upset you. What's the matter?" Kathy really blows her top. "It's not just Tommy. It's all of you. You are no better than the kids. I never get a minute to myself. Well, I'm sick of it. When is it my turn? When does someone do something for me?" Kathy Conlin is the victim of stress, which is obviously affecting her entire family. She is, indeed, pushing herself and is unable to control her life or her time. She assigns everything in her life equal priority, from pulling weeds to helping with homework. Kathy doesn't seem to realize that you can't do everything, and until she does, she will keep trying. She has recently returned to work. However, she hasn't accompanied this change with any adaptive changes in her life-style. Around the house she tries to accomplish exactly what she used to accomplish. She doesn't recognize that finally completing all household chores is an impossibility. There is always some job that really needs to be done. Kathy doesn't know how to identify her "prime time" and use it to the best advantage. She is doing her best—but she is never satisfied because she feels her best just isn't good enough. In short, Kathy is miserable and frustrated—and becoming more so each day. Little by little her family is beginning to suffer.

As life becomes more complicated and complex, we are faced with the necessity of streamlining our activities. The following questions will help you manage more effectively. The outcome will be a smoother-running, less stressful household that should allow you increased time to spend in one-to-one interaction with your child. The techniques are designed to reduce tension, so beware of the tendency to overorganize or to become obsessed with time.

Discover Your Management Ability

Do you know the value of an hour? You only have 24 hours in a day—168 hours in a week. In addition, your child's time is limited. Simple arithmetic reveals that if you arrive home from work at six and the child goes to bed at nine, you have only three hours together. Is it worth it to you to invest in a microwave oven, spend a little extra for carry-outs, or simplify your meals in order to gain precious time? Which costs more—the price of professionally laundered shirts or the time it takes away from your family when you do them at home? Can you afford a once-a-week cleaning lady? Before you decide, ask yourself: What toll is house-cleaning taking? Is it a task you dread all week that finally costs you a full day on Saturday to complete? Do you sometimes let it slide—only to feel it nagging at you, spoiling whatever supposedly fun activity took its place? How are you and your family subtly affected when the house is a wreck? Making your own curtains, furniture, cakes, and clothing is admirable—but what is their cost in terms of time and stress, particularly if you have a completion deadline to meet? Don't overlook your child—lessons and extra-curricular activities are important. However, ask yourself if your child is so overprogrammed that stress is a threat or family time is jeopardized.

All parents are unique, but many share the common need to simplify their life-style. Personally, I wouldn't be without my dishwasher, microwave, and commercial-type pressing machine. However, cleaning the house is one of my few sources of exercise, so I don't hire a housekeeper. Once you recognize the need to free more hours, the techniques used will depend on personal priorities and budget.

"Superparents"—who needs them? Perhaps your demanding life-style has earned you the title "superparent." Have you ever stopped to consider if you or your child actually values this distinction? "Superparents" vary in their ability to handle the resulting superstress before burnout. Few experience meaningful satisfaction from their lives or children. Ask yourself, "Just what makes me tick!" If you are compelled by a need to fulfill a set of idealistic roles as parent, spouse, employee, and community member, stop to examine the validity of your perceptions. For example, do you derive gratification from your position on the library board, or do you simply feel obligated to serve? Spreading yourself too thin can result in a pressured state in which you and your child are the losers. Select your optional commitments with care. I have personally adopted a philosophy of child-centered service projects. When I donate my time, my daughter is directly involved. I would rather serve as a room mother than sit on a school board. Your biggest problem may be that you choke on the word "No." If declining seems impossible or results in guilt feelings associated with not living up to some undefined notion of your responsibilities, consider if your model for coping is one you would want your child to emulate. Also, take heart—you will find that each time you squeak out a "No," it becomes that much easier the next time.

Can you spot the time wasters? Many parents lament the fact that their children's childhood is slipping away. They can't even seem to remember important developments in their children's lives—such as learning to sit up or talk. They wish there were more time to play with a Frisbee, fly a kite, or do some kiddie cookery. Most of us can find more time once we become proficient at identifying the time wasters in our lives.

The telephone can be a tremendous time saver, but is can also be a time waster. I have found, for example, that it is much more economical, timewise, to send written invitations to large family gatherings than to phone. By the time you exchange pleasantries and catch up on the news, it can take an entire day to invite relatives you haven't seen lately—and after all, isn't socializing the purpose of the get-together? Don't be afraid to limit your calls and to tell people you are busy—it's true, isn't it? When you have telephoning to do or calls to return, plan to do all your phoning at once. Just knowing that you have a number of other people to speak to makes it more natural for you to limit duration of conversations.

Television is a notorious time waster. Just stop and think about the many enjoyable, worthwhile activities that could be substituted for TV viewing. Is there a conscious choice involved, or does your family have a daily TV routine that has turned into near reflex action?

Consider your sleeping habits. Researchers find that many people can actually function quite well on less sleep than they are accustomed to getting. If you are sleeping in excess of eight hours per night, perhaps you are one of these people. Try gradually reducing sleep by setting the alarm one-half hour earlier. If you feel fine, in a week or two set the clock another half hour earlier. Continue until you sense you are at your limit.

Everyone has friends and acquaintances who invariably contribute to time wasting. When you know you have things to do, common sense dictates that you steer clear of those time-wasting situations.

Shopping can be a source of relaxation and fun, if shared by the family at a leisurely pace. It can also be a frustrating time waster.

If you find yourself in stores nearly every day, this area is one in which you can definitely trim some time. Resist those impulse shopping trips, and try to plan meals so you need only grocery-shop once a week.

A glass of wine with dinner has become more and more common in recent years. However, many parents find that all they feel like doing after dinner is having a few more glasses of wine. Time is a precious commodity. The hours between dinner and bedtime are few, and yet they are the only family hours in most households. If you find you are not in the mood for fun, conversation, or homework after the wine you drank to relax, why not postpone your relaxation until the children are tucked in bed?

Do you have a "time converter"? Everyone has the potential to use time creatively during those inevitable minutes spent tied up in traffic, waiting in line, or sitting in the doctor's office. Rather than generate stress by anguishing over the loss of precious moments, use them. Carry a note pad and pen or reading material. Use the time to mull over a problem or develop a plan.

If you spend a large portion of your day commuting, put that time to good use. If you drive, consider listening to instructional or foreign language tapes. Some people use the time to dictate into a recording machine. If keeping up with current events is a problem, listen to a news station rather than music.

Breaks and lunch often go unrecognized as a time reserve account. Only you can judge if they are rejuvenating or merely disruptive. Some people grab a quick bite and use lunchtime for exercise, a known stress-reducer.

Your family—a wasted resource? Many parents believe that increased demands outside the home should be balanced by an equal escalation of service to the family. They feel that since the decision to become more actively involved away from home was a personal choice, it should not result in the family assuming more responsibilities. These parents pick up after their children, press clothing, and prepare meals with an air of resignation. "Juggling stress" is generated, in which the parent fears that one day one of the balls will be missed and the others will come tumbling after. The entire family is affected by the tension, and the constant juggling leaves little time for important one-to-one communication.

Your family probably wants more of you and less of the juggler. Don't cheat them by refusing to share responsibilities. They can develop a sense of importance and learn valuable homemaking skills, if given the opportunity. Delegate authority, assigning jobs like unloading the dishwasher, watering the plants, and making beds. Even toddlers can perform regular, genuinely useful jobs. However, once you initiate the program, don't be inclined to relax your standards. Give some thought to your assignments and be realistic in your expectations and criticism. Does it really matter if the bed is a little sloppy? Let the family know how much you appreciate their assistance. Some jobs might be rotated or selected by lottery (try placing slips of paper in a jar and drawing at random). Choretime can also be a time for warm, uninterrupted conversation. Ask your spouse or child to join you while you do necessary household chores.

Does haste always make waste? If you tend to be a perfectionist or a procrastinator, you might want to consider the merits of jumping headlong into a job to just get it done. The stress generated by procrastinating is usually greater than the effort it takes to put the job behind you. Perfectionists also work under self-generated pressure. In certain areas high standards are not only admirable, but appropriate. However, when standards become a compulsion, they create unnecessary tension and drain time from more important endeavors. Who really notices if the chandelier is cleaned before each and every dinner party, or actually cares if your child's valentines are printed in perfect script?

When in doubt, do you throw it out? Everyone knows that just as sure as day follows night, no sooner do you get rid of something than you need it. However, consider the alternatives. As long as you keep that seemingly useless item, it will certainly remain useless. Therefore, in the interest of streamlining, I urge you to adopt a get-tough attitude when it comes to clutter. Clutter has a number of stress-producing characteristics. First, it creates an unsettled air. In addition, it makes it difficult to locate important items, which have been absorbed by the clutter. Last, clutter is evidence that you have let things get out of hand. It lurks in closets, drawers, desks, cabinets, and various other crannies—a tangible symbol of disorganization and neglect.

Mail, advertisements, newspapers, catalogs, and magazines should be handled as few times as possible. Immediately discard junk. Most of us never seem to get back to a partially read newspaper or magazine. Assess the likelihood that you will ever find time to continue your reading. If you truly wish to finish reading something, place it in a spot where you will be most apt to pick it up. If you suspect that there will probably be three more magazines or newspapers accumulated before you get more time to read—dump it. The catalogs you save as references should be judiciously selected and stored and should cover a wide range of merchandise—rather than specialty gift items. Once you order an item from a mail-order form, your name is often placed on a mailing list, and you can literally receive scores of catalogs. Look them over and then immediately order or discard.

The "souvenir syndrome" is another prime source of clutter. Used airline tickets, old theater tickets or playbills, inexpensive novelty items, or menus can make it impossible to find really important documents. If you enjoy verifiable evidence of your pleasant trip or experience, put your memorabilia into a scrapbook soon after you get home instead of letting it clutter up your desk for years.

Do you live by lists? Set aside a regular time for making a list of the day's essential phone calls, errands, projects, and jobs. Some people make their lists a day in advance for the following day, while others compile it over morning coffee. Have it your way—but get in the habit of making a list, 365 days per year. Those days when you really don't have much to do provide you with an excellent opportunity to accomplish nagging odds and ends—such as shortening those pants, writing that long-overdue letter, or finally looking into yoga lessons. Holiday stress can be minimized with lists. Jot down the items you must take to Grandma's party or the news you want to share during that long-distance conversation with Aunt Helen.

After you have completed your list, analyze it to discover possibilities for organizing and combining. For example, set aside a special time for all telephoning, or plan to combine trips by grocery-shopping on the way home from the dry cleaner.

When you are planning a party, you might conceivably prepare four lists: a shopping list (compiled with recipes at hand), an hors d'oeuvre list, a dinner list, and a schedule for party day—which includes the exact time you must place the lasagna in the oven or pick up the cake. These lists prevent the common frustration of finding some elaborate dish you forgot to serve, arriving at the bakery ten minutes after closing, or serving dinner at 11:00 P.M. because the frozen lasagna takes four hours to bake. Save the hors d'oeuvre and dinner lists for planning your next party.

Making lists will help you control your own stress, as well as reduce the chaos and confusion you infuse into your household when you are hassled. In addition, carefully planning your day will provide you with a very precious gift to share with your child—more of your time. However, remember the purpose of lists is to reduce stress, not generate it. Guard against the beginning listmaker's tendency to overschedule. Failure to realize daily goals is certain to demoralize you unless you accept the fact that you won't always be able to complete your list.

Your calendar—do you ever leave home without it? Busy parents often place themselves in impossible situations by making plans and promises without the benefit of a detailed calendar. Purchase a pocket or purse-size version that gives one full week to a page. Carry the calendar with you *constantly,* at home, on business, or during leisure hours, and *use* it. When the school distributes its yearly calendar, take time to record free days, parties, programs, conference days, and hot-lunch days (so you won't unnecessarily send a lunch). Each business and personal commitment should be noted. Jot down warnings, such as "Quarterly Report due in one week," "Insurance due in two weeks," "Time to schedule yearly physical," or "Club—my house next week." Auto maintenance, tax deductible contributions or other expenditures, and other information should be listed. Resist the temptation to trust your memory or to casually make any appointment without first checking your book. Find more time for yourself and family by efficiently scheduling appointments back-to-back when they take you to the same vicinity. Use your calendar in daily listmaking, and save it for a permanent record of the year.

Does your home come equipped with an office? Every household needs an office. Home office space may range in size from an entire room to a small corner. It should not be confused with an area in the home in which a family member works on business, although it may be incorporated into such an area. The home office should be set up to manage household business efficiently.

Your first step is to set aside an office area with space for writing and storage of important papers. Finding this area requires a high level of creativity since few homes have available extra space. Consider constructing a space in the kitchen or family room, or converting an old armoire or buffet. Look for space under a staircase, in a closet, or at the end of a hallway—and don't stop until you have found it, even if it means getting rid of some useless piece of furniture.

Next, discipline yourself and your family to conduct all business out of the office. Create files for all important papers, and act on these papers as few times as possible in the process of completion. Resist the temptation to establish a large number of highly specific files. Instead, files should be broad in scope. For example, keep all instruction manuals and warranties in one file, keep all paper work related to the dog in another, and file all information regarding taxes in a third. Bills should be filed together for payment at the same time. An updated directory of important names, addresses, and telephone numbers should be a permanent fixture. The office should also be equipped with a large calendar, and all family members should develop the habit of noting important dates as soon as they are announced.

Office supplies such as paper clips, tape, stapler, pencil sharpener, stamps, stationery, ruler and paper will be close at hand, ultimately eliminating hours of frustrated searching. However, you will have to enforce some rules and regulations governing their use and return.

Does your child have a record? Adults are not the only ones with carefully scheduled, busy lives. Children have deadlines to meet, programs to attend, lessons to take, and games to play. Your home office should include a file for each child in the family. As the child brings home the listing of dance rehearsals, schedule for soccer games, rundown of supplies for camp, or format for book report, it should be placed in the file. Adherence to this policy can prevent your child from missing obligations and save you the frustration of rooting through the garbage for that important piece of paper your child "left sitting on the table."

When my daughter was in preschool and kindergarten, I couldn't bear to toss out her work sheets or enchanting artwork. However, by the end of first grade I had accumulated boxes of these papers. I realized that the very packaging of these priceless souvenirs of her development made it highly unlikely that anyone would ever take an interest in looking them over again. I gritted my teeth and decided to establish one notebook for each academic year—to include representative samples of her most interesting work. Special projects, creative writing, art, and selected seatwork are included. The notebook encourages her to constantly evaluate the quality of her work and calls attention to progress and growth. In addition, it is a very attractive, easily handled remembrance.

When is enough, not enough? You can greatly enhance the efficiency of your household by laying in a supply of varied extras. Begin by having several sets of keys made. I wish I had a nickel for every set of keys that were lost by a toddler at play. I actually remember getting teary-eyed and kissing a set of keys I had been desperate to find. Keep an extra set of car keys in a magnetic box somewhere on the car for those inevitable times when you lock the keys inside. (It always seems to happen in rainy or cold weather when the children are crabby.)

Purchase extra greeting cards, wrapping paper, and gifts (especially when you find an item on sale). It is a lot easier to go to your gift closet for a child's birthday present purchased during January clearance sales than to go dashing to the store at the last minute.

The technique of stocking extras can work quite well in eliminating tension and stress. However, with some items—such as stamps, socks, toilet paper, panty hose, and disposable diapers—extra is never enough.

Are you a kitchen magician? A large percentage of any mother's at-home time is probably spent in the kitchen. Therefore, kitchen streamlining can result in greater efficiency and time savings. Most kitchens are overcrowded. Examine your countertops. Does each visible item serve a regular, useful purpose? A vase with dried flowers is attractive—but is it worth the space it commands? You might not want to be without your food processor—but do you use it often enough to justify assigning it permanent counter-top status? Look inside your cabinets. Any serving pieces, pots, or pans that have not been used within the past two months could probably be moved to a storage area in the utility room or basement. How about duplicates? Realistically, just how many graters or gelatin molds can you use?

Fancy cooking can be fun and delicious. However, it is almost always time-consuming. Explore the merits of cooking simpler dishes or making double quantities and freezing so that you get two meals for close to the time it takes to prepare one.

Running out of staples and key ingredients is always frustrating. Keep an ongoing shopping list in the kitchen and add to it whenever you discover you need something. Take it when you grocery-shop and begin a new list.

Does your car handle well? A certain amount of organization can make your automobile a happier place. A set of rules for car conduct should be clearly established, understood, and enforced. If the smell of decomposing french fries or the sight of a milkshake on your upholstery is unnerving—do something about it. Make a "no eating in the car" rule. If children riding unbuckled, in the front, or seated on the armrest make you apprehensive, it's time for another rule. Even the youngest can learn that roughhouse play and fighting are absolutely unacceptable. However, you may have to pull over a few times to make this message perfectly clear.

Many unpredictable situations can be handled with a minimum of stress if your car is well-equipped. You should have a simple tool set, container with a variety of coins, scissors, first-aid kit (with bandages), and a blanket. It is not a bad idea to carry sweaters for all family members. I can recall a number of family outings to overly cool restaurants and theaters that were spoiled by complaints of "I'm cold."

Is your house in order? Death or serious illness have among the highest stress-producing capability. Although you can do little to prevent their occurrence, you can avoid compounding the stress by being prepared for an emergency. Many individuals avoid discussions that center around estate planning and wills. They consider the subject morbid. I have even encountered a few people who refuse to write a will because of a superstitious belief that once they do, death will certainly follow.

No one is too young to begin planning for an emergency. Your first step is to seek high-quality legal advice. Preparing wills is among the least-expensive legal services available, and all families need one. The responsibility for financial matters should not center in any one family member. Both parents should be fully aware of the total picture. At least once a year an inventory of vital documents should be taken. The following should be reviewed and updated:

1. Will
2. Listing of insurance policies, policy numbers, and beneficiaries
3. Listing of stocks, bonds, and certificates of deposit
4. Listing of savings accounts
5. Listing of all real estate
6. Listing of all outstanding loans, mortgages, and taxes
7. Listing of social security numbers for all family members
8. Listing of all credit cards and their numbers
9. Original or photocopies of all titles, deeds, birth certificates, marriage certificates, military discharge papers, and so on

Death is an inevitability. However, a mature effort to ease your family's pain and agony can help cushion the loss. Tragedy is hard enough to deal with—why make it harder? In the process of getting your house in order you should find that your stress is replaced by a sense of calm and preparedness.

Do you defer it or deal with it? The common practice of prolonging the "doing" process by delaying action can create stress and strain, while accomplishment results in a sense of peace. Consider the hypothetical case of a well-intentioned wedding invitation.

The invitation arrives with the morning mail on March 1—with an R.S.V.P. requested by March 14. Dawn Cobb's first reaction is that although she should certainly attend her cousin's wedding, something else is planned for that evening. She places the envelope in one of her "holding places," and tells herself she will have to check her dates before responding. Several days later Dawn's closest office friend, Rita, asks her to baby-sit three weeks from Saturday. Dawn remembers the wedding—but is uncertain of the date. She tells her friend she will have to let her know. Rita asks again the following day, but Dawn has forgotten to check. The third day Dawn does remember the invitation on her way out the door. However, after tearing the house apart for three minutes she is unable to locate it and makes her train only after an illegal parking job and undignified dash down the boarding platform. When Rita asks her about baby-sitting on Saturday, she is too embarrassed to admit she still doesn't know. Wishful thinking takes over and Dawn rationalizes: "I am almost positive that wedding is on Sunday. I'll say I can take the baby." During the following week the R.S.V.P. creeps into Dawn's consciousness on several occasions—becoming more stress-producing and ominous each time. However, each time she thinks about phoning, there is a good reason not to. Suddenly, things virtually explode at work. Dawn works frantically just to keep up and arrives home late each evening, exhausted. On March 13 Dawn's son reminds her that she promised to make three-bean salad for his Boy Scout banquet the following week. Dawn suddenly realizes that the banquet coincides with her baby-sitting. She doesn't want to renege and disappoint Rita, so she decides she will just have to take Rita's four-month-old with them to the banquet. During the next week things at work only get worse, and in between the office chaos, Dawn dreads the impending banquet but realizes she has only herself to blame. Somehow her exhausted body manages to drag all the baby paraphernalia to the dinner, and she even feigns delight at the opportunity to show off the infant at this family event. She fulfills her obligation to her son and to Rita. She awakes on Sunday to the ring of the telephone. Her Aunt Ruth is livid. Not only did she fail to attend her cousin's wedding, she didn't even have the courtesy to respond. Dawn's only response is: "I'm sorry. I just totally forgot." Yet, she realizes that is no excuse at all. She vows to send a gift the same day—as soon as she finds the invitation.

Many of Dawn's problems would have been prevented if she had adopted the policy of dealing with important papers immediately. Time management and efficiency experts recommend that each time you handle a piece of paper you act on it, and the fewer times you handle the paper, the better. If Dawn had recorded the Boy Scout banquet in her appointment book the minute she received the notice, she could have immediately discarded it and trusted the daily check of her appointment book to remind her. When the wedding invitation arrived, Dawn should have handled it only once, by immediately reaching for her appointment book, recording all pertinent information, and answering the R.S.V.P.

Household turmoil, which generates stress for all family members, can be minimized by breaking the paper-shuffling habit of reading, rereading, and movement of mail from here to there. As you go through the mail, act directly on each and every piece. Junk mail, no matter how interesting, should be deposited in the wastebasket. Bills should be placed in a Bills file. Newsletters, brochures, or other lengthy material should be placed in a Pending file. Mail that requires a response should receive a response—immediately. When the children come home with forms to be completed or notices regarding special events, adopt the same policy. Act on them without delay, and save your child the unnecessary strain associated with failure to return the required field-trip permission slip or the unhappiness of missing out on a taffy apple because you both forgot to send the money.

Quantity Versus Quality

It has often been said that it is not the quantity of time spent with children, but rather the quality that counts. As a working mother I believe that it is possible to mesh work and parenting, and recognize the importance of making the limited time shared by parent and child count. However, I believe that raising a child does require a certain minimum amount of time. I am also concerned about the definition of "quality."

The Broman family's situation is worth consideration. Frank Broman leaves for work each morning before the children are out of bed. He is an up-and-coming executive and often works over-time—only to arrive home after the children are in bed. Jill Bro-man also works and drops the children at the sitter's before school, where they return after school and remain until 6:00 P.M. By the time Jill drives home, makes dinner, and does dishes, it is usually 7:30 P.M. One night per week she attends exercise class, and a sitter takes over. Two nights a month Frank attends board meet-ings for the civic association. On weekends the children are in-volved in gymnastics lessons, Sunday school, and children's church service. Jill Broman spends Saturdays shopping and cleaning. Frank Broman usually takes care of odd jobs and yard work, or plays racquetball. Saturday nights Mr. and Mrs. Broman reserve for themselves—usually having dinner out, catching up on the week's events. Sunday afternoons are spent reading the newspaper, taking a nap, or nursing a hangover.

Jill and Frank love their children. They provide top-quality med-ical care and wouldn't think of missing a PTA meeting or school program. Any single use of their time can certainly be justified. Everyone needs time to exercise, time away from the children, and so on, and so on. However, when all the pieces are put together, the final picture is one in which the children are rarely engaged in meaningful interaction with the parents. Jill's idea of quality is children's designer clothing, expensive toys, and looking the other way when children misbehave.

Fathers have long faced the problem of finding time for high-quality contact with their children. In years gone by, some experts even hypothesized that children spent more time with the tele-vision than with their fathers and probably television was having more impact. With the entry of more mothers into the work force, the problem is now shared. No one can assign an arbitrary mini-mum number of clock hours required for parenting each week. However, it appears obvious that one hour shared in front of the television each evening is not enough. Following are some ideas for improving the quality of time (often increasing the quantity simultaneously):

Take time to really look at your child. Notice signs of illness, emotional upset, weight gain or loss, poor grooming, or changes in development.

Spend more time listening. Ask about everything—from how things are going in school to how your child likes the lunches you are preparing.

When your child is facing a crisis, drop everything and offer support, understanding, and assistance in working through the problem. Let the child know he or she is more important to you than a job or community service.

Share laughter. Let your child show you how to be a child again and appreciate the humor in a silly joke or funny accident.

Try to see the world through your child's eyes. Delight in a first snowfall or romp in the pile of leaves you just raked.

Take up exercise that can be shared with your child. Cycle, swim, jog, or jump rope together.

Make dinner a special family time. Resist the temptation to alternate between local fast food establishments each evening. Discourage eating in shifts or in front of the television set and use the time around the table for family discussion.

Teach your child restaurant etiquette, and when you do dine out make it a family event.

Make shopping trips leisurely family excursions. Share in clipping coupons, planning meals, discussing prices, and considering nutrition. Top off the day with a stop for ice cream.

Use automobile travel time for discussion and planning instead of listening to the radio.

Work side-by-side to accomplish household chores.

Carefully consider any children's extracurricular activities that take away from precious family time. Attempt to schedule these activities when the child would normally be at a sitter's.

Be selective about any community service that does not directly involve your child. Instead, try coaching a team, running a children's club, or helping at school.

Refuse to give up prime evening time to work overtime or stop for a drink with friends.

Guard against parallel parenting, in which parent and child are engaged in the same activity (such as television viewing) without actually interacting.

Play hookey once in a while. Call in sick and take your child to a museum, for a hike in the woods, or on a picnic.

Remember the importance of starting the day right, which includes not only a good breakfast but also a warm, happy send-off. Always join your child at breakfast, even if you only have coffee.

Turn off television and play a game. When watching TV, discuss programming.

Plan family vacations. If you want some time away from the children, there are numerous ski lodges, cruises, camps, and hotels that run child care programs.

Find ways to involve your child in cooking, yard work, repairs, cleaning the basement, sorting through drawers, or giving a party. Suggest your child chat with you as you prepare a meal or clean up afterward.

Tell your child how you feel. Explain the reason for rules, punishment, and displeasure. Let your child know that nothing ever affects your love. Good kids sometimes do' bad things.

Give your child kisses, hugs, and handshakes.

Say, "I love you," every day.

Finally, remember that not all time spent with your child will be high-quality time. No parent manages perfectly, although you may know several who appear to. You will occasionally lose control of your time and your temper. You will feel incompetent, inefficient, and just plain tired. Although you realize that your toddler just wants to be close, you will be annoyed at constantly tripping over the child who follows you from room to room. You may resent the invasion of privacy when you are interrupted in the bathroom. Experts make time management sound easier than it actually is. However, it is possible if you work at it to become better organized, reduce household stress, and have more high-quality time to spend with your child in the process. Use this time to form the bond of special memories and to enjoy parenthood's unique rewards. I remember the thrill I experienced when fielding errors enabled my daughter to parlay a bunt into a home run in one of her first baseball games. Although her team was already winning 68 to 24, the run was a personal victory over her fear of competition and failure. Carly ran to me and said, "I'm so glad you were here to see me hit my first home run!" I was glad too.

Chapter Eleven

Cope with Child Care and Medical Care

An Ounce of Prevention

Keeping children healthy and providing care when they are sick or when you must be away are continual sources of stress for parent and child alike. If you have ever stayed home because you couldn't find competent child care, blushed with shame at having forgotten an important inoculation, been frustrated when you forgot half the questions you wanted to ask the doctor or dentist, or felt like pulling out your hair in the sickroom—read on. Because of their importance, this whole chapter offers specifics for preventing and eliminating these major sources of stress before they develop.

Selecting Child Care

Would you spend as much time selecting child care as you would selecting carpeting? Considering the importance of child care, I hope your answer is a resounding *"Yes!"* However, many parents select a nursery school simply because it is in the neighborhood or hire a sitter solely on the recommendation of a friend. The total time spent in considering the matter is less than it takes to drive to the local carpet store.

There are a variety of options open to the parent who must leave a child. Care can be arranged in the child's home, in someone else's home, or in a center. However, the selection process can be a source of stress for parents who are not sure what they are looking for. In addition, parents who later sense that the child is not in the optimal setting will be upset each time they exchange good-bye kisses with their child. This source of stress will increase, rather than decrease, with time—as mother or father lives with this vague sense of uneasiness, waiting for the ax to fall. The child experiences stress if the caregiver fails to meet important needs, provide a feeling of security, or create a home-away-from-home.

The millions of parents who work, continue their education, do volunteer jobs, or simply want some time for themselves share in their criteria for child care. They seek an attractive, safe, well-equipped setting—with adults who are genuinely warm, conscientious, and sensitive to the needs of their child. They are looking for a sound philosophy and educational program that does not conflict with their basic values and life-style. It should promote the child's total development through the use of a variety of interesting toys and learning materials. Convenience, flexibility of hours, and schedule of fees are obviously also major concerns.

Unless you are extremely fortunate and have a friend or relative nearby who agrees to provide care, making just the right arrangements can take days or even weeks. The process resembles finding that perfect house—in which you weigh a number of variables, such as location, cost, suitability, and basic appeal—and it can take just as long. Often parents who are looking for child care are simultaneously facing major upheavels in their lives. In an effort to solve at least one of their many problems, they trade a long-term prudent choice for the short-term satisfaction of being able to say, "Well, at least that's out of the way." Sadly, the stress generated by an unsuitable selection will eventually result in a drain of energy far outweighing that required to do it right in the first place. The improperly placed youngster will also experience stress that could have been prevented. This negative first exposure to child care casts a wide shadow, often creating a sense of foreboding even when the child is moved to a second, more appropriate setting. The child experiences stress-by-association that might have been avoided altogether.

The suggestions that follow will help you reduce the time, effort, and stress that accompany the child care decision.

Let Your Fingers Do the Walking

Your first step is to find out exactly what is available. You will probably be amazed at the alternatives that emerge from your research. Begin with a stack of index cards and the telephone directory. Check the Yellow Pages under Day Nurseries, Nursery Schools, Kindergartens, and Baby-sitters. On each index card, record the name, address, and telephone number. Next, phone your local school district. They can provide information regarding programs operated by the federal government, school system, or nonprofit agencies. Most communities have a department of social services, office of children's services, or bureau responsible for licensing that can provide a list of resources. Local churches occasionally offer services or rent their facilities for child care. If there is a college or university in your area, phone and ask if they operate a program. The Classified section of your community newspaper will include ads for child care. Ask other parents for their recommendations. If you are new to the area, stop parents in the supermarket or park. There is probably an organization for newcomers that can offer suggestions. Your pediatrician might have some suggestions, and there are even some hospitals with a center on the premises. Many park districts sponsor play groups or part-day programs. Check the bulletin board in your grocery store or Laundromat for possible sitters.

After you have identified all possibilities, set aside a morning for telephone inquiries. Phoning for basic information can help you weed out situations that are obviously unacceptable and avoids wasting time on visits to those sites. Begin each phone call by identifying yourself and the age of your child. Ask if they can handle another child. If the response is yes, ask if they would mind answering a few questions. Answers to the following will help you decide if you should visit:

1. Are you a licensed child care provider?
2. What are your hours of operation?
3. What are the age levels of children served, and how are they grouped?
4. What is your fee schedule?
5. How many children do you currently serve?
6. How many adults are involved, and what are their qualifications?
7. What types of meals are served, and who prepares them?
8. Do you provide transportation?
9. Can you describe your building and playground?
10. Can you describe what a typical day would be for my child?
11. When do you accept visitors?

Record all the information on an index card. Tell them you will call back for an appointment to observe. If they discourage you from visiting, file their card under Unacceptable. No child should be placed in a setting that the parent has not studied firsthand.

Don't be fooled by their claims that you will disrupt their routine. Reputable child care providers welcome an opportunity to show what they are doing.

Don't automatically exclude a program if there is a waiting list. It usually signals excellent care. You have nothing to lose by placing your name on the list. You might just be ready to move your child when your name finally comes up. After you have completed your calls, sort the index cards into categories:

Private sitters

Baby-sitting can be arranged in your home or in the sitter's home. This option is among the most expensive, although the cost per child is reduced if you have more than one child or share the sitter with another parent. The major advantages of a sitter hired for your home are convenience and highly individualized care. If the sitter works at his or her home, transportation costs, daily hauling of kiddie gear, and your child's discomfort while braving the elements should be contemplated. The prime disadvantage is that sitters can arrive late, get sick, or have personal business that interferes with responsibilities to you. However, if your need is for infant or before- or after-school care, private sitters may be the only choice. A good sitter is hard to find. Your best bets are relatives, elderly persons, retired teachers, students, or a mother with a child close in age to your own. Some families arrange to exchange room and board for child care services.

If your child is very young and unable to communicate effectively, the selection process becomes crucial. The only stress indicators will be your child's reaction when the sitter takes over and your instincts regarding the child's level of happiness and security. Unless you have full confidence in your sitter, uneasiness and constant delving for clues to give you some indication of what goes on in your absence are bound to generate stress.

If your child is school-aged and requires care before or after school, consider contacting a classmate's parent. Someone not actively looking for baby-sitting work might be willing when the child is on the same schedule as her own. There is no major disruption in routine—and that extra money always comes in handy.

Infant care   In recent years mothers have entered the work force progressively sooner after the birth of their children. This fact has produced a steadily increasing demand for infant care. Although the licensing requirements are stringent, a number of nonprofit agencies, as well as private nursery schools, have gone into the business and take children who are but a few months old. Because of the mandated ratio of adults per child, infant care is very expensive. However, despite the disadvantage of having to transport a baby with accompanying paraphernalia in all types of weather, distinct advantages exist. Since a number of caregivers are involved and programs are monitored by licensing agencies, parents often feel more secure about the quality of care than they are with sitters. Provisions for emergency medical care are clearly established, and parents can rely on the service—whereas a sitter who arrives late or not at all can complicate one's obligations.

Small group   This care is provided in a home setting. The number of children involved ranges from two to twelve. Some homes care for preschoolers, while others specialize in before- and after-school care. In many communities licensing is strictly enforced. There are rules about the number of children under two, under six, and under twelve for which the home can provide care. Physical, health, and safety standards furnish some measure of quality control, and certain qualifications may be required of the sitter. Not all homes are licensed, and licensing guarantees little beyond physical and health conditions. Some sitters simply cannot afford the expenditure necessary to bring their home into compliance. In considering an unlicensed site, if you do not feel totally confident—steer clear. Remember, there is a reason the sitter is not licensed.

Many small group arrangements do, in fact, provide all the comforts of home. The stress experienced by the child as a result of separation from parent is minimized because the new arrangement so closely resembles life at home. There is an intimacy and warmth that provides an atmosphere of support not found in a large group. The child is able to play and interact with other children. In addition, in the small group setting your child will probably be accepted with a slight illness or fever. The larger centers refuse to accept a sick child.

One of the biggest disadvantages of home-based care is the absence of a developmental program that promotes intellectual, social, emotional, and motor growth. The children often play among themselves—only rarely interacting directly with the adults. The sitter arranges few special activities, such as field trips, parties, or programs. Toys, materials, and playground equipment cannot compare with those in larger centers. Television viewing may constitute the bulk of the child's day, and the parent can expect to be regularly inconvenienced as a result of the sitter's illness or personal commitments.

Centers

Centers may be run for profit or may be nonprofit. They are found in schools, churches, park district facilities, or their own buildings. The number of children served can be as low as fifteen or can exceed one hundred, with children grouped into classes. There is no correlation between cost and quality. Some of the finest programs are sponsored by nonprofit groups or funded through special grants and are entirely free, or charge only nominal fees. Some of the most expensive private nursery schools offer the children the least in terms of staff, program, materials, and facilities. Money spent to hire additional help or to replace toys or furniture reduces the profit level. Other private operators are dedicated professionals, with years of training and experience. Your challenge is to find the program that best fits you, your child, and your pocketbook. Remember, child care expenses can be tax-deductible. Check out the requirements for claiming a tax benefit.

The biggest advantage in placing your child in a center is the program. Play, educational activities, meals, and naps are usually well planned. The staff has formal training, and your child will benefit from the knowledge of a number of qualified adults. Centers provide a source of reliable care. You can count on the program to open on time, and the absence of one staff member does not curtail service. After-school programs are available for school-aged children.

There are disadvantages associated with the larger group settings. First, if you have a very young child you must ask yourself, "Can my child cope with the stress of care away from home?" Centers offer less individualized care than sitters or small groups. The large group may overwhelm the child who is not used to numbers of people or sharing adult attention. If your child has been separated from you with no apparent stress, a center with lots of new friends and playmates might be ideal. Most large group arrangements operate between the hours of 6:00 A.M. and 6:00 P.M. If you work nights, require care extending beyond those hours, or are often delayed, the center is probably not a viable option—unless you find one offering twenty-four-hour service.

Part-time   Many schools and park districts offer part-time programs for preschoolers. Children enroll in the morning or afternoon session—two, three, or five days per week. Parents looking for time for themselves or for doing volunteer work might find this arrangement ideal. Costs vary—but are usually nominal. The part-time programs are extremely effective in reducing the childhood stress typically associated with kindergarten entry or full-time placement in a center. The child makes the necessary social and emotional adjustments during more easily tolerated, occasional short separations from home and parent. The child has fun with playmates, while simultaneously learning how to share toys, equipment, and the teacher. Respect for rules, acceptance of discipline and constructive criticism, and problem solving all come in easily swallowed doses. There are also part-time after-school programs operated by schools, community groups, and parks.

Baby-sitting clubs

Joining a group of parents sharing a need for baby-sitting may offer you another option. These clubs are organized in neighborhoods, colleges, and businesses. They are ideal for irregular child care needs and can prove effective on a more regular, rotation basis. For example, you might be able to exchange care with a fellow employee who works a different shift or is scheduled to fill your position when you are off duty.

School or company

Hospitals, universities, colleges, unions, and companies have all become interested in facilitating child care. These programs are often subsidized and offer high quality at low cost. If you are returning to school or accepting a new job, be sure you check what is available. A growing number of employers also have job-sharing programs, in which two employees split the responsibility of one position, each working part-time and caring for their own children in the interim.

After your cards are organized, consider if there are any entire categories you wish to exclude from your list of options. You may decide that your child is definitely not ready to cope with the large group center or that the cost of private baby-sitters is prohibitive. Move these cards into the category called Unacceptable. Next, go through the cards in the remaining categories, removing those which did not provide satisfactory answers to your preliminary questions. Place these cards in the Unacceptable section too. Do not dispose of the Unacceptable cards. In the event you encounter difficulty making a satisfactory arrangement, you might have to reconsider. Save all the cards for future reference or for a friend who is just beginning the process.

The next step is to visit the remaining child care options. Before you phone for appointments, get a large calendar and decide exactly what days and times you have free. Mornings are the best time to observe: children are not napping and are involved in the regular routine. You probably won't be able to visit more than two or three sites in a morning, since you will want to stay an hour and a half at the very minimum. Record each appointment on your calendar—and don't forget to compute travel time from one facility to the next.

Have Checklist—Will Travel

It is very easy to visit a child care site and leave with a rosy picture. Simply being surrounded by a roomful of cute, smiling children can lift your spirits. Although the toys, equipment, and materials are important, resist the tendency to imagine your child gleefully exploring these wonderful things, daily delighting in a sort of perpetual birthday party. Your child will maintain excitement over the materials at the child care site just about as long as it is maintained at home. "Things" soon become old hat. It is what is happening to children's social, emotional, physical, and intellectual development that you should concentrate on.

Talk with the director and teachers, but don't spend the entire visit in an office or waiting area. You may encounter an apparently dedicated professional who describes a fantastic program, but, as you watch the children in their daily routine, you note little evidence of this. Immediately following each visit record your impressions on the index card. Following are some questions to keep in mind as guidelines when interviewing different childcare workers. Be thoroughly familiar with each point and record responses immediately upon leaving.

PRIVATE SITTER OR SMALL GROUP CARE

1. What is the sitter's background?
2. What is the sitter's current situation (place of residence, family, reason for accepting employment)?
3. What does the sitter view as major child care responsibilities?
4. What might prevent the sitter from fulfilling these responsibilities?
5. Does the sitter have any medical problems?
6. Does the sitter drive?
7. How would the sitter discipline my child?
8. How does the sitter feel about assisting with my special needs (toilet training, providing care if I am delayed, transportation to lessons, helping with homework)?

9. How does the sitter feel about my restrictions (smoking, drinking, telephoning)?
10. How would the sitter handle a medical emergency?
11. What are the names and telephone numbers of three other families for whom the sitter has provided child care?
12. Would my child feel happy and secure with this person?
13. If care is to be provided in the sitter's home, is it clean, safe, convenient, and homey?
14. If care is to be provided in the sitter's home, will the meals be nutritious and tasty?
15. If care is provided in the sitter's home, how will my child fit in with the other children? Will they be kind to my child? Will my child receive enough attention?

INFANT CARE

1. How much individual attention, cuddling, and talking to will my baby receive?
2. What are the feeding arrangements?
3. How often are the babies diapered?
4. What provisions are made for allowing the babies to move and crawl?
5. What types of stimulation are provided for the babies?
6. Is the physical arrangement clean, safe, and large enough to permit movement and play?
7. Can the names and telephone numbers of three other families who have received child care be provided?
8. Are there attractive materials for manipulative play and motor development?
9. Would my child feel happy and secure in this arrangement?

CENTERS

1. Is the center convenient, attractive, clean, safe, and large enough to provide approximately twenty-five square feet for each child enrolled?
2. Is the center well stocked with a wide variety of toys, books, art materials, pets, plants, and learning aids—maintained neatly and in good condition?
3. Is the playground safe and equipped with a variety of well-maintained apparatus? (Note: Swings, monkey bars, open slides, and teeter-totters are extremely dangerous.)

4. Are there separate areas for different activities such as art, napping, housekeeping toys, blocks, puzzles, water play, riding toys, sand tables, dress-ups, cooking, and science?
5. How are discipline problems handled?
6. Are the children treated with affection, kindness, and respect?
7. Are the children happy and at ease?
8. Does the staff spend time talking with each child and providing individual attention?
9. Are the children given some freedom in pursuing their own interests?
10. Do the children move around freely and locate materials easily?
11. What special activities are planned—such as trips, programs, or parties?
12. Does there appear to be a planned program and daily schedule?
13. Does the place seem cheerful and organized or gloomy and cluttered?
14. Were the children well-behaved and able to handle conflicts?
15. How are emergencies handled?
16. Would my child feel happy and secure?
17. Would my child fit in with the other children? Would they accept my child and treat the child kindly?
18. What provisions are made for communicating regularly with parents?
19. Are student records kept?
20. Did the director provide the names and telephone numbers of at least three other parents using the center?

Narrowing the Field

By now you probably have zeroed in on one category of care and eliminated most of your options. You have the field trimmed down, and now face the final decision. Don't ignore your basic intuition. When it comes to your child, you are the ultimate expert. Many of your instincts aren't instincts at all, but a reflection of your deep understanding of your child's needs, interests, abilities, and personality. For example, if a place feels cold to you, don't brush off that impression. You will probably be stressed every time you leave your child in that setting—no matter how well-equipped the facility or educationally sound the program. Take plenty of time to study your accumulated information. Plan to sleep on it and to discuss the matter with someone. Weigh the convenience, cost, and program—but most importantly, ask yourself, "Where will my child be most happy and secure, while developing intellectually, socially, emotionally, and perceptually?" If you are not satisfied with any of the options, you may have to enlarge the scope of your search or, if possible, even reconsider your decision to return to work, school, or more active social life at this particular time. Remember, the child care decision is not irrevocable. If you sense your child is stressed, you can make new arrangements. Watch for the obvious symptoms of stress presented in Chapter One. The most positive evidence that you have made the correct choice is your child's desire to go to the child care site each day. You should never be too busy or too tired to ask your child for the details of what happened during the day. Listen carefully to anecdotes, and be alert for a decline in eating or sleeping. Examine samples of the child's work and find out what food was served. Be prepared for a few problems, and don't overreact. Any new child care arrangement requires adjustment on the part of the child, parent, and care provider, who must get to know the child's unique ways. There are a few basic measures you can take during the first days to reduce stress for everyone concerned.

The Child Care Debut

Prior to that important first day, it is important to discuss what is going to happen with the child. Tell the child why care is being arranged and what to expect. If your child is stressed by the mere prospect of being away from you, don't automatically begin re-evaluating your plans. Children can be tyrants, and no child looks forward to a parent's absence. It is usually unwise to involve the child in the selection process. Consider the case of Billy Haupt, who pushed for Alphabet Academy simply because he spotted a Big Wheels in the riding toys when he visited. When his parents opted for what they judged to be a higher-quality program, Billy was upset, angry, and disappointed. Although he ultimately accepted his parents' choice, his first days were marked by pressure and stress. Obviously, this all could have been avoided. However, after the choice is made, the parent should describe the arrangement or even take the child to see it. Tell the child about all the new friends, interesting materials, and fun activities.

Prior to the first day, check and see how long you will be allowed to stay. Hopefully, you can plan your schedule so that you don't have to drop the child and rush off. Many children are terrified when they are abruptly deposited and are suddenly alone. A brief period of understanding and support can prevent days of stress. If you will not be allowed to stay or will only be there for a short time, tell the child exactly what to expect. Indicate that you will talk to the teacher for a few minutes or watch the class and then leave. Reassure your child that you will be back and that the adult in charge knows exactly where you are and can always reach you.

It is important that you assume an upbeat, positive attitude. If this is your first separation from your child, you may indeed be more stressed than the child. I have often had to restrain myself from strangling a mother who arrives with a happy, excited child only to deeply upset the child with her maternal tears and a general aura of anxiety. Avoid rushing back for one more kiss, coming back unexpectedly to check on things, or peeking through the window.

Every child has special needs and unique ways. Share this information with the care provider before you leave. When you call ·for your child, be sure to ask how the child ate, if the child napped, if there were any problems, what the child enjoyed most, and what activities were conducted.

Emergency telephone numbers, a medical release form, and a change of shoes, underwear, and outer pants should be provided by the parent.

In the case of school-aged children the first day probably won't be as traumatic. However, it is important to find out what happened and to provide the child with a sense of being the most important thing in your life. No matter how old the child, coming home from school to an empty house can create the stress of loneliness and fear. Avoid the "after-school blues" by arranging for your child to receive care at a friend's home, or participate in a school, community, park, or YMCA program.

Are You the Doctor in Your House?

A visit to the general practitioner or pediatrician can be a harrowing experience for a child. Anticipating the embarrassment of undressing in front of strangers, and then being gagged by a tongue depressor, poked in the ears and nose with a lighted gadget, and finally struck by a horrible needle is understandably stress-producing. Some children manifest their nervousness by becoming unusually fidgety during the long reception-room wait. The annoyed parent, who can't figure out why a professional office always tells you to arrive at 2:00 P.M. when in fact they mean 3:00 P.M., is in no mood to cope with the child's restlessness. By the time parent and child enter the examining room, stress has taken its toll. The parent is so vexed that half the questions are forgotten. The child is experiencing fear, which can intensify the actual discomforts.

Many competent, efficient parents, who handle minor crises totally unruffled, leave their doctor's office feeling that the physician has failed them and that they have failed themselves. They are not satisfied with answers to questions, or worse yet, feel the foolishness of not having remembered to ask them. They have been made keenly aware of the physician's superiority but wonder if anyone is really worth five dollars per minute.

Children learn their fear of the doctor. Most medical experiences contain some measure of unpleasantness. Usually one of two negative situations exists: Either the child is sick and receives an injection, or the child is well and receives an injection. There are a few measures you can take to keep medical stress at a minimum. Following are some important don'ts:

DON'T tell your child there will be no shot when you know there will. Even if you think there is no injection scheduled, you are better off to say, "I don't think so, but we'll have to wait and see." Inoculations have a way of creeping up on you, and you may not think it is time for immunization when actually it is.

DON'T ever allow your child to be injected when the child is asleep or distracted. The child should not be shocked.

DON'T reassure the child later by saying: "That mean doctor! Mommy didn't know he was going to hurt you."

DON'T scold, slap, ridicule, or later punish a child who was restless, crying, or fighting at the doctor's office.

DON'T arrive at the waiting room with nothing to occupy the child's time. Come prepared with toys, books, games, or other items.

DON'T threaten to call the doctor if a child won't do something—like take medicine. Physicians should be portrayed as good, helping individuals rather than ominous torturors.

DON'T react to your child's injection or to bad news with a look of terror, repulsion, or sadness.

DON'T outshout your child. It will only generate stress and cause the child to cry louder to be heard.

DON'T tell your child something won't hurt when it will. Injections, certain treatments, and surgery are painful.

DON'T fail to reassure, calm, or even hold the child during injections or treatment.

DON'T hesitate to explain the reason for immunization, physical examination, or treatments. However, be careful about using words that are automatic stressors, such as *blood, cut,* or *stitch.* Even the term *blood pressure* can frighten a child.

DON'T overlook or forget to provide your own form of "lollipop" after it is all over. Your child should associate the visits to a doctor with something pleasant afterward. A stop for an ice cream sundae or the purchase of a small gift can go a long way toward minimizing the negative feelings that contribute to the stress reaction.

DON'T become upset if your child exaggerates or minimizes symptoms. If it is obvious to you, the doctor will spot it as well.

DON'T introduce your child to the doctor in a suspicious manner—for example: "Billy, this is Dr. West. She won't hurt you. She is a nice lady." Children naturally assume people they meet are nice and won't hurt them. Your mention of these words places the child on guard.

DON'T neglect to tell the child what to expect if you know that one of those inoculation guns will be used. Although the device is effective, efficient, and safe, its very appearance can strike terror even in older children.

DON'T dismiss the importance of the regular checkup, even when there is nothing apparently wrong with your child. It is important to have an opportunity to discuss growth, development, and health habits—when the child is not suffering the stress of illness. You may even consider making an appointment and leaving your child at home.

How to Talk Turkey with the Doctor

Your child's medical care involves a three-way relationship. Parent, child, and physician must all cooperate. The doctor with whom you have trouble communicating might get along just fine with your child. Conversely, your child might feel slighted by the physician who casually and freely chats with you, asking you questions that the child could easily answer.

It is an absolute necessity to prepare for a personal or telephone conversation with your child's physician. A bundle of parent stress can be avoided by having an index card and pencil in hand (not buried in the bottom of your purse or stuffed in a pocket somewhere). The card should contain the following (the last three items obviously apply only if the doctor is new and has not treated your child before):

1. Date symptoms were first apparent
2. Exact nature of the symptoms
3. Course the fever if any, has been running
4. Questions you want to ask the doctor
5. History of related past illnesses, including dates
6. Treatment of related past illnesses
7. Complications during related past illnesses

When the doctor is poking and probing, remain quiet—unless you are directly questioned. Don't pop in with answers to questions the doctor asks the child. A good medical person has a sixth sense when it comes to reading the subtle clues provided by children. Most children are refreshingly honest in describing their pains and illnesses.

Most doctors allow time for a brief conference after the examination is completed. They don't like to waste time on small talk, but will gladly give you all the time necessary to deal with the real issues. If you have questions you would rather not discuss in front of your child, request a private conversation. Use your pencil to record the answers to your questions, as well as all instructions. Refrain from discussing your other children who are not even present. If the doctor talks rapidly or uses terms you don't understand, don't hesitate to ask for the information to be clarified or repeated.

There are a few classical parent-stress reactions associated with parent-doctor conferences. If you are able to spot yourself in the following descriptions, don't be dismayed. At least you are one step closer to coping.

Never Satisfied   Some parents are never quite satisfied with the examination, diagnosis, treatment, or quality of care. They feel that their child merits special consideration and that the problem should have been handled better. Every child is unique, but assuming every childhood illness or problem is also unique is stress-producing.

Alarmed

We can thank the media for contributing to the making of this type of parent. Vivid accounts of unusual and deadly illnesses and diseases has led to a form of hypochondria, in which the parent is afraid to overlook any childhood ailment. The alarmed parent panics and immediately makes an hysterical call to the hospital or pediatrician.

Hostile

The hostile parent recognizes the necessity of doctors but deeply resents the entire medical establishment. It doesn't matter who the physician happens to be; the parent is alienated. The negative attitudes and lack of respect make every encounter stressful—for parent and child alike. Imagine a sick child's reaction to remarks such as ''That guy is nothing but a butcher'' or ''All those doctors really care about is golf.''

Neglectful

Many neglectful parents don't actually abuse their children, but the results can be the same. The parent faithfully promises to administer a particular medicine for two weeks or to participate in a form of treatment, only to stop at the first sign of improvement. The child suffers a relapse, and it is back to square one for everyone.

Not following directions is particularly dangerous when an antibiotic is being administered. The drug is discontinued before the recommended ten days, two weeks, or ''when the bottle is empty''; the germ has not been killed, merely arrested, and may return more virulent than before.

Panacea Seeking

In this day and age of medical breakthroughs and wonder drugs, some parents expect the doctor to be able to prescribe a pill to solve every problem from the common cold to learning disability. In reality, there is no quick remedy for a plethora of childhood illnesses and problems. The parent who refuses to accept this fact will spend considerable time and money running from doctor to doctor. I strongly urge parents to locate the finest care available and in important matters get a number of opinions. However, unjustified eternal optimism can generate incredible stress for parent and child.

Grandma or Doctor—Who Should You Call

Parents don't like to waste their money or the doctor's time unnecessarily, but no one wants to make a mistake when it comes to a child's health. That nagging question, "Should I call the doctor?" is often difficult to answer. If the child is obviously hurt or sick, there is no choice. It's those minor complaints that don't seem to go away and enlarge in your mind that are tricky. My basic philosophy concerning this type of situation is that although the child may not actually need assistance, my mental health does. Rather than experience hours of stress, I phone the doctor or hospital for my own sake. In the process, I am sparing my child exposure to the highly contagious stress reaction. However, it is not a bad idea to phone the child's grandmother or grandfather, or someone like them whom you trust, who has a knowledge of children. They may be able to identify the situation, diagnose the problem, and suggest a treatment. Another preliminary step should be consulting a good childhood medical encyclopedia. Once you decide to telephone, just who should you call? In our area I have found that if I need facts or help in determining if my child really needs medical attention, the pediatrics department of local teaching hospitals provide excellent, accurate, free information. During odd hours you can pick up the phone and be talking with someone in minutes, rather than waiting for an answering service to convey a message to your doctor. If you require more personalized information or possible medical attention, a call to your child's physician is required. When you do telephone, don't forget to have the previously mentioned index card and pencil close at hand. If you know you are going to need a refill on a prescription, be certain to have the prescription number and the name and phone number of the pharmacy at your fingertips.

Sickroom Savvy

In caring for a sick child or one who is convalescing, not only is it important to keep your own stress to a minimum, it is also important to maintain a stress-free environment for the child, since stress has been related to illness and recovery.

The following suggestions will make your job easier:

Realize and accept the fact that caring for a sick child will require time. You will temporarily have to let certain other activities and responsibilities slide.

Organize medical supplies. Place tissues, paper cups, medicines, thermometer, and other items in a small box so you aren't continuously scurrying from room to room.

Move a television into the room.

Use pillows or sofa cushions for propping.

Place a bell or whistle next to the bed so the child can summon you. Discuss the importance of calling for help only when absolutely necessary.

Get a lap tray or make one out of a large cardboard box.

Place the child's supplies in a cardboard box. A clipboard comes in handy.

Cover the top blanket with a sheet for those inevitable mealtime spills.

Use a discarded man's dress shirt, with collar cut off and sleeves trimmed, for a hospital gown in the illnesses accompanied by rashes and lotion treatment.

If the child can be moved, arrange a temporary bed on the couch or on a chaise longue. Frequent change of scenery can minimize stress.

If you must be away from the child, tell where you are going and when you will return. Set a timer in the sickroom.

Have a supply of games and craft kits on hand.

If the weather is mild, ask the doctor if the child can go for a ride in the car. If permissible, you can make a bed in the backseat.

If the child is eating well, provide favorite meals and special treats.

Arrange to get the child's assignments to avoid falling behind in schoolwork.

Get travel brochures and plan a real or imaginary vacation.

Involve the child in menu planning each day.

Place flowers in the room and on the meal trays. Even dandelions delight children.

If you have a miniature Christmas tree, let the child make decorations for it befitting the season. (Hearts for Valentine Day, springtime flowers, snowflakes.)

Buy a pretty china tea set and only use it for sickroom tea parties.

Use a cookie cutter to make interesting sandwiches or to mold vegetables or potatoes.

Involve the child in a charity project, such as making something for the local hospital.

No matter how good a reader your child may be, all children enjoy listening to parents read to them. Select a spellbinding mystery and read a little each day.

Provide the child with a scrapbook and old magazines. Decide on a theme, such as laughing faces—not just smiling.

A child who is allowed to become neurotic or spoiled will experience stresses that extend far beyond the illness. A little extra attention, coupled with an outpouring of love and interesting things to do, can provide real prevention.

Handling Hospitalization

In a recent study of children under stress, hospitalization ranked high. To combat this, many hospitals have initiated programs featuring pleasant noninstitutional surroundings, bright colored uniforms decorated with cartoon characters, well-equipped playrooms, prehospitalization visits, and provisions for parents to remain with their children overnight. Forced separation from the parent at a time when the child needs parent support the most can result in permanent emotional damage. Children under five are particularly susceptible. Anxiety can be reduced by telling the child the reason for the hospitalization (without going into unnecessary details about surgical procedures) and exactly what is going to happen. Children often place hospitals and haunted houses in the same category. Adults tell about Uncle Bill, who went to the hospital and died. They recount their own negative experiences in emergency rooms and in surgery.

Playing hospital at home is an excellent way to learn how to cope with hospitalization. You can role-play being admitted, taking the temperature, giving shots, having visitors calling the nurse, and parents' arrival and departure. Alternate the roles each time you play. Equally helpful are the children's books that deal with a hospital stay. If your child's hospitalization isn't immediate, wait until the event is imminent before discussing it. There is no point in generating stress months in advance. If your child is having surgery, it is very important for you to be there when the child awakes. Plan to stay the first few nights, at least, and alternate daytime visits with other family members so that the child has company as much as possible. Tell your child that a chaplain, priest, minister, or rabbi visits all patients. Some youngsters assume they are dying when they have such a visitor.

Once your child is hospitalized, play provides a comfortable focus and helps to reduce anxiety and tension. Children organize their lives around play. During World War II even in bomb shelters or concentration camps, children continued play activities. Tape up a sign or inform hospital staff of your child's special fears, nickname, food preferences, unusual toilet habits, and interests. Many of the suggestions for the home sickroom can be used in the hospital. Be particularly careful that when you leave, you tell your child you are going, rather than slipping away, and tell when you will return. Many children fear their parents are never coming back or that they themselves will never return home. Be careful about discussing problems with the doctor in the child's presence. Offer your child reassurance and the opportunity to express feelings, fears, and resentments. Maintain an upbeat attitude and avoid showing the child signs of your stress. Vent your emotions to someone close to you outside the hospital. Keeping it all inside can result in an uncontrollable spillover which, if witnessed by the child, can prove saddening and frightening. When your child returns home, don't be surprised if the child clings to you, develops a fear of doctors, or reverts to bed-wetting.

Immunizations—Who Needs Them?

Are all those shots to prevent polio, diphtheria, whooping cough, tetanus, mumps, and measles really necessary? Does anyone ever hear about someone actually getting some of these diseases anymore? The answer to both questions is yes, and until a disease is totally eliminated, immunizations are necessary. The only disease that has almost disappeared and therefore requires no vaccination is smallpox. Unless your child is traveling to Africa or the Far East, where cases are still reported, no inoculation is necessary. Measles, mumps, and rubella are still reported in significant numbers. Tetanus also remains a threat to the unimmunized. Polio, whooping cough, and diphtheria are rare, but exist.

Immunization is usually accomplished by injections, although polio vaccine is taken orally. Immunizations for polio, measles, rubella, and mumps give permanent protection. Tetanus, diphtheria, and whooping cough require regular boosters.

Injections are the major cause for doctor's-office stress. No one likes them. However, if the parent and doctor handle the situation correctly, the stress and pain are momentary. If the child is not assisted in coping, the mere thought of the doctor can result in tears and terror, even when there is no injection on the agenda. When taking the child for immunization, don't lie. Shots do hurt, but not unbearably so. Tell the child exactly what to expect, including the fact that it will hurt for just a moment, much like a real hard pinch. You should also be careful about telling children they will feel fine after it is all over. Children react differently, and approximately ten percent suffer fever and other ill effects following tetanus, diphtheria, and whooping cough inoculations. In most cases the reaction passes within a day, but can continue for several days. If your child has a prolonged reaction, inform your doctor. In the future smaller, more frequent doses might be administered. Measles immunization often leads to a reaction, which is apparent five to ten days later. The child might experience fever, enlarged glands, or a mild rash resembling measles. Any shot can result in a sore muscle. The federal and state governments, as well as local school systems and public health officials, have recently adopted a get-tough attitude regarding immunizations. In some locations children are excluded from school until proof of immunization is provided. Avoid parent and child embarrassment and stress by keeping up-to-date.

The following schedule of immunizations is a sample. Consult your doctor for specific recommendations.

CHILDHOOD IMMUNIZATION SCHEDULE

Age	Immunization	Your Child's Record
2 months	Diphtheria	_____
	Whooping cough	_____
	Trivalent oral polio	_____
4 months	Diphtheria	_____
	Whooping cough	_____
	Tetanus	_____
	Trivalent oral polio	_____
5 months	Diphtheria	_____
	Whooping cough	_____
	Tetanus	_____
	Trivalent oral polio	_____
15 months	Measles	_____
	Rubella	_____
	Mumps	_____

18 months	Diphtheria	_____
	Whooping cough	_____
	Tetanus	_____
	Trivalent oral polio	_____
4 to 6 years	Diphtheria	_____
	Whooping cough	_____
	Tetanus	_____
	Trivalent oral polio	_____
every 5 to	Repeat diphtheria	_____
10 years	and tetanus	_____

Brace Yourself for the Dentist

The basic guidelines and suggestions presented for medical care can be easily adapted to dental care. The child's first visit to the dentist should take place between the ages of two and three and should not include treatment. Your child can get acquainted with the dentist and perhaps watch as you have a checkup. It is important to approach a visit to the dentist with a positive, open attitude. Children should be told the truth and reassured—rather than coaxed, coerced, and criticized. A treat or reward following the visit adds a positive reinforcement.

A Pound of Cure

Despite your precautions children are found to suffer some ill effects of stress related to child care, medical care, or dental care. The child's hesitancy to repeat a stressful experience is natural. However, with your guidance the child can learn to rationally accept the sometimes unpleasant necessities of life.

Chapter Twelve

Manage, Support, and Relax

One of my most prized possessions is an old pocket-watch with an intricately carved case. Although it is over a hundred years old, I have found that it runs best when it is wound and used daily. When left tucked safely away, the oil congeals and the many tiny parts no longer operate smoothly. Also, unfortunately, I found out the hard way that if I wound the watch too tightly, the spring broke and the watch no longer ran. People are a lot like my watch. They need some daily stress to function smoothly. Too little stress can cause a kind of human congealing. But like my watch it is possible to get wound up too tightly, and then something has to snap.

In this chapter you will find some management, support, and relaxation techniques you can share with your child, as well as a few designed for parents. Since stress is an individual matter, stress control must similarly be individualized. What works for one child may prove totally ineffective with another. Therefore, you will want to experiment with the ideas presented here to determine the optimal approach for your child. But remember, stress management cannot solve problems once and for all. As your child grows and matures, the nature of the stressors affecting the child will change, as will susceptibility and the means for coping and managing.

Susceptibility to stress is partially determined by a child's physical condition. Perhaps you have had an experience similar to that of Helene Webster when she took Becky to visit friends who had never seen her toddler before. Helene had not the slightest misgiving about taking her two-year-old to the casual dinner party. Becky was always pleasant and well-behaved. However, that night she hardly recognized her own child. About nine o'clock Becky became unreasonable and demanding. Despite everyone's polite smiles even Helen realized that the child was acting like a spoiled brat. When Helen refused to allow her to play with a decorative brass elephant, Becky had a tantrum and cried until they finally went home. Becky normally adapted to new people and surroundings with little stress. However, when the trouble started, it was already over an hour past bedtime, and the child had a slight earache.

Most parents are familiar with the obvious "I've had enough" signs. The child looks tired. Eyes become red or develop dark circles, and young children often begin rubbing them. Some children become pale, while others look flushed. Many children have a Dr. Jekyll–Mr. Hyde personality when fatigued. They are unusually irritable, bossy, hostile, or sensitive. The slightest stressful provocation can leave them hopelessly engulfed in sobs and tears. Weary children don't even sound the same. They do more talking in a louder, higher-pitched, faster voice. Some children become overactive, while others show signs of exhaustion by stumbling, becoming hoarse and drowsy, and finally just falling asleep.

Children tire more easily than adults, and once they do, the hustle and bustle of social activities can produce stress. A spent child has little energy left for coping. Such typical childhood activities as parties, especially those involving children, loud music, dancing, or staying up late; sitting inactively or concentrating for a long period of time; strenuous exercise or continuous exposure to noise; high levels of competition in sports or games; and wild, unruly play such as wrestling or uncontrolled giggling, can leave a child frazzled. Some means for controlling stress is needed.

The management, support, and relaxation suggestions that follow have been researched and proven effective. You and your child must accept the fact that it *is* possible to manage stress. You must expect to succeed at the task. Sometimes individuals approach the techniques with an air of disbelief or suspicion. They tell themselves that the whole business is probably silly and they give stress management a halfhearted try, at best. If you expect to fail, you certainly will. Stress-management techniques must be learned. As with any new skill it takes time to become proficient. Neither you nor your child should expect overnight results. Stress management is a continual process, to be constantly revamped in response to new stressors, new experiences, and maturity.

If your child is currently taking any regular medication or suffers from epilepsy, diabetes, or any disease, check with your doctor before attempting the suggested techniques.

Stress Detection

Children rely on a number of techniques that temporarily provide relief from stress. They withdraw or retreat from the entire situation, turn to adults to solve their problems for them, cheat, steal, overeat, or try to exercise supercontrol over every stressor they face. There are even documented cases of alcoholism in students still in elementary school, and ten-year-olds are being treated for hypertension. This assortment of responses has little value when it comes to long-term stress management.

We are not always aware of the stimuli bombarding our children or their reaction to them. While some stressors are relatively obvious and easy to spot, others are hidden and complicated by the child's imagination, lack of experience, fear, or partial understanding of a situation. An imagined source of stress can stimulate a reaction as severe as, or even greater than, a real one. Early experiences and television are two breeding places for the hidden variety of stress. Take, for example, the case of Donald, who demonstrated an absolute phobia for cakes, pies, or anything with whipped cream. His aversion became apparent at his first birthday party, when he reacted with near hysteria to the sight of his cake. Uncontrolled behavior was highly unusual for Donald, and as the weeks went by, it was evident something about certain bakery goods terrified him. Finally, his mother got to the root of the problem. Donald was in the family room watching one of his favorite programs when she walked in and found him cowering in the corner of the sofa, whimpering. Wondering what was frightening him, she looked at the television just in time to see one of the pie-in-the-face routines. She said, "Donald, what's the matter?" but all he could do was close his eyes and whisper: "No more cake in the face. No more, no more!" Even after the source of his fear was discovered, it took several years for him to outgrow his aversion to cakes, pies, and whipped cream. Next time you spend an evening in front of the television set, periodically ask yourself how the viewing might be interpreted by children at different age levels, beginning with a one-year-old and continuing through the impressionable preadolescent years.

Past, unpleasant experiences, such as being frightened by a dog, can also be long remembered and produce stresses that mystify adults. When your child reacts wildly to the sight of a cat or bumblebee, try to recall an earlier related bad experience.

Remember that there is an explanation for nearly all behavior. Stop to recollect the sources of your own childhood stress, and you will find that in addition to the more ordinary types, such as test anxiety, you revive memories of:

Fearing storms, wind, tornadoes, floods, earthquakes, or fog.

Fearing your parents' deaths.

Fearing a fire at home or school.

Fearing insects, snakes, animals, electric appliances, or power tools.

Fearing water.

Fearing the dark.

Fearing people with obvious physical differences or handicaps.

Worrying about your height or size.

Worrying about staying alone.

Worrying about going blind.

Worrying about being retained in the same grade for the second year.

Worrying about wetting in class.

Worrying about getting lost.

Worrying about homosexuality or castration.

Worrying about sex.

Worrying about seriously hurting someone else.

Worrying about being criticized.

Suspecting that you were adopted or born out of wedlock.

Mourning the death or disappearance of a pet.

Detesting the fact that your parents made you kiss certain visitors.

Feeling uncomfortable around a drunken adult.

Feeling lost when your brother or sister left home.

Feeling inferior when you had to do something you were certain you did worse than anyone else.

Feeling unsettled because your house was torn apart by a move, redecorating, remodeling, or spring cleaning.

The preceding list includes examples of stressors that span the childhood years. Since stress is such a highly personal matter, it is not possible to clearly delineate a specific age for which the stressor is typical. Indeed, fear of snakes or water might be evident in a three-year-old or a thirteen-year-old. Remember, a stressor is not determined by age, but by the perception of a threat to personal well-being.

In order to build a stress-management system to last a lifetime, your child must first understand stress. It is amazing how quickly children pick up on the concept. My own daughter was six-years-old when I began this book. The subject of stress was often mentioned in our household and Carly soon became an expert. She was quite serious as she told me that she thought her brief morning stomachache was caused by the stress of going back to school after spring vacation. On a number of occasions she politely interrupted as I was reprimanding one of her cousins to ask, "Mom, do you realize that *you* are putting Mikey under a lot of stress?"

Once your child understands the nature and causes of stress, you should explain the importance of managing it for physical and emotional health. The child should be able to identify for him or herself when personal levels of stress are reaching the danger zone. Armed with some specific management measures for when the going gets rough, your child should be able to handle the normal stresses of childhood.

I Get By with a Little Help from my Friends

The therapeutic value of "getting it off your chest" has long been recognized by laymen and professionals alike. When stress has you near the boiling point, perhaps you regularly turn to spouse, relative, friend, clergyman, or doctor for help. If you've sought help wisely, you can receive valuable assistance. In other cases you are disappointed. You find that the other person really didn't understand or attempted to shield you from the problem, rather than aiding you in coping with it.

It is not always easy for a child to turn to others for help. Some children consider such a request as synonymous with failure, immaturity, or inability to handle one's own problems. Self-esteem is threatened. Sometimes the child looks for help in the wrong places or takes poor advice. Your job is to help your child realize that both adults and children often need help to work through stressful situations. An important part of stress management is recognizing when it is time to seek that assistance. Your child should recognize that the purpose of turning to others is to improve long-term coping ability. Obviously, it takes some skill to select someone who has something more than a sympathetic ear to offer.

Depending on your child's age and the lines of communication you have established, you will probably be a prime resource in the child's coping. You will find you provide a variety of different types of support. In some cases the child will need to have self-esteem reaffirmed. In other situations the child must be guided in problem solving or gaining new skills necessary for coping.

Your child's willingness to turn to you in times of stress will be largely determined by the tone you set. Take the following self-test and find out if you usually "turn off" or "turn on" your child by checking any behavior description that fits you.

TURN-OFFS	or	**TURN-ONS**
____ Rushing the child or talking for the child in order to hurry the conversation along		____ Showing your child you have feelings, too, by talking about your stresses
____ Half listening or muttering absentminded replies like "Um-humm" or "Oh, really"		____ Helping your child recognize and name feelings and emotions
____ Betraying the child's trust or confidence by divulging secrets without first getting the child's approval		____ Encouraging your child to express feelings by saying things like "How did you feel about that?" or "Tell me more about the problem."
____ Communicating disapproval or shock by facial expressions, gestures, or voice intonations		____ Showing you understand by restating what the child has said
____ Using words or concepts that are unfamiliar or irrelevant to the child		____ Looking straight into your child's eyes during discussion
____ Acting as though the problem is silly or unimportant		____ Making physical contact by holding the child's hand, hugging, placing an arm over the shoulder, or giving a pat on the back
____ Acting as though the child is incapable of dealing with the stress, but can count on you to handle it		____ Using relevant examples and relating specifically to the child, rather than dealing in philosophical generalities, such as "the importance of hard work for a good life"

Total Turn-offs_____   versus Total Turn-ons_____

An older child should realize, too, that resources exist beyond the family. Certain conditions may call for expert guidance and knowledge that the family simply doesn't possess, or the child might not be able to face someone very familiar. Make your child aware of the professionals, organizations, and crisis centers available. Managing stress can involve many varied channels for assistance. An evaluation of the situation and judgment of just who has the most to offer will determine what channel is used. Meanwhile, your child will learn skills that will enable him or her to provide support for others in times of stress.

What's in a Name?

There are some simple basic steps any parent can take to prevent or diminish everyday sources of stress—so basic, in fact, that they are often overlooked. Even the name a parent chooses for a child can contribute to stress. In a study conducted at Tulane University, students ranked names as either desirable or undesirable. Next, pictures of young women who had earlier been rated as equally attractive were each assigned a desirable or undesirable name. In a mock beauty contest, contestants with the desirable names, such as Kathy, received 158 votes, while the undesirably named girls, such as Gertrude, received only 39. In fact, in one college survey 46 percent of all students questioned were actually dissatisfied with their names. While it is not practical to rename our children, we can take into account other important aspects of the childhood environment.

A well-organized home, for instance, in which rules, expectations, and physical space are clearly and precisely designated can help prevent confrontations and unhappiness. If your toddler passes that wobbly table with the crystal vase on it twenty times an hour and the inevitable calamity occurs, who is to blame for the ensuing stress? And doesn't it make sense to avoid when you can such rejoinders as "I didn't know, you never told me" when something goes wrong.

A warm and secure family atmosphere fosters a child's development rather than hindering it, and the foundation for this atmosphere is preparedness. As a beginning teacher I learned the secret of maintaining classroom discipline. Productively busy students create few problems. This principle applies just as much at home. When children become bored and fidgety, they *will* find something to amuse themselves and the social acceptability of their choice is often questionable. The household equipped with rainy-day or sick-day projects or the flight bag that contains things to while away time traveling are such simple illustrations of preparedness as to be hardly worth mentioning, but so simple, they are often forgotten.

It is usually just lack of preparation and foresight, too, when parents send a youngster off to school in a coat with buttons and clasps the child cannot possibly handle without frustration and help, or dressed in a fashion that invites peer ridicule; or when a parent guarantees embarrassment for the child by failing to teach an important skill such as tying shoelaces. A happy child is one who has been prepared to cope with life's challenges, both big and small.

Stress is sometimes caused when the child is too intensely involved in just one major interest, so that all the child's self-esteem is linked to success or failure in that area. Broadening this base of interest helps the child maintain self-worth even in the face of a failure.

Physical activity is a very effective means for marking off tensions. Rest and diet are also important. Many children (like many adults) are prone to binge when under stress, to eat foods that are loaded with sugar or artificial additives and colorings, to which they can react adversely. Lack of sleep can magnify stress reactions. Irritability is increased and problems get out of proportion. This is surely common knowledge, but many parents seem to forget it when dealing with their own children.

The willingness and ability to drop everything and listen when your child approaches you with a problem is probably one of the most important basics of child stress prevention. Many an anxious child gives up when interrupted three times in three minutes. When the child is finished, let him or her know you understand. Some children do not want to unload unless they feel the time is right. If you sense your child is under stress, make an effort to give him or her your undivided attention at some point each day.

And if you find that a stressful situation has gotten out of hand and your child is on the verge of going out of control, do what comes naturally to a mother or father. Put your arms around and hug your child. Show your love!

The Child-Parent Coping Model

In coping with childhood stresses, child and parent can profitably interact. The following steps help to define the stressor and control the reaction:

**Step 1.
Get the
facts.**

Child and parent should painstakingly analyze what has happened to produce this stressful situation. In some cases merely compiling the facts eliminates the stress. For example, the child who is unhappy because her classroom teacher did not select her artwork for display in the art fair may not be disturbed if she learns that another teacher, whose opinion she does not value as highly, made the selections.

**Step 2.
Recognize
the prob-
lem.**

After the facts have been gathered, it is important for the child to verbally express the sometimes vague sense of stress experienced.

**Step 3.
Develop a
plan.**

After the problem is clearly stated, the child can work out a plan for reducing, eliminating, or controlling the stress. The plan might involve preventing future stress by withdrawing from the stress-producing situation, such as the Little League team. It might involve making a conscious effort to accept the situation. Usually the formulation of a concrete plan is stress-reducing in itself.

**Step 4.
Suggest al-
ternative
approaches.**

Once the primary plan has been formulated, several alternative approaches must be outlined. Failure to have a back-up plan will result in additional stress should the original plan prove ineffective.

**Step 5.
Discuss
progress at
regular in-
tervals.**

Your child will need a sounding board to help evaluate the progress being made in coping with the stressor.

**Step 6.
Evaluate
the original
plans.**

After a reasonable length of time, parent and child should confirm that the original plan (or alternative plan, if adopted) is on the right track and if it is not, the process must begin again. Perhaps the plan's failure was the result of erroneous facts, poor definition of the problem, or haphazard attempts at implementation.

Exercise

Few parents worry about their children getting enough exercise. Most children never stop moving. However, the situation changes as youngsters grow into adults. Exercise is extremely important in preparing the body to withstand the effects of prolonged, chronic stress, yet many adults do not get enough exercise. Therefore, it is important that your child begin early in life to regard vigorous exercise as more than a way to have fun. Direct teaching, but more importantly, your example, can help your child develop a lifelong commitment to regular exercise, which will provide a buffer against inevitable stress.

Some experts say that during stress exercise is effective in settling the body back down. Stress increases the body's flow of adrenaline, while exercise dissipates it. When your child is under a lot of pressure, some sort of vigorous activity, such as jogging, boxing, or tennis, can be very beneficial or as a much simpler alternative, stretching exercises are often recommended for relieving pent-up tensions. Following are several stretches to share with your child:

Reach for the sky, partner.	Put your arms up straight over your head and stretch until you "touch the sky."
Show that doorway who's boss.	Stand in a doorway, with both arms extended, and pretend you're trying to make the doorway wider, by pushing with both hands.
I dunno.	Stand up with your back very straight and hunch your shoulders up to your ears.
Ten little Indians.	Put your arms out straight in front of you, with both hands made into fists. Then, spread your fingers out as far as they will go and bring them back into fists.
Around and around it goes.	Stand with your arms hanging loosely at your side and roll your head forward and backward to make a circle.

Relaxation

One of the more important body changes caused by stress is muscle tension, which helps protect the body from injury and readies the individual for rapid movement or battle. Muscle tension today, however, is an outdated response that often results in headaches, backaches, and other discomfort.

You can help your child to recognize when stress is present by identifying the signs of muscle tension before things get out of hand, and to learn how to release this tension through relaxation. Experts recommend that after relaxation techniques are learned they be utilized not only during times when stress levels are climbing, but every day.

Before you begin, make sure you choose a quiet place where the atmosphere is peaceful and conducive to loosening up. Many of the following steps are adapted from Dr. Herbert Benson's *The Relaxation Response*.[1] Tell your child:

Step 1   Lie down in a comfortable position.

Step 2   Close your eyes.

Step 3   Breathe deeply through your nose.

Step 4   Beginning with your feet and working upward, first tense and then relax your muscles (feet, ankles, legs, hips, fingers, wrists, arms, back, shoulders, buttocks, neck, jaws, face, and eyes). Tense each muscle group for five seconds and then suddenly relax. Concentrate on the relaxed condition for at least twenty seconds before tensing the next group.

Step 5   After you have completely relaxed all your muscles, sit quietly for a few minutes.

Step 6   Breathe normally for two or three minutes before getting up.

Even when there is no opportunity to lie down, once your child is proficient at controlling the release of muscle tension, it can be done when the child is seated at a desk or on the school bus or waiting to participate in a game. Many people find that with practice they can relax without going through the tense-release sequence by simply breathing deeply and concentrating on releasing muscle tension and relaxing.

Yoga

Yoga has been steadily growing in popularity in recent years. Many yoga exercises are easily adapted for relaxing children. Remember that it isn't important for your child to assume perfect yoga postures. Instead, you should aim for relaxation; improved flexibility, posture, balance, and coordination; greater concentration; and nostril breathing. The following exercises are based on yoga. If you have studied it and know additional exercises, you may want to use them with your child.

Exercise 1   Sit on the floor in the yoga position (cross-legged, with heels on thighs). Extend both arms out straight in front of you. Breathe slowly in and out through your nose. Take a deep breath, making your chest get as big as you can, then let all the air out. Repeat three or four times.

Exercise 2   Lie on your back. Bring your knees up, as close as you can to your nose, then rock back and forth as far as you can.

Exercise 3   Sit on the floor with your legs apart. Bend from the waist and try to touch your head to the floor.

Exercise 4   Lie on your back. Arch your back and lift it off the floor, keeping your head and buttocks on the floor.

Exercise 5   Lie face down, on your stomach. Extend your arms out in front of you. Next, walk your hands slowly back toward your stomach, keeping your arms straight and lifting your head and chin toward the ceiling. Then slowly walk your hands back to the original position as you lower your chin to the floor.

Fantasize

Fantasizing is like taking a minivacation. It provides a needed rest for mind and body. Begin by telling your child to get in a comfortable position. Next, have him or her identify any tense muscles and relax them by breathing deeply through the nose and using the tense-release sequence previously discussed. Now instruct your child to pretend the eyelids are getting very heavy and to slowly let them close. Then tell the child to breathe deeply, concentrating on some pleasant picture created in the mind. This thought should create a warm, peaceful, comfortable feeling, and the same mental image can be used over and over again. Encourage your child to blend as deeply as possible into the imaginary scene and then to gradually let the picture fade. When it is gone, have your child count to five and open the eyes. After two or three stretching exercises, he or she should be ready to face the world again.

Be Prepared

Help your child to anticipate stressful situations and plan in advance how to cope with them. The stress reaction is often intensified because the child is caught unaware and unprepared. Much can be learned after the fact about coping. When your child tells you about a stressful situation, take time to rehash the events and to discover if the stress could have been avoided or handled more effectively. You might advise your child that when stress leaves one shocked or stunned, the best thing to do is recognize the condition and use some relaxation or breathing techniques to regain composure. Responding with first impulses is rarely a useful coping strategy.

Sometimes role-playing a situation can help tremendously in preparing your child to cope. You each take a part and attempt to' simulate the events that are likely to occur. Your child is given actual practice in coping.

Take a Deep Breath

I hesitated including this section among the stress-management techniques, not because controlled breathing is ineffective, but because young children who get carried away might temporarily upset their chemical balance. However, the Mesa, Arizona, school system has developed an easy, effective coping technique they call Kiddie Q.R. (quieting reflex), adapted by Elizabeth Stroebel from work done by her husband, Dr. Charles Stroebel, M.D., Ph.D., and currently professor of psychiatry at the University of Connecticut Medical School. When the quieting reflex becomes a habit, it can be used automatically whenever a stress reaction is apparent. It is simple to learn and takes only six seconds:

Step 1   Recognize the symptoms of stress.

Step 2   Deliberately relax your facial muscles, then consciously form a smile in which the corners of your mouth point upward toward your eyes. Concentrate on feeling calm.

Step 3   Take a long, deep breath.

Step 4   Exhale slowly, opening your mouth and letting your jaw droop. Repeat if necessary up to four times.

Meditation

Some parents are leery of meditation. They associate it with Far Eastern rites or religious cults and fear that meditating might result in a child drifting into a trance or becoming overly passive. Actually, meditation is a means for developing *greater* control over mind and body, while providing a release for physical and mental tension. Meditators appear to handle stress more effectively than nonmeditators and actually react less intensely. Research studies suggest that during stressful times meditators suffer fewer stress-related illnesses and bounce back more quickly. Recovery is extremely important in managing stress. If a child is already tense from previous stress when a new stressor is encountered, there will be a more intense reaction than would have occurred had the child been relaxed.

Unlike the other forms of relaxation presented, meditation trains concentration. Its object is simple—to temporarily free the mind; it is like closing up shop for a siesta. For a brief time you concentrate on some object or meaningless syllable (mantra) and get rid of the thoughts that can create stress. After meditation you feel relaxed, freshened, and better able to cope with stress. The serenity that accompanies meditation can give someone a different slant on daily worries. Practice is essential to derive the full benefits of meditation. For a child, meditating twice a day would be about right. Adults usually meditate for about twenty minutes at a time, but for children, age and activity level should determine the length of sessions. They can last only a few minutes.

It is the absolute simplicity of meditation that makes it so difficult for some people to do. Basically, all it involves is getting into a relaxed, comfortable position; remaining still; and concentrating. Some concentrate on a pleasant object in a quiet room, others focus on their heartbeat or breathing, while a third group repeats a syllable or sound such as "Mmmmmmmmmmmmmm" at regular intervals. Children and parents alike often resist just sitting and doing nothing. It almost seems un-American. At first your child may feel silly, or be easily distracted. It is natural for beginners to find their attention wandering. When distraction occurs, simply have the child refocus his or her attention. Tell the child to try not to keep mentally asking, "I wonder how I'm doing?" After you have initially explained the purpose of meditation and helped your child find a comfortable position and a technique that suits him or her, the child will be less distracted meditating in privacy. I once tried to teach a group of four seven- and eight-year-olds how to meditate. We sat on the living room rug and were soon joined by the dog. Each time we started, the children erupted in giggles, and they were continuously checking each other's progress. Repeating a mantra is, in itself, distracting for some children. Young children usually do better listening for their heartbeat or breathing.

Don't expect your child to become a whiz at meditation. Childhood meditating provides a readiness for the more total, adult meditation, but it's not for all children. However, if your child is able to get into the process, even for brief stretches, he or she will undoubtedly experience a sense of tranquility and satisfaction at having achieved control. The foundation of a potentially powerful stress-management technique will be laid.

Oh, What a Relief It Is

In addition to the routines previously suggested, there are a number of other ways that can prove equally effective for relieving tension. For although step-by-step approaches do have proven value, don't forget these wonderfully simple relaxation techniques that have been used for generations and are part of a childhood heritage:

Enjoy a good laugh, corny joke, or bit of silliness.

Find images in the clouds.

Observe fish swimming in a tank.

Hunt for a four-leaf clover.

Play some soothing music.

Take a leisurely walk.

Recite nursery rhymes and finger plays (children love repetition, and finger plays like Eencie-Weencie Spider help tense arm and hand muscles relax).

Read a favorite story.

Make up fairy tales.

Tell stories about your childhood.

"Shake it all out,"—vigorously shake arms, hands, body, legs, and head for a few seconds and then suddenly relax.

Daydream—the more outrageous the dreams are, the better!

Play rag-doll, in which the doll slowly comes alive and marches like a tin soldier and then gradually becomes limp. Once the doll is limp, no matter how you try—you can't make it become stiff again.

Let your child take a warm bath.

Look at family pictures.

Play hide-and-seek or any favorite game.

Listen to the rain fall.

Play with the cat or dog.

Plan a pretend vacation.

Eat something special and delicious.

Make popcorn.

Get away from it all—take a drive, go to a movie, take an overnight trip.

Go fishing.

Have a picnic.

Plan coping strategies, both practical and impractical, for the next time the stressor appears. Rehearse how to handle the stress.

Sit down and draw, doodle, or color.

Give your child a back rub or massage.

Tuck your child in for a brief rest, but don't increase stress by demanding the child sleep.

Stress Management for Parents

Although the suggestions presented on the previous pages are designed for children's stress management, many can be adapted or adopted by parents interested in controlling their own stress. Following are some additional stress-breakers that can provide relief from daily tensions:

STRESS BREAKERS

Exercise. Physical activity is recognized by experts as a valuable means for overcoming the ill effects of stress. A brisk walk, swim, jog around the block, or bike ride can give you a whole new look on life. Jumping rope is another quick, yet effective, source of vigorous exercise. Don't overlook dancing—disco, ballet, aerobic, jitterbugging, or whatever your preference.

Do Something Nice for Someone Else. The pleasure of giving can be highly therapeutic and force you to direct some of your attention away from yourself and your problems. Surprise your family with a special treat, bring a sweet roll or flower to someone at the office, or telephone a friend or shut-in.

Say Something Nice. Make an effort to compliment as many people as possible during the day. In the process, you will notice the many nice things about the individuals you encounter daily and will give you a more positive outlook on life.

Succeed. Pick three minor, yet nagging, tasks you have been postponing for weeks and accomplish them. Make that appointment with the dentist, throw those dingy kitchen curtains into the washing machine, and pick up the parts you need to fix the broken cabinet hinge.

Dump Something.	Discarding useless junk can be an invigorating experience.
Spruce Yourself Up.	Spend a little time, money, or both, to improve your appearance. Get your shoes or fingernails polished. Buy a new article of clothing or jewelry. Looking sloppy is always demoralizing.
Clean Up.	If your house, office, car, purse, or toolbox is a mess, take time to straighten it out. Disorganization and clutter tend to make you feel even more tense and uneasy, especially when you can't find anything.
Get a Change of Scene.	Get out of the house, go somewhere new for lunch, or take a new route home. Change into fresh clothing.
Force Yourself to Appear Calm and Cheerful.	Initially, you will feel like you are acting a part. However, you may find that if you can keep it up long enough, you begin to feel better and in better control.
Take a Hot Bath, Drink a Glass of Warm Milk or Cool Wine, and Go To Bed.	Some days are so bad, the best thing to do is end them. Take heart in the old adage, sleep on it— things always seem better in the morning.

It's Not Whether You Win or Lose, It's How You Play the Game

No parent can completely protect a child from all the inevitable stresses of growing up. The horror stories in the media—of crime, drugs, teen-age sex, runaway children, and the like—have made some parents overprotective. Their anxiety curtails the development of their children's independence and coping ability.

Fortunately, it is not so much the stressful events of childhood that determine how well-adjusted or happy a child becomes, but rather how parent and child cope with them. Children are imitators. If parents furnish an effective coping model, their children will unconsciously imitate this positive behavior. Children are also unconsciously influenced by the general atmosphere of the home. A free, secure, warm setting is ideal for helping the child handle stress successfully, while simultaneously contributing to the formation of a strong self-image. And, when it comes right down to it, self-image is the key to coping. It influences every aspect of your child's life, including interpersonal relationships, learning capacity, morals, and the dimensions of growth and change. It would not be an overstatement to say that a robust self-image is the single most important ingredient in a successful life. With your help, your child can use the stresses of childhood to build a sturdy self-image by learning to face the future with confidence.

Notes, References, and Further Reading

Chapter One—UNDERSTAND STRESS

NOTES

[1] Hans Selye, *The Stress of Life* (New York: McGraw-Hill, 1956), p. 84.
[2] Donald J. Sobol, *Encyclopedia Brown's Record Book of Weird and Wonderful Facts* (New York: Delacorte Press, 1979), p. 79.
[3] Robert L. Woolfolk and Frank C. Richardson, *Stress, Sanity, and Survival* (New York: Signet Books, 1979), pp. 74–75.

REFERENCES AND FURTHER READINGS

Cannon, Walter B. "The Influence of Emotional States on the Functions of the Alimentary Canal," *The American Journal of Science,* Vol. 137, (1909), pp. 480–487.

Lamott, K. *Escape from Stress: How to Stop Killing Yourself.* New York: G. P. Putnam's Sons, 1974.

Lazarus, Richard S. *Psychological Stress and the Coping Process.* New York: McGraw-Hill, 1966.

Levi, Lennart. *Stress. Sources, Management, and Prevention.* New York: Liveright Publishing Corporation, 1967.

McQuade, W., and A. Aikman. *Stress: What It Is, What It Can Do to Your Health, How to Fight Back.* New York: E. P. Dutton and Co., 1974.

Selye, Hans. *Stress in Health and Disease.* Boston: Butterworths, 1976.
———. *Stress Without Distress.* New York: J. B. Lippincott, 1974.

Smith, Lendon. *Improving Your Child's Behavior Chemistry.* Englewood Cliffs, N.J.: Prentice-Hall, 1976.

Stress. Free booklet distributed by local public relations department, Blue Cross, 1974.

Chapter Two—BE A COPING PARENT

NOTES

[1] T. H. Holmes and R. H. Rahe, "The Social Readjustment Rating Scale," *Journal of Psychosomatic Research, 11* (Elmsford, N.Y.: Pergamon Press, 1967), pp. 213–18.

[2] Thomas Gordon, *P.E.T.—Parent Effectiveness Training* (New York: Peter H. Wyden, 1970), pp. 321–327.

REFERENCES AND FURTHER READINGS

Friedman, M., and R. H. Rosenman. *Type A Behavior and Your Heart.* New York: A. A. Knopf, 1974.

McCamy, J. C., and J. Presley. *Human Life Styling: Keeping Whole in the Twentieth Century.* New York: Harper & Row, 1975.

Pelletier, Kenneth R. *Mind as Healer, Mind as Slayer.* New York: Delacorte Press, 1977.

Silverman, S. *Psychological Aspects of Physical Symptoms.* New York: Appleton-Century-Crofts, 1968.

Weiss, J. M. "Psychosocial Factors in Stress and Disease," *Scientific American* (June 1972), pp. 104–113.

Chapter Three—PLOT YOUR CHILD'S INDIVIDUALITY PROFILE

NOTES

[1] Alexander Thomas and Stella Chess, *Temperament and Development* (New York: Brunner/Mazel, 1977), pp. 222–258.

[2] Rita Dunn and Kenneth Dunn, *How to Raise Independent and Professionally Successful Daughters* (Englewood Cliffs, N.J.: Prentice-Hall, 1977), pp. 94–109.

REFERENCES AND FURTHER READINGS

Bloom, Benjamin S. *Human Characteristics and School Learning.* New York: McGraw-Hill Book Company, 1976.

Chess, Stella, and Jane Whitbread, *Daughters* (Garden City, N.Y.: Doubleday, 1978).

Cross, K. Patricia. *Accent on Learning.* San Francisco: Jossey-Bass Publishers, 1977.

Dunn, Rita, and Kenneth Dunn. "Finding the Best Fit: Learning Styles, Teaching Styles," *NASSP Bulletin,* Vol. 59 (October 1975), pp. 37–49.

———. *Teaching Students Through Their Individual Learning Styles.* Reston, Va.: Reston Publishing Company, Inc., 1978.

Joyce, Bruce, and Marsha Weil. *Models of Teaching*. Englewood Cliffs, N.J.: Prentice-Hall, 1972.

Messick, Samuel, and Associates. *Individuality in Learning*. San Francisco: Jossey-Bass Publishers, 1976.

Sperry, Len. *Learning Performance and Individual Differences*. Glenview, Ill.: Scott, Foresman and Company, 1972.

Thomas, Alexander, and Stella Chess. *Temperament and Development*. New York: Brunner-Mazel, 1977.

Witkin, H. A., et al. *Personality Through Perception*. New York: Harper & Brothers, 1954.

Chapter Four—RAISE A FREE CHILD

NOTES

[1] Margaret Mead, *Sex and Temperament in Three Primitive Societies* (New York: William Morrow and Co., 1963), p. 280.

[2] John Money and Anke A. Ehrhardt, "Rearing of a Sex-Reassigned Normal Male Infant after Traumatic Loss of the Penis," in *Sex: Male/Gender: Masculine,* ed. Jack Petras (New York: Alfred Publishing Company, 1975).

REFERENCES AND FURTHER READINGS

Bernabei, Rita. *Can You Tell Me How to Get to Sesame Street?* mimeographed. Columbus, Ohio: Ohio State University, 1974.

Carmichael, Carrie. *Non-Sexist Child Raising*. Boston: Beacon Press, 1977.

Chavetz, Janet Saltzman. *Masculine/Feminine or Human?* Itasca, Ill.: F. E. Peacock Publishers, Inc., 1974.

Dunn, Rita, and Kenneth Dunn. *How to Raise Independent and Professionally Successful Daughters*. Englewood Cliffs, N.J.: Prentice-Hall, 1977.

Epstein, Cynthia Fuchs. *Woman's Place*. Berkeley, Calif.: University of California Press, 1970.

Frazier, Nancy, and Myra Sadker. *Sexism in School and Society*. New York: Harper & Row, 1973.

Gersoni-Stavn, Diane. *Sexism and Youth*. New York: R. R. Bowker, 1974.

Greenberg, Selma. *Right From the Start*. Boston: Houghton Mifflin Company, 1978.

Guttentag, Marcia, and Helen Bray. *Undoing Sex Stereotypes*. New York: McGraw-Hill, 1976.

Harrison, Barbara. *Unlearning the Lie: Sexism in Schools*. New York: Liveright, 1973.

Hartley, Ruth E. "Sex Role Pressures and the Socialization of the Male

Child,'' in *Men and Masculinity,* ed. Joseph Pleck and Jack Sawyer. Englewood Cliffs, N.J.: Prentice-Hall, 1974.

Maccoby, Eleanor E., ed. *The Development of Sex-Role Differences.* Stanford, Calif.: Stanford University Press, 1966.

————, and Carol Jacklin. *The Psychology of Sex Differences.* Stanford, Calif.: Stanford University Press, 1974.

Mischel, W. "Sex Typing and Socialization," in P. H. Mussen, ed., *Carmichael's Manual of Child Psychology,* Vol. 2. New York: John Wiley & Sons, 1970.

Pogrebin, Letty Cottin. *Growing Up Free—Raising Your Child in the 80's.* New York: McGraw-Hill, 1980.

Rivers, Caryl, Rosalind Barnett, and Grace Baruch. *Beyond Sugar and Spice.* New York: G. P. Putnam's Sons, 1979.

Rubin, Jeffrey Z., et al. "The Eye of the Beholder: Parents' Views on Sex of Newborns," *American Journal of Orthropsychiatry,* Vol. 44, No. 4, 1974.

Sprung, Barbara. *Non-Sexist Education for Young Children.* New York: Citation Press, 1975.

————, ed. *Perspectives on Non-Sexist Early Childhood Education.* New York: Teachers College Press, Columbia University, 1978.

Stacy, Judith, Susan Bereaud, and Joan Daniels, eds. *And Jill Came Tumbling After: Sexism in American Education.* New York: Dell, 1974.

Stoller, R. J., "Effects of Parents' Attitudes on Core Gender Identity," *International Journal of Psychiatry,* Vol. 4, No. 57, 1967.

Vogel, Susan, et al. *Sesame Street and Sex-Role Stereotypes.* Pittsburgh, Pa.: KNOW, 1970.

Chapter Five—ACCENTUATE THE POSITIVE

NOTES

[1] Stanley Coopersmith, *The Antecedents of Self-Esteem* (San Francisco: W. H. Freeman and Co., 1967).

[2] Norman M. Lobsenz, "How to Raise Money-Wise Children," *Woman's Day* (October 1972), pp. 214–218.

REFERENCES AND FURTHER READINGS

Axline, Virginia M. *Dibs in Search of Self.* New York: Ballantine, 1960.

Button, A. *The Authentic Child.* New York: Book Press, 1969.

Damon, William. *The Social World of the Child.* San Francisco: Jossey-Bass, 1977.

Felker, Donald W. *Building Positive Self Concepts.* Minneapolis, Minn.: Burgess, 1974.

Laing, R. D. *The Divided Self.* Baltimore, Md.: Penguin, 1965.

Livesley, W. J., and D. B. Bromley. *Person Perception in Childhood and Adolescence*. London: Wiley, 1973.

Rogers, Carl. *On Becoming a Person*. Boston: Houghton Mifflin, 1961.

Uslander, Arlene. *Their Universe, A Look into Children's Hearts and Minds*. New York: Delta, 1976.

Chapter Six—ELIMINATE THE NEGATIVE

NOTES

[1] Lendon Smith, *Improving Your Child's Behavior Chemistry* (Englewood Cliffs, N.J.: Prentice-Hall, 1976), p. 46.

[2] Ibid. p. 44.

[3] Rochelle Albin, "Depression Appears to Afflict Thousands of Children in U.S.," *The New York Times* (March 31, 1981).

REFERENCES AND FURTHER READINGS

Albin, Rochelle. "Depression Appears to Afflict Thousands of Children in U.S., *The New York Times*, March 31, 1981.

Becker, Wesley C., and Janis W. Becker. *Successful Parenthood*. Chicago: Follett Publishing Company, 1974.

Hymes, James L. *The Child Under Six*. Englewood Cliffs, N.J.: Prentice-Hall, Inc., 1972.

Ilg, Frances L., and Louise Bates Ames. *Child Behavior*. New York: Harper & Row, 1955.

Kohl, Herbert. *Reading, How To*. New York: E. P. Dutton and Co., 1973.

Postman, Neil, and Charles Weingartner. *The School Book*. New York: Delacorte Press, 1973.

Prenatal Care, Infant and Child Care, Your Child From 6 to 17. U.S. Department of Health, Education and Welfare. Children's Bureau pamphlets.

Rice, Joseph P. *The Gifted: Developing Total Talent*. Springfield, Ill.: Charles C. Thomas, 1970.

Rosner, Jerome. *Helping Children Overcome Learning Difficulties*. New York: Walker and Company, 1975.

Salk, Lee, and Rita Kramer. *How to Raise a Human Being*. New York: Random House, 1969.

Stewart, Mark, and S. Olds. *Raising the Hyperactive Child*. New York: Harper & Row, 1973.

Torrance, E. P. *Creativity*. San Rafael, Calif.: Dimensions Publishing Co., 1969.

Wender, Paul H. *Minimal Brain Dysfunction in Children*. New York: Wiley-Interscience, 1971.

Witty, Paul H., ed. *The Gifted Child*. Westport, Conn.: Greenwood Press, 1951.

Chapter Seven—JOIN THE TEACHING TEAM

NOTES

[1] David Wechsler, *The Measurement and Appraisal of Adult Intelligence,* 4th ed. (Baltimore: Williams and Wilkins Co., 1958), p. 7.

[2] C. L. Burt, "The Inheritance of Mental Ability," *American Psychologist,* Vol. 13 (1958), pp. 1–15.

[3] H. H. Newman, F. N. Freeman, and J. K. Holzinger, *Twins: A Study of Heredity and Environment* (Chicago: University of Chicago Press, 1937), p. 251.

[4] Anne Anastasi, *Differential Psychology,* 3rd ed. (New York: Macmillan and Co., 1958), p. 299.

[5] Lester W. Sontag, Charles T. Baker, and Virginia L. Nelson, "Mental Growth and Personality Developments: A Longitudinal Study," *Monographs of the Society for Research in Child Development,* Vol. 23, No. 2 (1958), pp. 1–143.

[6] Henry C. Lindgren, Don Byrne, and Lewis Petrinovic, *Psychology: An Introduction to a Behavioral Science* (New York: John Wiley and Sons, 1966), p. 248.

[7] Abraham H. Maslow, *Motivation and Personality* (New York: Harper & Brothers, 1954), p. 96.

[8] Margaret Jo Shepherd, "Learning Disabled or Slow Learner?" *Teacher* (March 1975).

[9] Ben F. Feingold, *Why Your Child Is Hyperactive* (New York: Random House, 1975).

[10] Stuart M. Losen and Bert Diament, *Parent Conferences in the Schools: Procedures for Building Effective Partnership* (Boston: Allyn and Bacon, 1978), pp. 239–247.

[11] Ibid., pp. 19–25.

[12] Blythe C. Mitchell, *Test Service Notebook 13,* issued by the Psychological Corporation, New York.

REFERENCES AND FURTHER READINGS

Darwin, Charles. *Origin of Species.* London: Murray, 1859.

Doman, Glenn. *What to Do About Your Brain-Injured Child.* Garden City, N.Y.: Doubleday, 1974.

Fine, B. F. *The Wrong Teacher. The Wrong School. Underachievers: How They Can Be Helped.* New York: E. P. Dutton and Co., 1967.

Chapter Eight—RECOGNIZE MODERN-DAY STRESSORS

NOTES

[1] Alvin Toffler, *Future Shock* (New York: Random House, 1970), p. 304.

[2] Daniel Yankelovich, "New Rules in American Life: Searching for Self-

Fulfillment in a World Turned Upside Down,'' *Psychology Today* (April 1981), p. 74.

[3] "One Child, Two Homes,'' *Time* (January 29, 1979), p. 61.

[4] Ibid., p. 61.

[5] Yankelovich, *op. cit.*, p. 69.

[6] Alvin Ubell, George Merlis, and Jeffrey Weiss, *Al Ubell's Energy-Saving Guide* (New York: Warner Books, 1980).

REFERENCES AND FURTHER READINGS

Ainsworth, Barbara A. *Education Through Travel*. Chicago: Nelson-Hall Publishers, 1979.

Arnold, Arnold. *Violence and Your Child*. New York: Henry Regnery, 1969.

Atkin, E., and E. Rubin. *Part-Time Father*. New York: New American Library, 1977.

Bass, H. L., and Rein, M. L. *Divorce or Marriage: A Legal Guide*. New York: Prentice-Hall, 1974.

Gardner, Richard A. *The Boys and Girls Book About Divorce*. New York: Bantam Books, 1970.

Hazen, Barbara S. *Two Homes to Live In: A Child's Eye View of Divorce*. New York: Human Sciences Press, 1978.

Kessler, Sheila. *The American Way of Divorce: Prescriptions for Change*. Chicago: Nelson Hall, 1975.

Larsen, O., ed. *Violence and the Mass Media*. New York: Harper & Row, 1968.

Liebert, Robert M., John M. Neale, and Emily S. Davidson. *The Early Window: Effects of Television on Children and Youth*. Elmsford, N.Y.: Pergamon Press, 1973.

Murdock, Carol V. *Single Parents Are People, Too*. New York: Butterick Publishing, 1980.

Noble, J., and W. Noble. *The Custody Trap*. New York: Hawthorn Books, 1975.

"Raising Children in a Changing Society.'' The General Mills American Family Report, 1976–1977.

Rice, F. Phillip. *A Working Mother's Guide to Child Development*. New York: Prentice-Hall, 1979.

Richards, Arlene, and Irene Willis. *How to Get It Together When Your Parents Are Coming Apart*. New York: David McKay, 1976.

Schramm, W., J. Lyle, and E. Parker. *Television in the Lives of Our Children*. Stanford, Calif.: Stanford University Press, 1961.

Shepard, Morris A., and Gerald Goldman. *Divorced Dads—Their Kids, Ex-wives, and New Lives*. Radnor, Pa.: Chilton Book Co., 1979.

Singleton, Mary Ann. *Life After Marriage—Divorce as a New Beginning*. New York: Stein and Day, 1974.

Wheller, M. *No-Fault Divorce*. Boston: Beacon Press, 1974.

Chapter Nine—HEART TO HEART

NOTES

[1] Mary Ann Smith, Toby Landesman, and Jackie Smith, "Behavioral Symptoms of Adolescent Alcohol/Drug Abuse and Addiction," developed as part of the project: Students and Alcohol, the Professional Development Center of the Northwest Educational Cooperative.

REFERENCES AND FURTHER READINGS

Dywasuk, Colette T. *Adoption—Is It for You?* New York: Harper & Row: 1973.

Frailberg, Selma H. *The Magic Years*. New York: Scribners, 1959.

Grollman, A., ed. *Explaining Death to Children*. Boston: Beacon Press, 1967.

LeShan, Eda. *Sex and Your Teenager*. New York: Warner Paperback Library, 1973.

Meredith, Judith C. *And Now We Are a Family*. Boston: Beacon Press, 1971.

Mitchell, Margorie. *The Child's Attitude to Death*. New York: Schocken Books, 1966.

Montagu, Ashley. *Touching: The Human Significance of the Skin*. New York: Columbia University Press, 1971.

Neisser, Edith. *Mothers and Daughters: A Lifelong Relationship,* rev. New York: Harper & Row, 1973.

Pincus, L. *Death and the Family: The Importance of Mourning*. New York: Pantheon, 1975.

Pomeroy, Wardell B. *Your Child and Sex: A Guide for Parents*. New York: Delacorte Press, 1976.

Wasson, Valentina P. *The Chosen Baby*. Philadelphia: Lippincott, 1950.

Chapter Ten—GET YOUR ACT TOGETHER

REFERENCES AND FURTHER READINGS

Bacharach, Bert. *How to Do Almost Everything*. New York: Simon & Schuster, Inc., 1970.

Baldridge, Letitia. *Juggling: The Art of Balancing Marriage, Motherhood, and Career*. New York: The Viking Press, 1976.

Burton, Gabrielle. *I'm Running Away from Home, But I'm Not Allowed to Cross the Street: A Primer on Women's Liberation*. New York: Avon Books, 1975.

Callahan, Sidney C. *Working Mother: How Liberated Women Can Combine Work with Child Rearing*. New York: Macmillan Publishing Co., Inc., 1971.

Gilbreth, Lillian M. *Management in the Home: Happier Living Through Saving Time & Energy*. New York: Dodd, Mead & Co., 1959.

Habeeb, Virginia T. *The Ladies' Home Journal of Homemaking: Everything You Need to Know to Run Your Home with Ease and Style.* New York: Simon & Schuster, Inc., 1973.

Laird, Jean E. *Around the House Like Magic,* paperback. New York: Tower Publications, Inc., 1971.

Lakein, Alan. *How to Get Control of Your Time & Your Life.* New York: Peter A. Wyden, 1973.

Love, Sydney F. *Mastery and Management of Time.* Englewood Cliffs, N.J.: Prentice-Hall, 1978.

McCay, James T. *Management of Time.* Englewood Cliffs, N.J.: Prentice-Hall, 1959.

MacKenzie, R. Alec. *The Time Trap,* paperback. New York: McGraw-Hill, 1975.

Pogrebin, Letty Cottin. *Getting Yours.* New York: David McKay Co., 1975.

Uris, Auren. *Executive Housekeeping: The Business of Managing Your Home.* New York: William Morrow & Co., 1976.

Yates, Martha. *Coping: A Survival Manual for Women Alone.* Englewood Cliffs, N.J.: Prentice-Hall, 1976.

Chapter Eleven—COPE WITH CHILD CARE AND MEDICAL CARE

REFERENCES AND FURTHER READINGS

Altshuler, Anne. *Books that Help Children Deal with a Hospital Experience.* Publication No. (HSA) 77-5402, Department of Health, Education and Welfare, Bureau of Community Health Services, 5600 Fisher's Lane, Rockville, Md. 20857.

Consumers Union. *Health Guide for Travelers.* Orangeburg, N.Y.: Consumers Union.

Curtis, Jean. *Working Mothers.* Garden City, N.Y.: Doubleday, 1976.

Green, Martin I. *A Sign of Relief: A First Aid Handbook for Childhood Emergencies.* New York: Bantam Books, 1977.

Greenleaf, Barbara K., with Lewis A. Schaffer. *Help: A Handbook for Working Mothers.* New York: Thomas Y. Crowell, 1978.

Levine, James A. *Who Will Raise the Children? New Options for Fathers (and Mothers).* New York: Lippincott, 1976.

Levitan, Sar A. and Karen Cleary Alderman. *Child Care and the ABC's Too.* Baltimore, Md.: Johns Hopkins University Press, 1975.

Norris, Gloria, and Jo Ann Miller. *The Working Mother's Complete Handbook.* New York: E. P. Dutton, 1979.

Roby, Pamela. *Child Care—Who Cares?* New York: Basic Books, 1973.

Sills, Barbara, and Jeanne Henry. *The Mother to Mother Baby Care Book.* New York: Avon, 1981.

Sullivan, S. Adams. *The Father's Almanac.* New York: Doubleday, 1980.

Chapter Twelve—MANAGE, SUPPORT, AND RELAX

NOTES

[1] Herbert Benson, *The Relaxation Response* (New York: William Morrow & Co., 1975).

REFERENCES AND FURTHER READINGS

Davis, Adele. *Let's Eat Right to Keep Fit,* rev. ed. New York: Harcourt Brace Jovanovich, 1970.

Downing, George. *Massage and Meditation.* New York: Random House, 1974.

Eastman, Peggy. "Six Second Fix for Stress," *Self* (January 1981), pp. 18–20.

Hittleman, R. *Richard Hittleman's Introduction to Yoga.* New York: Bantam, 1969.

Iyengar, B. K. *Light on Yoga,* rev. ed. New York: Schocken, 1977.

Yogi, M. M. *Transcendental Meditation.* New York: Penguin, 1969.

Index